W9-DBM-977

On the Spanish-Moroccan Frontier

Henk Driessen

The encounter of Europe, Asia and Africa in the Mediterranean basin has given rise to a culturally rich world; a world created by two millennia of warfare and conquest, trading and cultural diffusion, confrontation and accommodation. Combining a historical with a social-anthropological approach, this study of Melilla, a Spanish enclave in Eastern Morocco, offers an insight into these processes on the local, microscopic, level. A fascinating picture emerges of how people, representing the main traditions of the Mediterranean world: Christians, Muslims and Jews, came to live together, confronted each other and worked out a *modus vivendi*, although one marked by ambiguity and tension, often resulting in conflict. The study follows the development and consolidation of this stronghold on the Spanish-Moroccan frontier, its transformation into a trading post and base for colonial penetration and, finally into a multiethnic enclave. It conveys impressions of life, past and present, in a city betwixt and between Europe and Africa, addressing at the same time questions concerning frontier and ethnicity, ritual and power.

Henk Driessen is Associate Professor in Cultural and Social Anthropology at the University of Nijmegen.

EXPLORATIONS IN ANTHROPOLOGY
A University College London Series
Series Editors: Barbara Bender, John Gledhill and Bruce Kapferer

Jadran Mimica, *Intimations of Infinity: The Mythopoeia of the Iqwaye Counting System and Number*

Tim Ingold, David Riches and James Woodburn (eds.), *Hunters and Gatherers*
  Volume 1. *History, Evolution and Social Change*
  Volume 2. *Property, Power and Ideology*

Barry Morris, *Domesticating Resistance: The Dhan-Gadi Aborigines and the Australian State*

Pnina Werbner, *The Migration Process: Capital, Gifts and Offerings among Pakistanis in Britain*

Bruce Kapferer, *A Celebration of Demons* (2nd edn)

Thomas C. Patterson, *The Inca Empire: The Formation and Disintegration of a Pre-Capitalist State*

Joan Bestard Camps, *What's in a Relative? Household and Family in Formentera*

Forthcoming:

Alfred Gell, *The Anthropology of Time: Cultural Constructions of Temporal Maps and Images*

Max and Eleanor Rimoldi, *Hahalis and the Labour of Love: A Social Movement on Buka Island*

Terence Turner, *A Critique of Pure Culture*

Guy Lanoue, *Brothers: The Politics of Violence among the Sekani of Northern British Columbia*

On the Spanish-Moroccan Frontier

A Study in Ritual, Power and Ethnicity

Henk Driessen

BERG

New York / Oxford

Distributed exclusively in the US and Canada by St. Martin's Press, New York

DT
329
M4
D75
1992

First published in 1992 by
Berg Publishers Limited
Editorial offices:
165 Taber Avenue, Providence, RI 02906, USA
150 Cowley Road, Oxford, OX4 1JJ, UK

© Henk Driessen 1992

British Library Cataloguing in Publication Data
Driessen, Henk
   On the Spanish-Moroccan frontier: a study in
   ritual, power and ethnicity. – (Explorations in
   anthropology)
   I. Title   II. Series
   305.86

   ISBN 0–85496–702–8

Library of Congress Cataloging-in-Publication Data
Driessen, Henk.
   On the Spanish-Moroccan frontier : a study in ritual, power, and
   ethnicity / Henk Driessen.
      p.   cm. — (Explorations in anthropology)
   Includes bibliographical references and index
   ISBN 0–85496–702–8
   1. Melilla (Spain)—Ethnic relations.   2. Melilla (Spain)—Social
life and customs.   3. Melilla (Spain)—Religious life and customs.
4. Rif Mountains Region (Morocco)—Ethnic relations.   I. Title.
II. Series.
DT329.M4D75   1992
305.8'00964'2—dc20   91–33239
                                                          CIP

Printed in Great Britain by
Billing and Sons Ltd, Worcester

Contents

List of Tables, Maps and Illustrations

Tables

Maps

Illustrations

Between pages 4 and 5

Between pages 110 and 111

Preface

Fifteen years ago I became interested in the complexities of Spanish-Moroccan relationships while I was conducting field-work in southern Spain, though my research topics were quite different at that time. The traces of Muslim Spain in monuments, architecture, agricultural technology, vocabulary, and art attracted my interest and imagination. I listened to the stories about the Rif War and the actions of Rifian soldiers who helped to conquer Popular Front towns during the Spanish Civil War. I heard about 'festivals of Moors and Christians', mock battles between Cross and Crescent, which were enacted as part of patronal feasts in many Andalusian towns. I witnessed how mothers invoked the 'Moor' as a bogey when training their children, and I observed how countrymen reacted to Moroccan peddlars who visited their villages and towns selling watches and leatherwork. They were often treated with mistrust and sometimes ridiculed. In short, the 'Moor' serves as a model against which Andalusians express and affirm their own identity. In many ways the 'Moor' is an exemplar of what Spaniards are not, an inferior alien, yet he is also close and familiar, part of the cultural heritage. It was this paradox that intrigued me most.

After having completed my dissertation and specialised in Mediterranean ethnography, in 1984 I went on to research one of the two Spanish enclaves in Morocco where the 'Peoples of the Book' share a small territory. I was prompted by both the peculiarities of the place and by questions of a pan-Mediterranean nature. This book bears the mark of both these sources of inspiration, being neither a monograph in the conventional sense, nor a study with a sharply demarcated problem and argument. It deals rather with a collection of connected themes with a common focus in the life of the enclave past and present.

The research would have been impossible without prior knowledge of Spain and Morocco and familiarity with Moroccan ethnography and Spanish archives. I worked for six months in Melilla and also made some brief field trips into the city's hinterland. My main field language was Spanish.

This study was written while I was a fellow at The Netherlands Institute for Advanced Study in the Humanities and Social Sciences (NIAS) which provided an excellent ambience. Here I also participated in the working group on the 'comparative study of ritual'. I have very much profited from discussions and generous comments offered by the members of this group: Anton Blok, Don Handelman, Jan Heesterman, Zdzislaw Mach, Jonathan Parry, Kristofer Schipper, and Frits Staal. Anne Simpson carefully and patiently processed the manuscript and corrected flaws in grammar and style. Stephen Mennell kindly offered his valuable help as an editor. William Christian was of great assistance in inspiration and practical matters. I express my deep gratitude to all these friends. I also thank the copy-editor, Mr. Lewis, for many useful suggestions and corrections.

Many people in Melilla deserve special thanks. Without their generous help I would have lost my way in the enclave. The municipality offered hospitality and statistical data. Señor La Hoz helped me find my way in the municipal archive and library. Manolo Soria, dedicated photographer and self-taught ethnographer, shared with me his intimate knowledge of Melilla and Rifian society. Francisco Saro, Jesus Salafranca and Juan Diez provided many insights in local history. Leon Levy introduced me to the Jewish community. Mohand Moh and Mustafa Abdelqadr were of great help in finding my way among the Muslims. Alfredo Nuñez introduced me to the Spanish Foreign Legion and the Cabrerizas quarter, and Kishu Ghamandas to the Hindu community. To protect the privacy of all other informants I have used pseudonyms and altered some of the details of illustrative cases. I would like to record my thanks to them all.

This book is dedicated to Willy Jansen and Miriam Driessen.

Part I

The Hispano-African Frontier in History

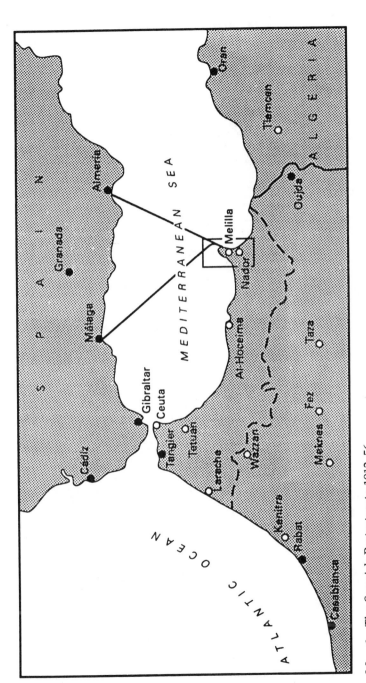

Map 1 The Spanish Protectorate 1912–56

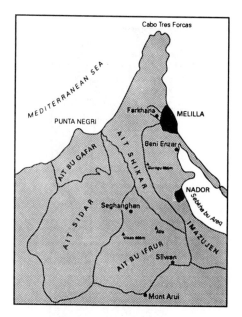

Map 2 The territories of the Iqar'ayen tribes, Melilla's hinterland

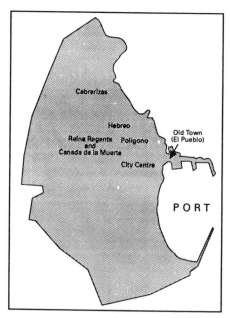

Map 3 The position of some of the barrios mentioned in the text

1 Rifian traders, their caiques beached. In the background the *presidio* (circa 1900; Archivo Municipal de Melilla. Sección fotografica)

2 Spanish officers talking with Rifian leaders (1912, A.M.M.)

3 Spanish guests from Melilla at an important Rifian wedding (1916, A.M.M.)

4 Colonel Francisco Franco Bahamonde – future dictator of Spain – leading his weather-beaten legionnaires as shock troops in the recovery of territory lost to Rifian rebels in the Melilla area (late 1921, A.M.M.)

5 Young Rifian painter's representation of Abd al-Krim's uprising against the Spanish Protectorate. The legendary leader with rifle and Koran; Spanish flag burning in front of fortified Rifian farmstead (early 1980s)

Chapter 1

Introduction

This is a book about an enclave society. It tells the story of how people representing the main traditions of the Mediterranean world were caught in a web of interdependencies in a small corner of this world, how they confronted each other, and how they worked out *modi vivendi*. The scene of action is Melilla, a Spanish sea-port in eastern Morocco. The narrative and discussion follow the emergence and consolidation of a stronghold on the Hispano-African frontier, its transformation into a trading port and base for colonial penetration, and finally, into a multiethnic enclave.

This study is in a sense Janus-faced. It conveys ordered impressions of life, past and present, in a city betwixt and between Europe and Africa, and at the same time addresses questions that go beyond the specific locale to the heart of contemporary anthropology. Much of the endeavor goes into striking a balance between the seemingly trivial detail and the momentous general problem. Many anthropologists are haunted by this paradox; they represent themselves as being involved in the study of mankind while conducting fieldwork in highly specific miniature settings. Most fieldworkers feel the tension this paradox generates both during the research and when writing up the material. So let me first point out how the general issues this study addresses emerge from the research setting.

The Anthropologist in the City

Anthropologists seem to have a special predilection for studying marginal phenomena. This is certainly true for what is called urban anthropology, much of which consists of studies of ethnic, predominantly marginal enclaves in metropolitan society. So even when anthropologists eschew the periphery and choose urban centres for their fieldwork, they mainly work in the fringes. In fact, contemporary urban ethnography does not differ much from the studies on subcultures of marginal people in Chicago of the 1920s.

The present state of the art reveals two major trends. First, the mainstream of urban anthropology is simply ethnography of social microcosms and subcultures in cities (cf. Caulkins 1980), taking into account the city at large to varying degrees. Second, a small minority of anthropologists working in cities aim at investigating the city as a social form in and for itself. Representatives of the latter trend deplore the predominance of the former trend. For instance, Ulf Hannerz (1980: 5) sees 'the flocking of urban anthropologists to the ethnic enclaves of our cities' as an 'evasion'. In my view both approaches of the city are equally valuable. They presuppose and complement one another, although only on condition that one important prerequisite is fulfilled. Ethnographers *in* cities should pay analytical attention to the nature of the interface between the microcosm and the city at large. Anthropologists *of* cities, in their turn, should try to take into account the relative autonomy of the various microcosms of which the modern metropolis consists. One of the aims of this study is precisely to combine a sketch of the parts with a view of the whole.

A well-known feature of the Mediterranean world is the existence of cultural enclaves of dispersed minorities such as Armenians, Greeks and Jews (cf. Adams 1981). This is particularly true of port cities which have been populated successively and often simultaneously by distinct ethnic groups. This condition makes them privileged places for studying processes of cultural confrontation and accommodation. Less well-known, however, is the existence in these ports of colonial enclaves where the major ethnic groups of the wider region live together. These are of special interest to students of Mediterranean history and ethnography in general and to students of ethnic politics in particular. Melilla is a case in point.

In spite of the recent trend towards the urbanisation of anthropological fieldwork, there are very few studies of Mediterranean ports available.[1] The general reason for this, of course, is that anthropological research is still largely geared to participant observation in small, well-ordered communities. From this stems the predominance of ethnographies of microcosms within cities lacking a view of the whole. Even in order to acquire a more than impressionistic sense of the city as a context for the study of specific sub-communities or well-defined problems, one needs more research tools than are available in conventional community studies.

My research strategy was very much a form of *bricolage*. I made extensive use of municipal census material dating back to the last quarter of the nineteenth century and a wide range of other statistical data. This quantitative material provided the skeleton for substantial ethnographic and historical data derived from the selective reading of the local daily newspaper, archival documents, and from oral history. This enabled me to draw a picture of the general evolution of the city and its barrios over a period of roughly one century. More specifically, I used this mixture of written and oral sources for tracing the trajectory through time of the Jewish, Muslim and Hindu communities and their interactions with the Spanish Catholic inhabitants.

The daily newspaper, available in bound volumes for the period between 1903 and 1980, proved an invaluable source of information in several respects, both for the present and for the past. It was not only useful as a source for the *faits divers* of public life, but also provided me with a means of selecting major topics for interviews and discussions with informants, for triggering off their collective memory, and for cross-checking written and oral data. Of course, a newspaper is a cultural product of special periods and groups, and consequently biased; as such it is therefore a source of information on the self-images of the Spanish-Catholic population, of their perceptions of history, and their images of the minority groups. Handled with care, it is a source of strategic importance in a large, complex and heterogeneous society.

I also did a lot of participant observation, worked with key informants from all ethnic groups, attended special occasions and gatherings, and conducted two sociographic studies of barrios. In Melilla, as in most of the Mediterranean world, bars and cafes are the most important foci of male sociability, regardless of social class and ethnicity. So bar crawling was a major field strategy, not only for making but also for maintaining rapport with informants. I spent almost half of my time in Melilla standing in bars where I talked and listened to men. I decided, largely on the basis of prior experience, that for several reasons formal survey research would not be very rewarding in a city like Melilla. It is intrinsically boring. It is very hard to make

appointments with informants in private space to conduct standardised interviews, private space being more private here than
in Western Europe. Most inhabitants are not used to question-
naires and are justifiably suspicious of official-type paperwork,
which severely limits the reliability of survey studies. And,
finally, simple conversation in 'natural' settings is more in-
formative and pleasurable.

   This is also a study in ethnography and history. The first part
deals with the past, making brief excursions into the present,
whereas the second part is largely about the present with regular references to the past. Good ethnography should be informed by history, because society is in constant flux and
culture is continuously being constituted. Continuity and dis-
continuity should have equal analytical weight.[2] For anthropologists who take time and process seriously, history is more than
an extra source of data. Just as the present informs the past, the
past should inform the present. In this book I employ a micro-
historical perspective, that is a perspective that mainly deals
with local processes.

   This book is also indirectly a contribution to the history and
ethnography of the Rif, the mountain chain of northern Morocco which stretches along the Mediterranean sea from west of
the Straits of Gibraltar to Melilla in the east, a zone inhabited by
Berber peasants. It does so from the perspective of a Spanish
city which has been a compelling presence in this area for almost
five centuries. This basic fact has not received due attention in
the ethnography of the Rif, although the enclave has influenced
Rifian society enormously.[3] For instance, five tribes in the immediate hinterland of Melilla forged a confederacy in order to
deal with the Spanish threat. In Chapter 2 I examine several
forms of interaction across the Hispano-African frontier. On the
other hand, Melilla would never have survived as a Spanish
enclave without varied and complex contacts with the tribal
hinterland. This brings us to the major theme of the book.

Frontier and Ethnicity

Between the tenth and thirteenth centuries Melilla acted as a
fortified trading-station between Muslim Spain, the North Italian city-states, and the trans-Saharan traffic from Timbuktu. It
started to decline in the late thirteenth century as a result of

dynastic struggles between the sultans of Fez and Tlemcen. When the Spanish occupied Melilla, it had already been abandoned and partly destroyed. Parallel to the Christian advance in Muslim Spain, Spanish Christians as well as Arabs and Berbers began to perceive the Hispano-African frontier as a dividing line between civilisation and barbarism. On the Christian side, this vision became firmly established in the course of the thirteenth century when several links between crusade and mission had developed. A recent study (Kedar 1984) has shown that in Pope Innocent IV's doctrine, crusader warfare and conversion of infidels became connected with each other. According to this doctrine, forcible conversion was not allowed, but crusades aimed at paving the way for missionary work received the Pope's blessing. On the Muslim side, the perception of the Hispano-African frontier became stronger as the Christians advanced. The Spanish seizure of strongholds on the Maghribian coast — Melilla was in fact the first — fixed the frontier. Throughout its Spanish occupation Melilla has frequently been besieged, yet it has continued to act as an important port of transit for European merchandise, including arms. Rif Berbers came with their agricultural products to the market held outside the town, or in the drill square during peaceful interludes.

Historians disagree on the degree of permeability of the Hispano-African frontier. There are basically two points of view. Fernand Braudel (1976) is the pre-eminent exponent of the view which stresses the ecological and cultural unity of the Mediterranean area. He pays close attention to the intermingling of Mediterranean societies, to cultural transfer and diffusion. Andrew Hess (1978), on the other hand, maintains that the division of the Mediterranean world into two rigidly defined spheres, the Turko-Muslim and Latin-Christian, is the dominant feature of its history from the sixteenth through to the mid-nineteenth century. In Chapter 2 I argue that the frequency and variety of contacts across the frontier justifies speaking of one overlapping society of Spaniards and Berbers. When in the course of the nineteenth century the Hispano-African frontier shifted further inland under pressure of European imperialism, both Melilla and Rifian society were radically transformed. This transformation is sketched in Chapter 3. Jews played a vital role in this process, a point that is further elaborated in Chapter 5.

Anthropologists have increasingly become aware of the connection between ethnographic knowledge and power. Said

(1978), among others, set the trend with his seminal critique *Orientalism*, arguing that Western representations of (pre)colonial societies and cultures were an instrument for domination. This argument has been further developed in the so-called 'experimental ethnography', which includes a critical re-examination and demystification of early ethnographies (cf. Marcus & Cushman 1982, Marcus & Fisher 1986, Clifford & Marcus 1986). Chapter 4 recounts how the Spanish domesticated the Rif by mapping and ordering it ethnographically. In other words, the ethnographic endeavour was part of the Spanish appropriation of Rifian society and culture.

As a result of Spanish colonisation of northern Morocco, Melilla became increasingly a multiethnic society with internal boundaries. The first boundary to emerge was between Catholics and Jews, who had helped to transform and extinguish the outer frontier. The history of the encounter of Catholics, Jews and Muslims (the Hindus are a case apart) in Melilla shows that the persistence of ethnic distinctions is predicated upon the interplay of avoidance and interaction.[4] The different ethnic groups have maintained rather strict boundaries in a complex process of conflict and co-operation that have resulted in a fascinating society.

Much of the literature on ethnicity is dominated by the assumption that the persistence of ethnic boundaries implies diversity between groups and homogeneity within them (cf. Cohen 1974, 1981b; Epstein 1978). This supposition is at odds with the dynamics of ethnic politics. One way to show this is to focus on the way social class divisions within ethnic groups bear upon the presentation and management of external boundaries.[5] This is discussed briefly in Chapters 8 and 9. Another way is to show how categorical distinctions become blurred in the margins of society, which is described in the final Chapter on legionnaires, prostitutes and young toughs who constitute a distinct local community, an enclave within the enclave.

Ritual and Power

Ritual is the second theme of this study and intimately related to the first. To put it bluntly, probably over-stretching the concept, ritual is a short-hand term for acts which individuals or collectivities carry out when boundaries are crossed. In Chapter 2

I examine several instances of crossing the frontier which are hedged about with rites. Apostasy and the mutilation of enemy corpses are extreme cases. The use of flags and sounds in transfrontier communication, of commensality and all kinds of formalities are more common examples. The Jewish festival of *mimuna*, which I analyse in Chapter 5, is a very instructive case. It accentuates the ambiguities inherent in the structural position of the Jews and acts out the contradictions of inter-religious contacts. In Chapter 8 I address the question of how ritual operates in inter-ethnic encounters, arguing that the crossing of ethnic boundaries is ritualised and that ritual serves the accommodation of interests.

In the second part of this book I deal with the major theoretical question of how ritual is linked to power. In line with both Durkheimian and Marxist traditions, anthropologists have long conceived of ritual as epiphenomenal, circumstantial, and ephemeral, stressing what ritual mirrors or expresses, predominantly in the religious domain. This is what one might call the cosmetic view of the role of ritual and ceremonial in the dynamics of domination and subordination. This view has impeded adequate understanding of the power of ritual.

Recently, anthropologists and historians have shown that ritual forms have a momentum of their own.[6] One of the early examples is Evans-Pritchard (1949), who in a detailed account shows how an Islamic order established itself among the Bedouin tribes of Cyrenaica, how it became politicised as a reaction to Italian colonial penetration, and how it was transformed into a centralised political structure, in which the ritual and political order became one. In his book on nineteenth-century royal rituals in Bali, Geertz (1981: 120) argues that '. . . pageants were not mere embellishments, celebrations of a domination independently existing: they were the thing itself.' While this book contains valuable insights into the links between ritual and power, Geertz overstates the case of the state as a ritual construct at the expense of the state as a structure of power. Bloch (1986, 1987) recounts how the grand royal ceremonies of the proto-state of Madagascar were themselves elaborations upon the extensions of everyday rites, making the important point that this emergence from ordinary life gave royal ritual its compelling force. The relations between power and ritual are thus dialectical. Dominance and subordination are clothed with rites which in their turn generate power, inducing all kinds of social and political activities. Power reveals itself in ritual performances and celebrations. People use rites, sacred as well as secular, to legitimise, reinforce, express, challenge and change the distribution of power.

These rather abstract introductory statements will be illustrated with case material in Part Two. Chapter 6 examines a state ritual, a ceremony of the national flag, the overt substance of which is Spanish domination and solidarity. In Melilla funerals and post-funerary rites are the most guarded of rituals which mark and maintain ethnic boundaries. I argue in Chapter 7 that the cult of the cemetery not only reflects the anxieties of the Spanish-Catholic population, but also helps to alleviate them. Chapter 8 explores degrees of ritualisation in ethnic interaction in relation to class differentiation, and Chapter 9 shows how ritual forms break down in a situation of extreme conflict. But let me first conclude this introductory chapter with a brief description of the setting.

The Enclave

The ports of Melilla and Ceuta and the islets of Peñón de Velez de la Gomera, Alhucemas and Chaffarinas are the last surviving relics of the Spanish empire. Together they cover about thirty-five square kilometers, and are populated by 130,000 people, of whom about 50,000 are Muslims (Kettani, 1986: 185). These societies are unusual in the way that other anomalies in the modern political order such as Hong Kong, Singapore, Macao and Gibraltar are. Since 1961 the ports and islets have been claimed by Morocco, while successive Spanish governments have defended the 'Spanishness' of these miniature territories for geopolitical and nostalgic reasons. They have argued that these territories belonged to Spain long before the emergence of the Moroccan state.

Melilla is a small port on the Mediterranean coast of Morocco held by Spain since the end of the fifteenth century. The old town — a former citadel, garrison and penal settlement — stands on a rock jutting into the sea, while modern Melilla is built on the surrounding hillsides. The centre, which has both the air of a colonial city in decay and of a thriving cosmopolitan bazaar, occupies the lower part of the enclave.

A treaty that ended the brief war of 1859–60 between Spain

'and Morocco granted the Christian victors a slightly extended zone of occupation around the chock-a-block fortress town. In 1863 Melilla was declared a free port and became a base for the commercial penetration of Morocco and Algeria. At the beginning of this century military expeditions entered the enclave's hinterland and when in 1912 the Spanish Protectorate was established over northern Morocco, Melilla became its eastern capital. After this interlude of territorial, economic, and demographic expansion, it once again became an introverted enclave-society of twelve square kilometers, locked in by the sea and fenced off from the hinterland with barbed wire, giving it a claustrophobic atmosphere. In this multiethnic society, religion has remained an ascriptive criterion of prime importance, notwithstanding the fact that for the majority of the inhabitants religion is not so much a matter of faith and compliance with religious precepts, as an integral part of their ethnic identity and a focal component of their sense of personhood. One third of the 64,000 inhabitants[7] are Muslims of Rifian origin, of whom only a small minority hold Spanish nationality. More than 12,000 Rif Berbers, many of whom were born in the enclave, are classified as Moroccans by the city administration. Apart from their semi-official card of residence they have no formal status and enjoy virtually no civil rights. Few of them have Moroccan documents, and only 1,500 have an official employment permit. Illegal Moroccan immigrants, for example those who do not even hold a card of residence, are estimated at 3,000. From time to time the police hold *razzias* and send these illegal residents back across the border, but they often return under the cover of darkness.[8]

There is also a tiny community of approximately 100 Hindus of Indian origin, only half a dozen of whom have chosen to adopt Spanish citizenship. Although small in number, they are very powerful and own the most successful commercial houses. They, in fact, control the massive flow of Far-Eastern luxury goods produced in Hong Kong, Japan, Singapore, and South Korea, and channel this flow through Melilla to the Iberian peninsula and North Africa. They constitute a fairly closed endogamous community.

Within the Spanish-Catholic or Iberian segment of the population there is a sub-community of about 150 gypsy families who form a distinct ethnic group. This group specialises in hawking and construction work and is treated with disdain by the established Spanish residents. Finally, there are 1,100 Sephardic Jews, descendents of the Moroccan Jews who settled in Melilla between 1860 and 1930. Almost all of these have adopted Spanish nationality. They are mainly traders and professionals who belong to the middle class.

The enclave is also a garrison city of strategic importance which adds another dimension to its peculiarity. The 7,500 soldiers and 1,500 officers and NCO's — one military man to every seven civilians — provide the population with an important source of income. As may be imagined, however, the existence of a group of thousands of men without women inevitably creates problems.

As a free port and border city Melilla has a large floating population. Most soldiers serve a sixteen-month term before returning home. Peninsulars come to buy tax-free cigarettes, liquor, watches, tape and video-recorders, and visit their relatives in the city and army. Foreign tourists and Moroccan migrant workers use the city as a port of transit. Each day thousands of border people, who have a permanent residence in the hinterland, pour into the enclave. For generations the source of income for these people has come from both sides of the border. They bring eggs, vegetables, grain, meat, fish, fruit, milk, and water into the city and return home with purchases of blankets, shoes, batteries, gasoline and electronic luxuries. They do not come only to trade, but use the many amenities available; they drink beer and liquor, go to the cinema, bingo, doctors, and prostitutes. Mention must be made of the dozens of beggars, mostly women with children, who are more or less tolerated. There is one common attraction for all these transient people — the smell of money.

In a sense Melilla is a parasitical society and it is common knowledge that much money is made outside the law. There are fewer controls here than in peninsular Spain. Many come to make quick money, invest their savings overseas, and then leave. Since 1956 there has been a considerable exodus. Within twenty-five years more than 25,000 Spanish inhabitants have emigrated to the motherland, while thousands of Jews left after Morocco gained its independence in 1956.[9] However, thousands of unskilled Rifians have since settled in Melilla.

Given its geopolitical status, economic condition and ethnic complexity, life in Melilla is precarious. Morocco maintains its claims to the enclave as an integral part of its own territory.

Many politicians in Madrid consider it a colony which costs too much and should be retroceded to Morocco. Economically, the enclave exists only at the whim of King Hassan II. The pulse of public life is intimately tied to the permeability of the border. Beneath the surface, tensions are brewing between Spanish-Catholic inhabitants and Muslim Berbers, as was demonstrated in the race riots in 1986.

Many permanent inhabitants live with their backs to Morocco. This is especially true for those Spanish residents whose parents and grandparents were born in Melilla and who consider themselves true *melillenses*. They are ready to defend the Spanishness of their city. They look across the Mediterranean to the 'Peninsula' as they consistently call Spain in order to indicate that they are part of Spanish society. They feel threatened by sporadic problems at the border and by what they call the 'March of the Tortoise',[10] the slow yet persistent invasion of Rifians who lack documents of all kinds and who are thought to upset the delicate economic and demographic balance of the enclave. These established people are largely middle-class merchants, civil servants, and skilled workers. They constitute the backbone of colonial society.

Ethnicity, which is mainly defined in terms of religious affiliation, is the main divisive force in local society. Although Catholics, Jews, Muslims and Hindus are in constant contact with one another, such interaction is largely centred on economic matters. In the areas of kinship, politics, religion, and regular social contact there is a high degree of ethnic apartheid. Even those Muslims and Jews who have adopted Spanish nationality and belong to the well-to-do section of the populace, are considered and treated as second-rate citizens by the dominant Catholic segment.

Melilla is in many respects a schizoid society: European and Oriental, cosmopolitan and parochial, liberal and intolerant, affluent and poor. The major social problems are the high rate of unemployment and illiteracy, a serious housing shortage and excessively high rents, deficient sanitation and the existence of overcrowded slums. The Rifian immigrants suffer most from these social shortfalls and are forced to rely on self-help. This is in broad strokes the kind of society which will be discussed in the following chapters.[11]

Chapter 2

The Permeability of the Frontier

One fruitful way to study the dialectics of meaning and power in religion is to focus on the role of belief and cult in the building of states and empires. The defensive frontier of Catholicism in the Mediterranean area from the sixteenth to the mid-nineteenth century is an intriguing and illustrative case. Along this line of Spanish strongholds on the Barbary coast, two empires — in essence two enemy religions — confronted one another. Both Muslims and Christians employed notions of barbarism and impurity to degrade the non-believer. Even the same abusive term (*perro, kalb*) was used on both sides. Official state policies required the maintenance of attitudes of religious intransigence. However, on the ground there were continuous and varied contacts between Muslims and Christians in which the key notion of the unbeliever as barbarian was frequently played down.

The Presidio as a Frontier Institution

In 1492 the Nasrid emirate of Granada, the last bastion of the Moors on the north-western Mediterranean shore, fell into Christian hands. This crucial event in the history of the Mediterranean area boosted the crusading euphoria (the *guerra divina*) against Islam. The Spanish monarchs received the Pope's blessings and financial backing for expansion in North Africa.[1] Five years later the crusade was carried to the southern shore of the Mediterranean with the seizure of Melilla. This was an easy conquest as the town had been abandoned by its inhabitants because of longstanding warring between the rulers of the cities of Fez and Tlemcen over the possession of the town and its port. From that year to 1510 a series of key ports on the Maghribian coast followed, Mers el-Kebir, El Peñón de Vélez, Oran,

Bougie, and Tripoli. While the crusading spirit of pious Isabel of Castile and her ecclesiastical advisors was the main force behind this expansion,[2] two pragmatic considerations settled the conquest. Pirates scoured the Mediterranean and threatened trade with Morocco which had never until then been interrupted in spite of hostilities. At this time Barbary corsairs were still fighters in the Holy War against the Christians (Julien 1970: 206, 274).

The second reason was one of internal politics. After the fall of Granada many ruling-class Muslims had left Spain or converted to Christianity. The larger part of the working population, however, remained and continued to cling to its religion and way of life. Towards the end of the fifteenth century intolerance *vis-à-vis* the Muslim minority rapidly increased. The powerful Fray Francisco Jiménez de Cisneros, cardinal and future regent to Spain, became the champion of forced conversion. In 1499 he ordered copies of the Quran and other Islamic works to be burned. Many Muslims were forced to renounce Islam.

In 1500 the first Muslim revolt broke out in the city of Granada and spread to the surrounding mountains. The rulers of Spain began to fear an alliance of the rebels with Barbary corsairs and their Turkish protectors. The conquest of Oran, Mers el-Kebir, and Peñón de Vélez must be seen as a strategy to prevent this coalition. In southern Spain religious opposition stiffened, and compulsory baptism was imposed by royal decree on all Muslims living in the Kingdom of Castile (of which Andalusia was a part). The converted Muslims came to be known as *Moriscos*. These 'New Christians,' however, persisted in practising Islam. After new revolts, subsequent deportations and resettlement of *Moriscos* in other parts of Castile, they were finally expelled from Spain in the early seventeenth century.[3] The failure of assimilation and the fate of Jewish and Muslim minorities indicate how strongly the formation of Spanishness rested on Catholicism and xenophobia.

The Turkish threat coupled with the rebelliousness of the *Moriscos* and the increasing activities of Barbary corsairs all contributed to the erection of a string of *presidios* along the Maghribian coast as defensive outposts of Catholicism. In documents they are referred to as *fronteras de Africa*. The Maghreb was essentially African in the Spanish mind and was thus primitive, alien, and barbaric. In the course of the sixteenth century the Spaniards increasingly restricted themselves to a system of limited occupation. They transformed the conquered ports into formidable strongholds, *presidios*, which were a combination of citadel, garrison and penal settlement. These served mainly as havens for Spanish ships and observation posts for monitoring the movements of the Turkish fleet and Barbary corsairs.

Since its occupation on behalf of the noble house of Medina Sidonia the *presidio* of Melilla had been progressively fortified. The settlement itself was a small cluster of houses around a chapel. In the middle of the sixteenth century the garrison amounted to between 300 and 400 soldiers, while the civil population consisted of 200 people, labourers, two dozen slaves of both sexes, 100 children, sixty married women, and a dozen prostitutes.[4] However, in the course of the sixteenth century it became an increasingly expensive and vulnerable outpost of the Spanish empire. Food, fresh water, materials for the construction and maintenance of fortifications and houses, ammunition, soldiers, convicts, workers, prostitutes, cloth and fish came by sea from the port of Málaga. Since the Mediterranean was infested with corsairs, life in the *presidio* was precarious. The expense of maintaining Melilla became so heavy a burden for the Medina Sidonia that in 1556 they were forced to transfer their fief to the Crown of Castile.[5] During the reign of Philip II the reinforcement and expansion of the citadel was accelerated. Its location on a steep rock high above the sea combined with technical superiority in artillery and fortification made Melilla an almost impregnable stronghold. However, bringing in supplies was its weak spot.

In the second half of the sixteenth century Spanish interests began to shift away from the Mediterranean towards northern Italy, the Low Countries, Portugal and the New World, while the Ottoman policy was reoriented towards Persia and the Indian Ocean (Braudel 1976 II: 1185). As the centre of European gravity gradually moved northwards, the Maghreb became more and more detached from Europe. The Mediterranean became peripheral to the main thrust of Western European interests which in the seventeenth and eighteenth centuries was the Atlantic. Mediterranean trade, though still important, was overshadowed by the Atlantic slave-trade (Thomson 1987: 45). This shift in the world economic system was in a sense foreshadowed and sealed in the Spanish-Turkish truce of 1580. The age of crusades was over and the Latin-Christian/Turko-Muslim frontier remained more or less fixed until nineteenth-century colonial penetration. In Braudel's apt words, piracy became a 'substitute for declared war' between Islam and Christendom.

This swing in international policies had a profound impact on Melilla. It meant that the *presidio* found itself increasingly isolated and forced to rely on its own resources. From the late 1620s onwards the governors of the stronghold incessantly complained in their letters to Madrid about shortages of men, fresh water, firewood, food-supplies, clothes and ammunition. Maladministration, endemic conflicts between the quartermaster, parish priest, engineer-architect, and captain general, desertions, low morale, famine, and plague constituted more serious threats than recurrent raids by corsairs, Berber hillmen and sieges by the Sultan's troops. Life in the *presidio* was one of genuine hardship. Pay was low and irregular, work hard, and the atmosphere was both claustrophobic and monotonous. Consignment to Melilla virtually meant deportation.[6]

One of the main customs of the *presidio* was the raid (*jornada* or *razzia*) on Rifian hamlets in the surrounding countryside. There were various motives for these planned sorties. They were sometimes necessary for survival, as, for instance, when supply ships arrived late or did not arrive at all. This, in fact, was a frequent occurrence and the citadel's population could survive only by roaming the hinterland in search of grain, fruit, cattle, firewood, and salt. Ambitious and greedy captains-general sometimes made dangerous sorties to collect booty and slaves. Raids were also punitive expeditions into the settlements of Rifian frontiersmen, who constantly annoyed the *presidio*. However, such raids were sometimes carried out under the guise of the 'crusading spirit' which presented a method of overcoming boredom and creating excitement. The *razzia* was both a cause and a consequence of the hostility between Melilla and its hinterland.

The eastern Rif was a peripheral region, albeit never entirely isolated from the Moroccan state. In fact, it has long been important to Morocco's rulers because of its strategic location at the crossing of two important trade routes, from the Sahara to the Mediterranean and from the Atlantic through the centre of Morocco to the rest of the Maghreb. Moreover, it constituted a border zone between the empire of Morocco and the Ottoman empire to the east. In spite of the significance of the Rif, the tribes were never effectively subjugated and incorporated into sharifian Morocco. At many periods in the history of this inhospitable area, central authority over the Rif was merely nominal. Only at infrequent intervals did sharifian troops arrive to collect tribute and levy tribesmen for laying siege to Melilla.[7]

The peninsula on which the Spanish enclave is situated was the homeland of five Rifian tribes, who constituted the confederacy of the Iqar'ayen. This inter-tribal league was probably created as a reaction to the presence of Christian intruders.[8] It is likely that Islam became popular and militant in these parts of Morocco precisely because of Christian aggression, which was also felt to be a threat to the integrity of the Muslim faith. The reaction often took a religious form and was led by holy men, miracle workers and warrior saints (Julien 1971: 217; Rabinow 1975: 5–8).

The hinterland of Melilla is strewn with shrines of Muslim saints or marabouts, several of whom, according to oral tradition, fiercely opposed the Christian presence in Melilla. They were extraordinary men, who by virtue of their descent from the Prophet Muhammad and of their personal qualities, were considered to be chosen by Allah to intercede on his behalf in human affairs. They were endowed with *baraka*, supernatural power, as a result of their special tie with God. From time to time marabouts made their appearance among the tribes of the Iqar'ayen to preach Holy War against the infidels and rally tribesmen for an attack on the *presidio*. The best documented case is the assault on Melilla led by a marabout named Muhammad ben Alal in 1564. Early that year the captain general was informed by Rifian confidants and frontiersmen who came to sell their products in the *presidio* that a marabout was preparing for a raid. This religious leader had spread the message among the Rifians that his *baraka* and their faith would enable them to take the stronghold without a blow being thrown. They would be immune to Christian bullets and by reciting prayers, they would cause the gates to open automatically at their approach.

The captain-general made plans for an ambush. When the marabout arrived with his followers at the gates of Melilla, they found them open. The excited Berbers penetrated the stronghold and were subjected to a surprise attack. About 150 of them were killed. Two months later the marabout tried to attack the stronghold for a second time, but on this occasion he was supported by 2,000 armed hillmen. Again they were entrapped and more than 200 Rifians were killed and 400 taken prisoner.[9] However, the great majority of Rifian raids were small-scale operations and less spectacular than that described above.

Sometimes the explicit motive for mutual raids seems to have been the desecration of shrines. The following incident is recorded in the parish archive:

> *November 4, 1631*: The Moors succeeded in entering the parade square and pillaged the chapel of the Virgin of Victory, trying to carry off the image and when this turned out to be impossible, they took away the crowns of the Virgin and the Child, a crucifix, the jewels and cut off [the statues'] hands so they could also take the rings [two days later the priest relates that the sacred jewels had been ransomed. — H.D.].[10]

This incident fed a legend that still circulates among the Catholic inhabitants of present-day Melilla. One version has it that one night twelve Moors penetrated the ancient chapel of the Virgin, removed Her image from the platform and tried to carry it away. In spite of their concerted efforts, they were unable to move the image even by an inch. The church bells suddenly began to toll the call to arms. The panic-stricken Moors attacked the statue with their daggers, cut off three fingers of the Virgin's right hand and took to their heels.[11] This story has become part of Catholic lore and serves to prove the powerful protection of the patron saint and the superiority of Catholic faith.

The garrison in turn carried out several raids on the shrine of Sidi Wariach, the spiritual patron of the Iqar'ayen, located in a tiny hamlet some three kilometers from the stronghold. In 1737, for instance, a *razzia* left the shrine partly ruined.[12]

Catholicism on the Frontier

Archival data on everyday religious life in the *presidio* are scarce and scattered. The available evidence suggests that the authorities took great pains to uphold an image of a policy in which the cross stood behind the sword. One gains the impression from the documents that references to religion were intended to convey the message that Catholic devotion was of great consequence in *presidio* life.

The parish of Melilla fell under the jurisdiction of the diocese of Málaga. One of the main tasks of the bishop was the recruitment of the two priests who ministered to the spiritual needs of the garrison, the convicts and the civilians. This seems to have been a difficult task in view of the harsh conditions of Melilla. Sometimes compulsion and punishment were necessary to find candidates for this job (Mir Berlanga 1983: 50). The bishop also took great interest in the conversion of Moors, a matter that will be dealt with below. Direct intervention in the activities of the priests, through visitations, seems to have been rare. This may have been due to the isolation of the enclave and the difficulty of communication.

The installation of captains-general included a ceremony, called *pleito homenaje*, during which the incoming governor swore to defend 'the Mystery of the Pure and Clean Conception,' to which the parish church was devoted. This church was constructed under the aegis of the Capuchins in the second half of the seventeenth century. These friars, who had founded a small monastery in the *presidio*, took great pains to promote the devotion of the Immaculate Conception and placed the church under the patronage of the *Immaculada* (Blasco López 1987, Bravo Nieto 1987).

The arrival of the Capuchin monks set off a lasting competition with the secular clergy who promoted the devotion to *Maria Santissima de la Victoria* (The Virgin of Victory), one of the numerous invocations of the Virgin, proclaimed by Pope Pius V after the victory in 1571 of Christendom over Islam in the battle of Lepanto. How her image — a sixteenth-century product of the Granada school of religious imagery — and her cult were introduced to Melilla is not known. From the late sixteenth century onwards the chapel of the stronghold was dedicated to her cult. Originally she was particularly popular among the military and naval men, but in the course of the eighteenth century she overtook all other devotions in the *presidio*.

The Virgin of Victory's rise to prominence coincided with the most critical era in Melilla's history. The enclave was constantly being subjected to Rifian raids and from 1774 to 1775 suffered an almost fatal siege by the Sultan's troops.[13] At about this time, the idea of abandoning Melilla was gaining headway in Madrid. There were continuous shortages of the necessities of life as Spanish governments left the African *presidios* to their fate, which contributed to low morale in the community. The Virgin of Victory, a symbol of a glorious past, probably came to embody the frontiersmen's last hope.

Accounts of miraculous interventions by the Virgin in situations of acute crisis — famine, storm, plague and siege —

abound in eighteenth-century records. The following note made by a parish priest in 1752 is exemplary:

> One of the ships of the *Plaza* found itself surrounded by three hostile caïques [light boats used by the Rifians. — *H.D.*], but it managed to escape. The crew attributed this to the intervention of Our Lady of Victory, upon whom they had called for help in that dangerous moment; and when they arrived at the port they ascended barefooted in procession to the church as an expression of gratitude.[14]

Four years later the Virgin was finally proclaimed patron of Melilla during a solemn ceremony:

> Does this *Plaza*, its natives and inhabitants promise and swear for themselves and their families perpetual firmness of devotion to the Holiest Mary, Our Mother and Lady of Victory, ratifying the ancient conferment and legitimate possession of this title of patron in the mode that has been laid down? Yes we swear (. . .)[15]

The Virgin and other saints were symbolic weapons in the struggle with the infidels.

Almost the complete toponymy of the *presidio*, the streets and parts of its fortifications were blessed with sacred names and icons, as, for instance, 'the Bastion of Conception,' the 'Gate of Santiago,' the 'Promontory of San Lorenzo,' and 'San Antón street.' The documented and oral history of Melilla reveals above all that at times of crisis religious sentiments and strategies were strong. But how profound was religious experience in daily existence? How rigid were religious observance and control in a remote outpost of Catholicism, where sheer survival was the prime concern, and where many residents represented the worst elements in Spanish society?

Metropolitan Spain did not have a high opinion of the quality of religious life on the frontier. Throughout the sixteenth century Melilla's reputation in religious matters was plainly negative (de Castries 1921 I: xxviii). This was probably partly due to extreme incidents such as the case of a priest who in 1556 took part in a plot to kill the captain-general and surrender the *presidio* to the enemy. The conspiracy was discovered, the priest sentenced to death and executed (Mir Berlanga 1983: 50). From time to time tensions in the relationships between military and religious authorities came into the open, as in the case of a zealous priest who protested against the custom of concubinage and prostitution and who was finally expelled from the enclave (de Castries 1921: I, xxiv). The gulf between religious ideals and prescriptions and the harsh reality on the frontier forced the military authorities to close their eyes to the breaking of religious rules.

Presidio practices sometimes openly clashed with the rules of metropolitan Spain. For instance, between 1606 and 1631 many of the Rifian captives taken during raids were forced to renounce Islam and undergo the rite of baptism. The bishop of Málaga reacted by prohibiting forced conversion (de Morales 1909: 63, 66–7). In the course of the eighteenth century, the government in Madrid intervened in several instances on behalf of Rifians who had been baptised against their will (idem, 179). It does not come as a surprise that towards the middle of the eighteenth century Spanish politicians in favour of abandoning the *presidios* employed arguments of a religious kind. In the words of a governmental commission:

> it is not convenient to our religion to maintain them [the *presidios*], for the cult is being celebrated better in Spain than in those places where iniquity, laxity of customs and scandal visibly reign, apart from the fact that there are very few Moors who embrace our religion, while 198 of our men have been made their slaves over the last ten years.[16]

The 'abandonists' cleverly exploited the profound anxiety for the loss of Christian souls to Islam. The Ibero-African frontier was anything but a watertight religious barrier.

Desertion and Apostasy

From the last quarter of the sixteenth century onwards, the seizure of captives, usually called slaves, began to replace open warfare between Turks and Christians.[17] This issue dominated diplomatic contacts between Barbary and Christian states for the next few centuries, until it was used by the French as one of the justifications for invading Algeria in 1830. For both Muslim and Christian corsairs and privateers the taking of captives represented a substantial part of their booty. The traffic in ransoms and the exchange of captives and goods created a new commercial circuit in the Mediterranean area (cf. Braudel 1976: II, 888).

The seizure of Christian slaves became an acute problem to Spain given its geopolitical position. In fact, one of the reasons for the erection and maintenance of the *presidios* had been to counteract corsair activity. Ironically these enclaves actually exacerbated the problem of Spaniards in Muslim captivity, as a considerable number of Spanish captives originated from these places (Friedman 1983: 48). The prisoners can be roughly divided into two categories, those who were seized during sorties, and convicts and soldiers who deserted to the Muslims. The latter was the larger category and also the most interesting from an anthropological point of view, because the deserters knew that by crossing the frontier they betrayed their religion and society.

In the course of four centuries more than 20,000 men fled from Melilla only to be captured by the Rifians. Many of them apostatised, settled down among the tribes and married Berber women (Fernández de Castro y Pedrera 1919: 118). Desertions were mainly motivated by hardship, the tyranny of *presidio* governors, low pay, poor rations, prolonged military service, and penal servitude. The runaways believed that life among the Muslims could not be worse than *presidio* life. Moreover there was the hope that they would eventually manage to cross over to Spain.

Rifian frontiersmen who seized deserters from Melilla were supposed to hand them over to the Sultan as they were considered slaves of the Moroccan state. However, since central authority and control in the Rif was generally weak or nonexistent, deserters were rarely sent to Fez or Meknes. They were usually sold to Algerian slave traders. This was the fate of the following runaways:

> 1756: eighteen convicts [called *desterrados*, exiled, or *presidiarios* — H.D.] succeeded in breaking out, carrying off as a hostage a captain of the garrison. All of them were taken prisoner by the tribesmen who sold them for 460 *reales* each to the Algerians. The captain perished. Rifian frontiersmen delivered his corpse to the gates of Melilla in return for money.[18]

It was a widespread custom to return the corpses of Christians to the *presidio* for ransom money. Catholics attached great value to giving deceased captives a proper burial for the salvation of their souls. In these cases the final rite was also a ritual of re-incorporation into the community of the faithful.

Sometimes the Rifians took the deserters to the Sultan:

> 1777: two convicts went over to the Moors, who took them to

Meknes, where Sultan Sidi Muhammad invited them to foreswear their faith. When they refused, he handed them over to the Franciscan mission and later allowed them to return to the *presidio*.[19]

The Sultan's decision to give them back their freedom was probably a gesture of goodwill at a time when peace negotiations were being held between Spain and Morocco. Usually, deserters did not receive such benign treatment. They were rarely returned to Spain.[20]

There are also many documented cases of fugitives being tortured and killed on the spot if they were seized by the Rifians:

1826: At ten o'clock in the morning the convict Juan Pedrera broke out to frontier country from the site called La Estacada. He was immediately seized by the Moors who killed him and cut him into pieces. [ritual mutilation of Christian corpses was a common practice among the tribes of the Rif — H.D.]

1829: The corpses of M.L.S., A.C. and J.P., convicts who had deserted, were found hanged in *campo moro*.[21]

1834: The Moors seized various convicts who had been outside the walls to collect greenery for the day of Corpus Christi. They were slaughtered on the spot and split open from top to bottom, hanged and burned in sight of the *presidio*. The governor ordered the convicts to make a sortie and pick up the remains of their comrades; however, they were terrified and refused, whereupon the commander ordered them to shave off their whiskers as a sign of cowardice. This and urging of sergeant Antonio López Roldán made them react. They went out, drove back the Moors and recovered the bodily remains.[22]

The fate of most fugitives is simply unknown as in the following case:

1848: Three hundred convicts made a sortie without success; nineteen of them deserted and many lost their weapons.[23]

The Redemptorist and Trinitarian monks who were sent to Morocco and Algeria to redeem Christian captives had a vested interest in depicting their condition as negatively as possible, with the aim of arousing sympathy for the Christian slaves and thus ransom money to buy them back. The myths of the cruel treatment of captives and forced conversions, created and perpetuated by the accounts of these monks, were mostly taken at face value and played an important role in arousing Christian zeal against the Infidel (Thomson 1987: 26–7).

The widespread notion among contemporary Spaniards that Christian captives were constantly being pressed to become Muslims does not seem to be justified. Deserters who became slaves of the Moroccan state were not permitted to convert to Islam while still enslaved, since they were not regarded as trustworthy and their economic value was reduced or lost when they apostatised (Friedman 1983: 47,77). Rifian Berbers, however, often adopted deserters who expressed a wish to go over to Islam. The number of absconders who apostatised, married a Rifian woman and became members of a tribe is not known. Only at the beginning of Spanish colonial penetration of the Rif were several cases of captives and deserters who 'had gone native' discovered. Consider the following cases:

> In the early nineteenth century a fisherman from Tarifa called López was seized by corsairs on the coast of Western Morocco. He passed through several Berber tribes till he was finally adopted by the Ait Bu Gafar in the vicinity of Melilla. He converted to Islam, took the name of Mimum and married a local woman. His first son, Dudu ben Mimum, took service in the *Tiradores del Rif* [the first voluntary corps of native soldiers in the service of Spain, founded in 1859 — H.D.] and fought at Tetuan during the war of 1859–60. After the war he returned to his native tribe.
>
> In the 1920s a man called 'El moro Joaquín' was a popular figure in Melilla. Born in Aragón, condemned to ten years of *presidio* for manslaughter, he deserted, apostatised and was adopted by a leader of the Ait Waryaghar in the central Rif, one of whose daughters he married. He assumed the name of Muhammad Si Bukar [the name of his patron and ritual father — H.D.]. During the pacification war of the Rif (1919–25) he acted as a go-between for the release of Spanish prisoners in the hands of Abd el Krim. After the war King Alfonso XIII pardoned him and he received permission to visit his mother in Aragón.[24]

I examined 156 documented cases of desertion for the period 1820–1855.[25] The overwhelming majority of runaways were common criminals who had been condemned to eight or ten years of penal servitude for such offences as 'blasphemy of God and the Virgin' (ten years), highway robbery (ten years), cattle rustling (eight years), the 'theft of silverware from the cathedral of Seville' (ten years), homicide (ten years). Political prisoners among the convicts rarely attempted to break out.

The first measure taken when a case of desertion was discovered was to ring the bells 'que designa hombre al moro'
('signalling man to the Moor'), which communicated to the
Rifian frontiersmen that a man had escaped. They were re-
warded when they returned deserters to the *presidio*. A report
was written of the circumstances, possible accomplices etc. The
most interesting passages in these reports concern the procedures followed when an absconder was returned or gave
himself up. Let us consider two cases in detail:

> In 1820 a convict named Manuel Rodriguez managed to escape to
> 'campo infiel'.[26] Born in Valencia, condemned for robbery, he ar-
> rived at Melilla in 1817 at the age of twenty-one. More than a year
> after his desertion he reported to the guards at the gates of Melilla as
> 'Catholic, Roman, and Apostolic.' The report emphasises that he
> 'was dressed in the Moorish fashion'. He was subjected to long
> cross-examinations by officers and the priest who were eager to find
> out whether he had apostatised. The procedure included a medical
> examination of his private parts in order to find out if he had been
> circumcised. When it turned out that this had not been the case,
> Rodriguez was acquitted of 'having committed the crime of renuncia-
> tion or at least that he has not been marked as a renegade by way of
> circumcision.' He told the authorities that he had been sold to a
> master who 'kept telling me that another Christian had embraced his
> sect and all rites and ceremonies according to Moorish law (. . .)
> However, I never stopped being a Christian, commending myself
> constantly to Our Lord and to the Queen of Angels, Our Holiest
> Mary'. When asked by his master whether he was a Moor or Christian,
> he kept repeating that he was a Christian, an answer which pro-
> voked bastinados. Finally, he was sold to another master to whom he
> lied that he had been circumcised at Fez. From that day he pretended
> to be a Muslim. After having learned from a Moor in the service of
> the American Consul that the King of Spain had declared a general
> pardon for deserters, he awaited his opportunity to escape to the
> *presidio*.

> In 1825 Lorenzo Cerda, a thief of twenty-three, was condemned to
> ten years of penal servitude in Melilla. The same year, while tilling
> the land in the outer precinct, he managed to escape. Seven years
> later he returned, and was placed in quarantine for six weeks. When
> asked why he had deserted, he replied 'because of bad thoughts.'
> The Rifians who had seized Cerda sold him to a landowner who put
> him to work in his fields. The runaway declared that he soon
> regretted his deed and planned to return to the 'bosom of Christian-

ity'. But, he claimed to have been circumcised by force, although, as he told his interrogators, he had opposed this operation violently. The Moors were convinced that he now had become a Moor and would never dare to return to his former colleagues of the same faith. 'My wish to return to the true faith grew stronger and stronger (. . .) and I never expelled from my mind (*imaginación*) the prayers which I have recited since my childhood. I refused to devote myself to the orations which the Moors tried to teach me.' He stated that he prayed daily in secrecy. Finally, after many years, he managed to escape and gave himself up to the garrison of Melilla. The Ecclesiastical Court ruled that in view of 'clear and definite statements by the deserter on having apostatised our Sacred Religion, when he underwent, as he told, the operation carried out by the Moors according to their rites and customary for those who abjure the faith, and in view of the fact that he was violently subjected to this operation, we impose on him the usual penances.' The military court, in its turn, decided to extend his servitude by five years. Some months later Cerda again took to the Moors. An eye-witness had seen him talking with two Rifians who took off in the direction of Farjana [a village some three kilometers from Melilla — H.D.].

It was considered of prime importance when deserters or captives returned to Christian territory to establish whether they had apostatised. Religion defined the essence of personhood. The interrogators primarily focused on bodily proofs of renunciation. Circumcision simply marked them as Muslims. It was only of minor importance whether renegades had embraced Islam of their own free will, or had been forced to do so. The Ecclesiastical Court was not really interested in the other parts of the rite of initiation into Islam, such as shaving the skull, the major ritual ablution (*ghusl*), the declaration of faith which simply involved the recitation of 'There is no God but God and Muhammad is His messenger,' and the festive meal.

Sometimes renegades mentioned one or more of these elements, apart from adoption by a Muslim patron, the acceptance of an Islamic name, and the wearing of Moorish attire. Rarely did the interrogators pursue these points. Unfortunately, we do not know what the 'usual penances' involved, because they were never specified in the reports. We do know, however, that the return of ransomed captives was celebrated with great religious pomp. The case of deserters was, of course, different because they were perceived as traitors to Christianity.

The second case reveals the ease with which convicts switched sides. It is very probable that their motives in converting to

Islam were purely opportunistic, for they must have been aware that by abdicating their own faith they could improve their living conditions. There were also some spectacular cases of conversion, as, for instance, the case of the Francisan monk Anselm Turmeda of Catalonia, who during his captivity, embraced Islam and started a career as a Muslim saint. One of the implications of renegation was the transfer to the Muslim world of European skills, in particular with regard to navigation and warfare. When Moroccans did encourage conversion, this applied to deserters or captives who had valuable skills to offer (cf. Friedman 1983: 89).

The number of Muslims who became Christians was considerably lower. Again there are two different classes of converts, those who were seized during raids and subsequently enslaved and those who sought refuge in Melilla. Eighteenth-century documents make a distinction between 'free' and 'enslaved' converted Muslims:

> 1724: Manuel Nicolás, free New Christian, received the Holy Baptism which he asked when in mortal danger; it was administered to him without solemnity.
>
> 1756: Death of Maria Gertrudis, born in Cazaza [a village near Melilla — H.D.], where she had been made a captive. She was baptized and married to a soldier.
>
> 1812: A Moor took refuge in this *Plaza* together with his daughter, fleeing from his own people, and both embraced our Religion, the latter was named Maria del Carmen Gúzman who married lieutenant Federico Martín.
>
> 1834: Two Moors took refuge in this *Plaza*; one of them returned to frontier country, while the other became a Christian. He was sent to Málaga for further religious instruction.
>
> 1835: Death of Don Fernando Carlos Benjaimut, second lieutenant, catechumen and renegade of the Mohammedan sect, baptized in the city of Ceuta, married to Sedima.[27]

At times Muslim captives were forced to convert to Christianity, a practice usually condemned by Spanish civil and religious authorities, as the following cases show:

> At the beginning of the eighteenth century a Rifian informer in the service of the captain general was badly wounded. Since it was feared that he would die, the priest was called to baptise him. However, when the man recovered and expressed the wish to return to his native tribe, the captain general refused to let him go. The case

was finally brought before the court in Madrid and in 1710 the King decreed that he had the right to return to his own people.

Some years later, the King wrote a letter to the captain general arguing that 'it is not right that Moors who come to the *Plaza* in the confidence of being treated benignly, are being enslaved. If they have not chosen to become Christian out their own free will, they must be set free.'[28]

Central authority showed itself much more tolerant towards Muslims than its representatives at the *presidio*, a fact that caused bitter rancour among its inhabitants.[29]

Another strategy of christianisation was the adoption of Rifian children. This practice persisted well into the nineteenth century as the following cases show:

In 1859 a mariner starts a procedure to adopt an orphaned Muslim boy. Several 'Moors of the frontier land' appear before the notary to declare that the boy has no parents or other kin. The mariner promises that the boy will be 'educated according to the Christian doctrine of our religion and will be baptised.' One month later the boy is returned to his 'native land.' All attempts to christianise him have failed ('because of a profound obstinacy on the part of the African'). Moreover, in the meantime an uncle has come to claim the boy.

In 1862 a merchant appears before the public notary expressing his wish to adopt a Moorish girl of about eight years old, whom he plans to send to Málaga 'in order to educate her in our customs, teaching her our sacred religion and make her a Christian.' The Moorish interpreter of the *presidio* declares that he knows the girl as an orphan, while the child herself indicates that she is willing to go to Málaga.[30]

Initiation to Catholicism was in one respect simpler than conversion to Islam. Whereas circumcision was the focal rite of passage in Islam, in Christianity it was baptism. In another respect it was more complicated, since more emphasis was placed upon 'education in the Christian Law' for which catechumenes were sent to Málaga, obviously a rite of separation and incorporation. The converts also adopted a Christian name, usually that of their godparents, and Western dress. It is significant to note that on both sides of the Mediterranean conversion automatically entailed naturalisation, which indicates how intimately religious identity was linked to political status. The first case I could find of naturalisation without conversion was in 1863 when 141 frontiersmen of Farjana, Ait Shikar and Ait Sidar, and four Jews from Tetuan collectively applied for Spanish citizenship without giving up their religion. After ample inquiries into their background their request was granted in a ceremony in which they had to pledge allegiance to the Queen of Spain: 'the Muslims by turning their face to the east, swearing by Allah, Muhammad and the penalties of the Quran, and the Jews by their God and what they consider to be their Holy Scriptures.'[31] The Rifians were only interested in getting a passport, which they needed for travelling to the Oranie in Algeria to work on the farms of French colonists, while the Jews planned to settle in Melilla for business. This case points at the diminishing role of religion in the definition of citizenship and the gradual emergence of Spanish tolerance for alien religious belief and practices.

Breaches in the Frontier

Whereas in Spain all Muslims were indiscriminately called *moros*, the inhabitants of the *presidio* distinguished several categories. The main class was *moro fronterizo* as opposed to *moro del rey*, frontiersman or Rifian and Arab under the Sultan's rule respectively. A second distinction was that between *moro de paz* and *moro de guerra*. 'Moor of peace' and 'Moor of war'. The boundary between these categories was rather fluid. Peaceful, subjected Muslims who had traded with the enclave for years, could easily turn into enemies and vice-versa. In the late 1850s, for instance, warriors of the neighbouring tribe of Ait Sidar harassed the enclave for days. Then several of the aggressors changed their attitude overnight and became traders who entered the town peacefully to conduct commerce. In order to teach them a lesson, the governor had them lashed and driven out of town.[32] In 1859 members of several tribes who had attacked the garrison in preceding years enlisted in the first native unit of the Spanish army recruited for the war in Western Morocco. Finally, there was a category of Moors who lived in the *presidio*, mostly as enslaved captives. A number of them were used as *moros de rescate* or ransom Moors, for there were periodic exchanges of captives at the gates of Melilla. A special category was that of *confidente*, informer, spy or confidant, who also acted as interpreter.

While raid and counter-raid, a form of negative reciprocity, was a basic institution of frontier society, trade or balanced reciprocity was even more important. Although frequently forbidden by the central authorities of Morocco and Spain, commercial exchanges between Melilla and the neighbouring tribes had always been an integral part of life on the frontier. Even the powerful Sultan Isma'il (1672–1727), whose long reign brought political stability and some measure of central control over the Rif, was unable to enforce his ban on trade between the *presidios* and the surrounding tribes. As early as the sixteenth century Spanish coins and vocabulary circulated widely among Rifians (cf. de Castries 1921 II: 14–32). *Moros de paz* were usually permitted to enter the outer precinct of the stronghold daily to sell their produce, mainly grain, olive oil, fruit, vegetables, chickens and sheep. When relationships with the tribes were particularly tense, trade took place at the gates of the outer bastion. Commerce was only infrequently interrupted by sieges and raids.

Throughout its history, Melilla acted as a refuge or sanctuary for those Muslims who were persecuted or who fled tribal feuding and civil war. Some of these refugees went over to Christendom. At times Muslims also paid fraternal visits to the *presidio*. The following case was rather exceptional:

> 1782: 'The crown prince Abd-er-Rahman, son of Sidi Muhammad [Sultan of Morocco — H.D.], entered the *plaza* with five of his servants. He was profusely entertained and showed a great liking for alcoholic drinks. This visit was very exceptional, for Muslim princes are forbidden to enter Christian towns.'[33]

Muslims were also aware of the superiority of European medical science for there are many instances of them asking for medical treatment in the enclave:

> 1807: An important frontiersman asked for medical assistance, which was procured for him in exchange for four cows, thirty sheep, and four quintals of olive oil.[34]
>
> 1848: Frontiersmen were shooting at the *plaza* when they abruptly ceased fire and hoisted the 'flag of parley'. Thereupon a Moor of the Sultan approached the *plaza* and manifested that he was ill and wanted to enter hospital. The commander told him that they first had to stop hostilities and hand over the deserters. But when his comrades did not agree, fire was reopened.[35]

During periods of hostility the garrison and its adversaries communicated through shots and the *bandera de parlamento* (flag of parley, to indicate that they wanted to negotiate) and the *bandera de paz* (flag of peace or truce). This flag code was rarely abused. The following is a most uncommon incident:

> 1839: the Moors hoisted the flag of parley and asked for negotiations with the governor; when the latter presented himself, they started to fire at him.[36]

What we tend to see as contradictions in the dealings between Muslims and Christian frontiersmen are in fact breaches in the frontier, which grew wider and wider as the nineteenth century wore on. The pressures of European colonialism, together with civil war in Morocco and intra and intertribal feuding in the Rif, helped to bring about a profound transformation of the His-pano-African frontier. Both Spanish and Moroccan authorities perceived and represented the Spanish-Moroccan frontier for more than four centuries as a hard and fast line of division between 'civilisation' and 'savagery', a divide that was mainly defined in terms of religion. In daily life, however, it was a zone of interaction between two different cultures, which, in spite of religious antagonisms, knew very well how to deal with one another in various ways.

As I have tried to show, there was considerable movement across the frontier, which suggests that the *presidio* and its neighbouring tribes in fact constituted a single frontier society. Both parties in this society were far removed from the centres of power, ideology and control, and dependent upon each other in several respects. This created room for other than hostile modes of communication. Thus at the fringes of Catholic and Islamic society boundaries of religious practice failed to coincide neatly with the boundaries of language, polity and economy.

Chapter 3

From Presidio to Trading Post

We have seen that trans-frontier dealings between Melilla and the Iqar'ayen frequently occurred, in spite of religious and cultural differences, mutual hate and endemic hostility. On the other hand, long-distance trade between the Andalusian ports of Málaga and Cádiz and the coastal tribes of northern Morocco was much more irregular. But, in spite of its irregularity, this trade could be extremely important. For instance, one of the crucial factors in the rise to power during the seventeenth century of the Alawites, the present dynasty of Morocco, was the control it gained over the trade between Morocco's deep South and the Mediterranean. Guns and ammunition were purchased from European merchants in exchange for goods from the southern oases and Western Sudan (Fogg 1940: 94; Abun Nasr 1971: 226; Brignon *et al.* 1967: 239–40).

Melilla acted as a landing-place for European merchandise. The Spanish and Moroccan states usually considered this trade to be smuggling, although they lacked the means to ban it. From time to time the Sultans sent punitive expeditions into the Rif when they learned of illegal selling of cattle and barley to European merchants (cf. Houdas 1969: 194–5). The smuggling of weapons, ammunition and tobacco to the Rif constituted a constant preoccupation for successive Spanish governments (cf. de Castries 1921: I, 49–50, 52–54; II, 14–16, 25, 32, 475, 480).

The locally circumscribed trade between the *presidio* and the tribes of the hinterland was mainly dictated by Melilla's immediate subsistence needs. However, when in the course of the nineteenth century the competition between the European powers for access to the Moroccan market became increasingly aggressive, Melilla was drawn into a wide international network of commerce. As the only port of importance between Ceuta in the West and Oran in the East, Melilla became a major base for colonial penetration. In the course of the shifting of the Ibero-

African frontier both Melilla and Rifian society were radically transformed.

Spanish Expansion and Rifian Resistance

Ever since Spain gained a foothold in Morocco, the relations between them had been strained, constantly alternating between open confrontation and delicate entente. Diplomatic ties were frequently threatened by endemic piracy and the failure of the central power in Morocco to bring the tribes of the northern fringe under lasting and effective control. The first half of the nineteenth century witnessed an increasingly massive and aggressive commercial invasion of Morocco by Britain and France. Spain resented the virtual monopoly England had obtained over Morocco's foreign trade and feared the growing influence of France on internal Moroccan affairs from French Algeria.

Around 1850 some politicians, military leaders and merchants began discussions in Madrid about the need to define and further Spanish interests in the 'dark' continent. When in 1859 local tribesmen attacked new fortifications at Ceuta, Spain was presented with an excuse for direct military intervention. Spanish troops crushed tribal forces and occupied Tetuan in February 1860. Morocco had to settle on unfavourable terms in a peace treaty signed in May 1860. Apart from huge financial compensation, the treaty provided for the extension of Ceuta and Melilla, and the stationing of Sharifian troops in the vicinity of the enclaves to prevent attacks by local tribes.

This treaty marked the beginning of a period of rapid decline in Morocco's economy and state power. The growing dissidence and subversion in the areas beyond the central Atlantic plain contributed to a rapid decline in state revenues. In the last quarter of the century the trans-Saharan trade — a major source of income for Morocco — was reduced drastically, mainly because of the European penetration of West Africa from which much of that trade originated.[1] Within a few decades Morocco had been caught in a web of mounting loans and debts spun by the major European colonial powers.

The 1860s saw the emergence in Spain of the so-called *Africanismo*, the Spanish manifestation of a general European ideological current aimed at the exploration of the territories and peoples of Africa and a civilising mission in this continent through trade (cf. Morales Lezcano 1984: 43ff). In 1876 the *Real Sociedad Geográfica* was founded, which devoted much attention to Africa. Seven years later the Spanish Society of Africanists and Colonists was formed. This society consisted largely of missionaries, especially Franciscans who did some missionary work in Morocco, army officers and businessmen. The first Spanish colonies in Africa, Rio de Oro (Spanish Sahara) and Rio Muñi (Spanish Guinea) were formally occupied. The *africanistas* advocated a policy of using the *presidios* to establish a special link between Spain and Morocco, turning the neighbour into a client state, while at the same time undermining British, French and German interests. Sharifian expeditions sent from Fez to the northeast to compel the Iqar'ayen to pay their taxes were generally received well by the authorities of Melilla. It became a policy to regale their commanders with gifts (cf. de Morales 1920: 149).

The Moroccan troops stationed at Qasba Silwan near to Melilla were unable to control the local tribes, let alone prevent them from assaulting the *presidio*. In 1878, for instance, tribesmen revolted against the regional representative of the Sultan, looted his residence, killed his son and two brothers, and obliged him to flee (idem: 134). From time to time the bey had to seek refuge in Melilla (cf. de Morales 1909: 335, 337). Local tribes strongly resented the customs barrier which the Sultan had established between the Spanish enclave and their own territories.

After a series of violent incidents in the 1880s, the Spanish decided to build new fortifications in the territory acquired under the 1860 peace treaty. The construction of a fort only a stone's throw from the sanctuary of Sidi Wariach, the spiritual patron of the Iqar'ayen, provoked new hostilities against the enclave. In 1893 a brief but bloody war ensued between Spanish troops and tribesmen (cf. Llanos y Alcaraz 1894). Iqar'ayen oral tradition claims that Spanish soldiers desecrated the shrine by urinating against it. This serious incident almost provoked an armed conflict between Spain and the Sultanate. Morocco had to allow the Spanish to station troops outside the boundaries of Melilla, which was the first step in military expansion.

In the early twentieth century Morocco was further weakened by civil war. In 1902, Bu Hmara, a pretender to the Sultanate who claimed to be Mulay Muhammad's brother, was proclaimed Sultan in Taza. Supported by the French and most of the tribes in the Taza region, he was able to conquer northeastern Morocco, crushing the Sharifian forces, the remnants of

which had to take refuge in Melilla. In 1903 Bu Hmara established his headquarters at Qasba Silwan and for the next five
years Iqar'ayen remained under his control. Spain, which remained neutral, saw its *presidio* flooded by thousands of Jewish,
Rifian and Arab refugees. When Bu Hmara sold mining concessions to Spanish businessmen in 1907 around Wixan in Ait
Bu Ifrur territory, the Iqar'ayen who had supported the Pretender turned against him and finally drove him out.[2]

Meanwhile the European powers defined their areas of influence. In 1904, Britain agreed to allow France a free hand in
Morocco, while Spain and France agreed to divide the country
into a French and Spanish zone of interest. Spain accepted the
north between the Muluya river in the east and the city of
Larache in the west. These arrangements were respected in the
Treaty of Algeciras in 1906 and finally resulted in the declaration
of the French and Spanish Protectorates in 1912.

At first, Spain followed a policy of 'peaceful penetration' in
imitation of General Lyauty's strategy. The 'barbarian or semi-
barbarian peoples had to be civilised by means of trade'.[3] While
Spain tried to implement this policy between 1900 and 1907 by
remaining neutral in the Moroccan civil war, it soon became
obvious this policy was doomed to fail. The local newspaper of
Melilla, for instance, was constantly creating an atmosphere to
justify direct military intervention. It applied the term *moro*
mostly in a malignant sense as infidel, barbarian, rebellious, and
untrustworthy. It published endless and detailed reports on
'acts of Rifian barbarism' and 'cruel warfare' and laments about
the 'insecurity of roads, banditry and anarchy' in the Rif. The
newspaper was a powerful instrument in producing and repro-
ducing colonial fantasies about Rifian wildness, which indicate a
mixture of contempt and fear. Thus by 1907 the policy of 'peaceful penetration' had given way to the policy of 'bread in one
hand and the stick in the other' (cf. Lobera Girela 1912: 155).

In 1908, General Marina, military governor of Melilla, seized
Restinga, a trading post founded by the French with permission
of Bu Hmara, and left in its place a Spanish garrison, 'happily
accomplishing the first deed of Spanish expansion in Africa,' as
a contemporary chronicler put it (de Morales 1920: 38). In the
meantime Spanish labourers proceeded with the construction of
a railway between the mines of Wixan and the port of Melilla.
When in 1909 local tribesmen attacked these works, killing
seven labourers, Spain had an excuse to invade and occupy the

entire Iqar'ayen area. Between 1909 and 1911 the first extensive pacification campaigns were conducted in the eastern Rif to protect Spanish mining concessions against Rifian assaults.

Tribal resistance was led by Sidi Mohand Ameziane, the last warrior saint of the Rif. He belonged to a holy lineage in the territory of the Ait Bu Ifrur tribe not far from Wixan where the Spanish had started to mine iron ore. The shrines of this lineage, the *zawiya* of Seghanghan, constituted one of the most sacred sites of the Eastern Rif. Sidi Mohand was the last and most prestigious *sharif* of this lineage, not only because he displayed all the qualities of his forebears but also because of his heroic role in Rifian history. Stories about his courage and the miracles surrounding his exploits are still told in the Rif.[4]

I will deal with Sidi Mohand's political career at some length because he represents the traditional Rifian leadership which became extinct after the establishment of the Spanish Protectorate. He was born in the Ait Bu Ifrur tribe in the 1860s. As a member of a prestigious sacred lineage, he was destined to become a local leader who participated in all important ceremonies of the tribal council, and who acted as a mediator in intra- and inter-tribal feuding. He was an intelligent man with a strong character, a talent for persuading and organising people, and with a great love of his native region. Trade brought him regularly to Algeria where he became very popular among Rifian migrant workers. For reasons of security these men preferred to travel with him from their homelands to the Oranie where they worked on colonial farms, for nobody dared to attack a caravan led by this *sharif*. In the spring of 1909 Sidi Mohand began to preach resistance at tribal councils and weekly markets and rallied support for attacks on Spanish mining and railway works.

Spanish troops succeeded in occupying the Iqar'ayen territory at the close of 1909, following some fierce fighting. Confronted with superior Spanish troops, heavy losses and dissidence within his own ranks, the warrior saint had to retreat behind the river Kart in the west. In the summer of 1911 he had gathered enough warriors and arms to resume raids on Spanish convoys and property. Sidi Mohand was always to be found in the forefront of any battle, often engaging in hand-to-hand fighting. His daring and legendary courage, together with the fact that he escaped death several times, earned him the reputation among Rifians, that his *baraka* (supernatural force) made him immune to Christian bullets.[5]

Finally, in the summer of 1912, on a reconnaissance expedition, Sidi Mohand and his fighters met with a large Spanish force. When he saw that the majority of Spanish soldiers were *regulares* — Rifians in the service of the Spanish colonial army[6] — he tried to approach them giving signals that he wanted to confer. However, he was neither recognised nor were his signals understood. The *regulares* opened fire and Sidi Mohand fell mortally wounded, killed by men from his own people.[7] After his death, Rifian resistance lost its momentum and crumbled. Another decade passed before a new leader was able to rally the Rifian tribes to a common cause once again.

It took the Spanish more than fifteen years to establish effective control over the rest of their Protectorate. Beyond the river Kart to the west, the Rif was an isolated region, inhospitable and largely uncharted by Europeans. The hostile landscape, lack of roads, dispersed settlement pattern, fragmented political structure and the strong sense of honour and independence of the Berber inhabitants, made it extremely difficult to colonise the Rifian heartlands. The Spanish were only able to make very slow military advances by erecting makeshift camps which were, however, difficult to provision. At the same time, the colonial authorities continued to seek out prestigious local leaders (*hombres de prestigio*) whom they tried to bribe into becoming *amigos de España* by offering them all kinds of privileges.

One of these men was Si Mohand 'n Si 'Abd al-Krim, son of a local *fqih* and *qadi* of the Ait Waryaghar in the central Rif.[8] This leader maintained contacts with merchants and officers of the small island of Alhucemas, which had been occupied by the Spanish since 1673. His younger brother was one of the first Rifians ever to receive Western education. 'Abd al-Krim first received traditional education at the local Quran school at Tetuan and at the famous *Qarawiyin* in Fez before he attended Spanish school in Alhucemas, where he also served as an interpreter. In 1906 he was sent to Melilla for further education and soon became editor of the Arabic section of the local daily newspaper. His friendship with Spanish officers, especially Colonel de Morales, Director of the Central Office of Native Affairs and a local historian, enabled him to rise rapidly to the rank of *qadi* for the entire eastern Rif. He gradually came to resent the corrupt, inefficient and rapacious way in which the Spanish managed their Protectorate.

Influenced by the Young Turks movement and by the Islamic

Reform movement of Salafiya, he began to write anti-Spanish articles for which he was jailed. However, he was reinstated in office after serving his prison term. When he heard about plans to occupy the entire Rif he asked permission to return to his homeland where he began to rally support for resisting the Spanish advance. In the early summer of 1921 he eliminated Spanish advance posts all the way back to the gates of Melilla, killing or capturing more than half of the Spanish occupation army. The city was defended by the Ait Shikar, the only tribe that remained loyal to the Spanish, and rescued by shock troops.

'Abd al-Krim became the leader of one of the first nationalist independence movements of the Arab world. He represented a new type of leadership, a modern guerilla chief and nationalist politician. He drastically reformed Rifian society along Salafiya lines and turned against popular Islam, the maraboutic cult and local customary law. It took the Spanish army five years of fierce struggle before it was finally able, with French support, to destroy 'Abd al-Krim's Republic of the Confederated Tribes of the Rif. In May 1926 'Abd al-Krim surrendered to the French, and by July 1927 Spanish Morocco had been fully pacified.

Spain, itself a poor country ravaged by political turmoil, used the Protectorate principally for a training ground for its army, and secondarily for the extraction of iron ore. Only in the late 1940s were serious efforts made to initiate a development plan for the area.

When Spain resigned its Protectorate in 1956, it left a poor infrastructure and an impoverished, largely illiterate population. After an abortive uprising against the central government in the late 1950s, Rifians began to emigrate *en masse* to Western Europe. Today, the north-eastern zone of Morocco is one of the most depressed areas of the country.

Life on the Frontier

When the 'War of Africa' between Spain and Morocco ended in 1860, the *presidio* had a population of 1,874, of whom 1,500 belonged to the garrison and penitentiary. Among the civilians there were sixty 'foreigners'. This frontier society was overwhelmingly male. Spouses of officers, domestic servants and prostitutes number 172 (cf. de Morales 1909: 596). These people lived a hard and monotonous life within a small, compact and heavily fortified area.

In 1864 the first step was taken to open up the *presidio*. Spanish citizens (called 'nationals') were permitted to take up residence freely, *solteras* (unmarried women) included. Increasing commercial activity began to attract Spanish and Jewish immigrants. By 1880 the civil population had almost doubled and the number of female inhabitants increased considerably.[9] The old town was too small to accommodate the newcomers, so the military authorities gave permission for the construction of new dwellings beyond the old walls of the fortified settlement. Over the next five years the civilian population almost doubled once again, and included 1,023 'nationals' (528 women) and 153 'foreigners' (72 women). Of these only 300 were born in Melilla. The majority were immigrants from the eight Andalusian provinces, with over half (264 out of 427) coming from Málaga; 112 came from Castile, and the remainder were Jews from Tetuan.[10] Almost 400 inhabitants were living in the rapidly growing trading barrio of Mantelete, which grew up opposite the port. In 1886 this barrio consisted of 113 wooden shacks, twenty-seven shops and workshops, thirty-two taverns, four cafes, nine brick-and-plaster houses and two iron sheds (cf. de Morales 1909: 599).

The population continued to grow at an accelerating pace, mainly due to heavy immigration. By the turn of the century it amounted to almost 6,000 civilians, 2,750 officers and men, and 380 exiled convicts.[11] Several new provisional barrios sprang up far beyond the walls of the old town. In 1904 King Alfonso XIII paid an official visit and laid the first brick for the construction of a new port. This was an important symbolic act in two respects. He was the first Spanish king to set foot in Melilla, emphasising by his visit Spain's new colonial ambitions. The ceremony also marked the beginning of a new era in the history of Melilla. Two years later the penal colony was closed down, another symbolically charged event. The local authorities celebrated the removal of this ugly stain from their society as part of a civilising mission.[12]

The civil war that divided Morocco from 1902 until 1908 brought thousands of Rifian, Arab and Jewish refugees to Melilla. In 1905, there were still 3,400 Rifian and Arab and 200 Jewish refugees living in provisional encampments.[13] Most of these destitute people had to be fed by the local government and constituted a heavy burden on the municipal budget. All the Jewish refugees became permanent inhabitants.

Bu Hmara's granting of mining concessions to Spanish businessmen in 1907 marked the beginning of a true urban and demographic explosion. That year the *Compañia Norte Africano* was founded in Madrid and Melilla with a nominal capital of ten million pesetas to initiate the mining of lead in the enclave's hinterland. In 1908 the *Sociedad Española de Minas del Rif*, based in Madrid, Bilbao and Melilla, invested a nominal capital of four million pesetas in the exploitation of iron ore mines at Wixan. (Morales Lezcano 1984: 187). The latter was to become the major limited liability company of northern Morocco. A recently-opened office of the Banco de España coordinated the flows of investments and profits from the companies.

The military occupation of Melilla's hinterland, the railway and mining works, and the pacification campaigns attracted a wave of new immigrants, mainly from Andalusia. The enclave was flooded by thousands of labourers, hundreds of artisans, small tradesmen, saloon keepers, adventurers and prostitutes. They followed in the wake of the military convoys brought over to Melilla to protect the exploitation of ore mines and to consolidate Spanish authority in the newly conquered territories. Local entrepreneurs feverishly built new barrios of wooden and corrugated iron shacks, mostly in the shadow of the military barracks, to house the stream of immigrants. The rapid expansion of the garrison, which had to be provisioned, was a major factor in the growth of economic activity. The pulse of economic life came to be intimately linked to the size of the military population. By 1920 the civil population of Melilla came close to 40,000 (see table 3.1).

This population was living in eighteen barrios. The breakdown according to religion and nationality illustrated in this table shows that Melilla was becoming a pan-Mediterranean, cosmopolitan society.

The large-scale war of pacification of the 1920s gave a new impetus to population growth. In 1925 the garrison of Melilla reached its greatest level with 41,110 soldiers and officers. After the pacification of the Rif it decreased to 14,000. The civil population, however, continued to grow rapidly, from 52,000 in 1925 to 61,000 in 1930 and 71,000 in 1935.[14] Further increases between 1935 and 1945 were mainly due to the rise of the birth rate and the decline of the death rate, especially of infants, together with a steady influx of Rifians. The population reached its peak in 1945 with 86,500 and then began to drop slowly.[15]

Towards the end of the nineteenth century the occupational

Table 3.1   De facto population according to the Padrón of 1917, Archivo Municipal de Melilla (*A.M.M.*)

	male	female	total
Spaniards	15,897	17,728	33,625
Jews	1,480	1,423	2,903
Muslims	153	81	234
French	38	70	108
English	3	4	7
Germans	2	6	8
Americans	4	13	17
Swiss	3	4	7
Turks	2	3	5
Portuguese	1	2	3
Cubans	39	36	75
Indians	12	–	12
Italians	–	4	4
Norwegians	3	–	3
Chileans	2	3	5
Total	17,639	19,377	37,016

structure was in the process of complete transformation. Within a brief period of time it had changed radically as the following brief comparison between 1882 and 1907 shows.[16] In the early 1880s the professional population still consisted largely of military artisans and convicts. There were twenty-one civil servants, four priests, a doctor, a pharmacist, a notary, four teachers, twenty-three artisans (bakers, shoemakers, barbers, bricklayers, a miller, a carpenter and a tailor), five seamen, two fishermen, ten casual labourers, seventy-one traders, twenty-one female domestic servants, three gardeners and two property owners. Twenty-five years later the municipal census listed more than 150 different occupations. Casual labourers, who numbered more than 600, were by far the largest occupational group, followed by artisans with a predominance of bricklayers (163) and eighty-four carpenters who found plenty of work thanks to the construction boom. Twenty-two barbers and sixty-three shoemakers served the population. More than 400 men were listed as trader, testifying to the rapid growth of the commercial sector. The bureaucracy was staffed by almost 100 civil servants. The presence of 226 female domestic servants and 130 seam-

stresses indicates that the town housed a substantial bourgeoisie.

Melilla's economic hinterland increased vastly with the establishment of the Protectorate. The abolition of the customs barrier
and the intensification of mining and agriculture boosted the
volume of trade, as we will see below. In fact, Melilla became
the capital of the entire Rif up to the Muluya river and economic life was geared to transit trade and service. Apart from
some small food-processing and artisanal workshops, there was
little development in the industrial sector. Due to the massive
influx of unskilled and illiterate workers from Andalusia, Murcia
and Valencia in the 1920s, the proletariat grew disproportionately
large. Unemployment became a grave problem and gave rise to
serious class tensions in the early 1930s, mainly in the Catholic
and Jewish population.

The rapid and unplanned urban growth, and the harsh primitive capitalistic ambience generated all kinds of social problems. A
large proportion of the immigrants consisted of uprooted people,
especially those who came from the Iberian Peninsula. The
mixture of religious and ethnic groups characteristic of frontier life
in the first decades of this century created profound social tensions. First, there was the basic problem of widespread poverty.
Thousands of immigrants, unable to find regular employment,
lived packed together in caves and wooden hovels. This problem
was exacerbated in the first decade of this century by the large
number of refugees. In 1905 the press announced that it was
becoming the rule for two or three families to share one room of
ten metres square:

> living under conditions of horrible promiscuity, without separation
> of sexes or ages, suffering from a lack of hygiene and posing moral
> dangers.[17]

A special section of the daily newspaper was reserved for accounts
of, and laments about what was called 'the plagues of our city':
theft, violence, prostitution and alcoholism. From records
for the year 1912 I counted 288 cases of physical assault, brawls
and fighting registered by the police.[18] It is important to observe that newspaper reports almost always specified the creed
and nationality of the people involved. Given the statistical
predominance of *paisanos* (civilian compatriots, that is Spaniards), it is not surprising that they were involved in the vast

majority of incidents: 166 violent confrontations were exclusively between Spaniards, many of them between spouses and
with neighbours, which should probably be attributed to overcrowded housing; twenty cases concerned Jews only, and a
further twenty-eight cases involved Muslims only; the police
intervened in thirty-three fights between Spaniards and Rifians,
fourteen between Jews and Rifians, and eleven between Spaniards and Jews; there were four reports on fights in which
Spaniards, Jews and Rifians were all involved; and finally, in
twelve cases the participants were not specified.

This is of course a very crude indication of the level of conflict
in Melilla. The figures do not, for instance, include brawls which
involved soldiers, for these would be dealt with by the military
police and received no publicity. Since a large part of the population had to rely on self-help, it is quite probable that in many
instances conflicts were settled without police intervention. In
any case, the reported incidents were grave enough to provoke
action from both the police and newspapers. To introduce some
measure of comparison, it is worth looking at figures for 1930.[19]
In that year 405 cases of physical assault were recorded by the
police, apart from 135 'scandals' (disturbances of the public
order) listed separately. Setting these figures against the 288
cases computed for 1912, it is important to take into account that
the population had increased by more than 24,000 over this
period.

We may also get a glimpse of life in a booming town if we
compare the level of prices to the rate of daily wages. Reliable
figures are available for 1917 (see table 3.2).[20]

The data display a number of striking aspects. Differences
between official minimum and maximum prices are relatively
great for meat, chickpeas, eggs and wine, which must be
counted among the more luxurious foods. The fact that wages
for children are mentioned separately means that child labour
was prevalent. Wages for Rifian labourers were considerably
lower than for Spanish labourers, a product of the widespread
view that their level of productivity was proportionally lower (in
other words they were considered to be lazier than their Spanish
counterparts). The average annual rent for a working-class
dwelling amounted to 210 pesetas, while a middle-class house
cost 875. No complicated econometric exercises are required to
deduce from these basic facts that a proletarian family with five
children could barely survive on the husband's labour power

Table 3.2   Prices of basic necessities and daily wages, 1917

Products	Minimum price	Maximum price	(Pesetas)
bread	0.55	0.70	(per kg)
pork	3.00	3.50	(per kg)
rice	0.60	0.80	(per kg)
chickpeas	0.65	1.50	(per kg)
sugar	1.10	1.35	(per kg)
eggs	0.90	1.50	(per dozen)
wine	0.55	1.80	(per litre)
olive oil	1.50	1.80	(per litre)
milk	0.70	0.70	(per litre)
Daily wages (Pesetas)			
Category	Male	Female	Children
miners	3–5	–	1–1.25
spanish workers	3–4.75	0.75–1.25	
seamstresses	–	1–2.50	–
Rifian workers	2–2.75	–	0.50–1.25

Source: Junta de Arbitrios, 1917–18 Biblioteca Municipal de Melilla

alone, even if he managed to get work for most of the year. This inference is sustained by taking into account the extent of municipal charity.[21]

The municipal council defined the continuous influx of poor immigrants from Andalusia and Murcia, in particular abandoned women with their children, as one of the most serious problems from 1916 onwards. It was estimated that about 3,000 families, approximately 15,000 persons, depended upon regular municipal welfare. Another 20,000 persons needed occasional help, especially at times of seasonal unemployment. In sum, in the late 1920s almost three quarters of the total population of Melilla needed municipal charity from time to time in order to survive. The city authorities admitted that they were unable to meet these needs. The alternative was to send as many unemployed immigrants as possible back to their original regions: 790 people were expelled in 1927, 1,285 in 1928, and a further 1,072 in 1930.

Poverty hit the Spanish population almost as hard as the Rifians. In fact, the majority of the Spaniards in Melilla and the Protectorate were only slightly better off. But there were catastrophic years when harvests failed in both the Rif and western

Algeria. In 1921, for instance, famine and the Rif war drove
thousands of Rifian women with children into Melilla and Spanish
military camps to beg. One journalist wrote the following lines
in the local newspaper with that matter-of-fact paternalism
current at this time:

> The spectacle which we witness in our city, villages and military
> camps is too pitiful for us not to make an extreme effort to prevent
> those we protect dying of weakness through lack of food.

There was some official food distribution among the 'natives',
but this was only a drop in the ocean. In April 'one Rifian is
dying of famine almost daily.'[22] Even more devastating were the
drought and famines of 1945–6, the worst in the oral and
recorded history of the Rif. In those years thousands of Rifians
left their homes to look for food and work in Tangier and
Tetuan.[23]

A wide gulf developed between the people who lived in the
fashionable city centre with its Barcelona-styled buildings,
apartment blocks, casinos, Grand Theatre, cinema, stores,
clubs, avenues and park, and the poverty-stricken workers in
the outlying *barrios*. In 1930 more than 1,800 people were still
living in caves and shacks.[24] The class divide cut through ties
cemented by regional origin. However, ethnic affiliations were
much stronger than class loyalties, although a small number of
powerful Muslim and Jewish merchants were more or less
incorporated into the Catholic bourgeoisie, while a small core of
radical Jewish workers came to play an important role in the
formation of socialist and communist trade unions and political
parties. There were a number of violent strikes in the early 1930s
and a few pockets of armed working-class resistance when on
July 17, 1936 the elite units of the Protectorate army initiated
their revolt against the Popular Front. After two days the leftist
militants had been wiped out completely.[25]

A Booming Trading Post

While commercial exchanges between the *presidio* and its hinterland until 1860 had been largely determined by the immediate subsistence needs of the enclave, they began to increase
dramatically in the second half of the century. Expansion of

trade was conditioned by two major factors. First, the transformation of the *presidio* into a free trading port attracted Spanish businessmen from the industrialising parts of Spain, the Basque Country and Catalonia, and Jewish merchants from Tetuan, Tangier, Gibraltar and Oran. The latter were important agents of commercialisation as they had capital, strategic networks and language skills at their disposal. Secondly, the agrarian regime of the eastern Rif had reached its limits. The rudimentary cultivation techniques and the scarcity of arable land in the Iqar'ayen area together with a relatively high population density, drove many Rifian peasants out of agriculture into trade and seasonal labour migration.

From the 1870s onwards thousands of Rifians left their homes in early May to work as field-hands on the fertile latifundia of the French *colons* in the Oranie. When they returned in August or September they had plenty of cash to buy imported goods in Melilla. In the early twentieth century, when port facilities at Melilla had been improved, an increasing number of these 'swallow immigrants', as they were called by the city authorities, travelled by boat to Oran. On May 5 and 19, 1905, for instance, 5,175 Rifians embarked on the Melilla ferry to join in the grain harvest in western Algeria.[26] A Spanish source estimated that at this time between 7,000 and 8,000 Iqar'ayen participated in this seasonal labour flow, a very high proportion of a total population of between 55,000 and 65,000 tribesmen (cf. Fernández de Castro y Pedrera 1911: 37).

Prior to the establishment of the Spanish Protectorate, the Iqar'ayen had a small network of rural markets (*suq-s*) which were part of a wider regional network of which Melilla increasingly became the hub towards the end of the nineteenth century. Frontiersmen called Melilla 'Themrirth', literally 'place of gathering'. The mosque and market constituted the centre of gravity of the fragmented Rifian society, foci for the relatively isolated and scattered hamlets. The open markets were held weekly at a fixed place and time. Besides being a place for the exchange of goods, they were centres where legal and political affairs were conducted and information shared. They acted also as centres of tribal control and integration.[27]

The most important *suq* was the Sunday market of the Ait Shikar because of its proximity to, and good communication with, Melilla. More than 2,000 tribesmen and a large number of Spaniards congregated here weekly to trade in grain, wool, hides, sheep, salt, cotton, mules and cattle. This market acted as a *entrepôt* for cattle being exported to Spain through the port of Melilla (idem. 44). The fertile valley of Ait Shikar provided Melilla with vegetables and fruit. The other markets were the Monday market of Farkhana, the Wednesday market of the Ait Shikar, the Thursday market of the Ait Bu Ifrur, and the Friday market of the Imazujen. The highest concentrations of Rifian traders were to be found among the Ait Shikar and Imazujen, especially the tribal fraction of Farkhana, who had long mastered Castilian. These people acted as middlemen, buying up chickens, eggs, vegetables, hides and cattle in the interior markets and reselling these products in Melilla.

When hostilities hampered open trade, there were always Rifian traders who were prepared to come under cover of darkness by land or sea to sell food. On normal days the opening of the market was sounded by the tolling of the church bells. After the tribesmen had entered the *presidio* the gates were closed and all rifles collected by the guards. Commerce was strictly supervised and was only permitted in the market between 8.00 and 10 a.m. and 4.00 and 5.00 p.m. Rifians who came by sea had to disembark at one of the coves. During the 'War of Africa' no tribesmen were allowed to enter the *presidio*, and had to trade at the ramparts opposite to the port (cf. de Morales 1909: 579–80). When in 1863 the restrictions on trade were lifted, this location became the most important marketplace for the remainder of the nineteenth century.

During the 1870s and 1880s Melilla began to attract such a large volume of commerce, both of imported commodities and local products for export, that the merchants of Tangier and Fez and the French in Algeria feared losing control over their market. Mouliéras (1895: 180) estimated the number of caravans that arrived at Melilla at 100 a year. These varied in size from 100 to 500 pack animals per caravan, many of them coming from the south to buy guns, ammunition, tea, cotton, sugar, and ironware. Delbrel (1911: 61) relates how traders of the Ait Shikar travelled to the large market of Taza where they sold English cotton and candles which they had bought in Melilla, and brought back cattle which were then exported to Marseille. Even caravans from Algeria came to buy goods at the new port of trade where the prices of sugar, tea, cotton, and candles were 15 percent lower than in Oran (idem, 156). These data are confirmed by Llanos y Alcaraz (1894: 349) who observed that many caravans travelled as long as sixteen days in order to provision themselves in Melilla. This source also provides data for the local trade between the city and its hinterland. In 1892 tribesmen sold poultry, eggs, honey, wax, hides, wool, vegetables, potatoes, fish and cattle worth approximately 360,000 pesetas, while they spent about 5 million pesetas on tea, sugar, candles, cotton, ironware, olive oil, petrol, soap, tobacco, sweets and medicine.

At the turn of the century the volume of trade in imported goods between Melilla and Morocco and Western Algeria began to decrease as a result of the erection by the French of tax-free *depôts* along the Algerian-Moroccan border (cf. Gallego Ramos 1909: 362–3). French competition was serious enough to cause consternation among the merchants of Melilla.

In 1912 Cándido Lobera — a former army officer, powerful political boss, mayor of Melilla, founder-owner of the daily newspaper, and exemplary *africanista* — devoted a book to what was called 'the problem of Melilla'. His analysis of the problems involved in the colonisation of the Rif is sound, and I shall cite from his influential booklet at length. He pointed out the great imbalance between imports and exports: in 1910 Melilla imported goods worth 43 million pesetas (a tenth of which were imports from Morocco); exports amounted to a meagre 3,400,000 pesetas with goods worth 184,600 pesetas going to Morocco (1912: 113–4). Olive oil was the only Spanish product sold widely at the rural *suq*-s. Great Britain maintained a virtual monopoly over trade in cloth, soap, tea and candles, while French sugar was most popular in the Rif. The Germans tried unsuccessfully to win the Rifians over to using their sugar, for 'el rifeño es rutinario,' 'knowing that his father bought "Leon" and "Camello" (French brands), so he will continue to do so' (idem, 121–30). Jewish merchants controlled the transit trade with the Rif, using sugar as a bait to sell other products. Most of the wares sold in Melilla changed hands at Marseille prices.

Lobera points out that the Rif hardly produced enough for its own subsistence. In order to remedy this condition he advocated agricultural colonisation of the fertile plains by Spanish farmers. The true wealth, however, did not lie in agriculture but rather in the mineral deposits. He concluded that the problem of Melilla had two aspects. First, the city's hinterland was gradually shrinking because of French expansion towards the Muluya river, and, second, by the large-scale dealings in contraband by the central Rifian tribes which could not be subdued by peaceful means. Military intervention was thus the only solution; 'the army as the precursor of civilisation.' His book concludes with the famous statement about the linchpin of Spanish colonial policy: 'when the Ait Waryaghar have surrendered, peace will reign in the Rif' (idem, 153–4). The Ait Waryaghar's refusal to comply with this provided an ironic counterpoint to this statement.

From 1915 onwards the export of iron ore mined at Wixan by the Compañia Española Minas del Rif (CEMR) came to dominate the Spanish colonial economy as the following table shows:

Table 3.3   Import and export of iron ore through Melilla 1905–30 (in 1,000 tons)[28]

Years	Import	Export	Export of CEMR ore alone
1905	16.0	0.46	–
1915	106.0	95.03	74.1
1920	87.0	435.53	320.0
1925	168.08	400.39	279.8
1930	140.96	828.25	602.4

The pacification of the Rif had two important consequences. First, a decline in imports as a result of the drastic reduction of the garrison (from 41,110 in 1925 to 14,300 five years later) and a rise in exports, mainly of iron ore. Throughout the period of the Protectorate the CEMR remained the largest commercial company and employer in Spanish Morocco.

I will conclude this chapter by touching upon the question of how the transformation of Melilla from a *presidio* into a free port and colonial centre affected Rifian society. Since the impact of Spanish colonialism has been studied in detail for an Arabic-speaking tribe in the eastern region (Seddon 1981), I will confine my comments to a summary of the major changes with regard to the Iqar'ayen. These amount to what Eric Wolf (1973) has called a 'triple crisis'. The ecological crisis, which was already manifest in the pre-Protectorate era in the lopsided relation between population size and subsistence resources, further deepened because of an explosive population growth. Death rates, especially infant mortality, were reduced considerably by the spread of medical care — Spanish medical posts were set up in every tribal area — improvement of hygienic conditions, and the suppression of blood feuding. At the start of the Protectorate the Iqar'ayen amounted to between 55,000 and 65,000 people. In spite of the Rif War and the Spanish Civil War, in which many Rifians died, the population of the confederacy had doubled by 1940:

Table 3.4   Size of the Iqar'ayen tribes (in absolute numbers) and density per square kilometre, 1940

Tribe	population size	tribal territory	inhabitants per square km.
Ait Sidar	26,606	380.65	69.9
Ait Bu Ifrur	24,378	201.26	121.2
Ait Bu Gafar	9,139	62.74	145.6
Ait Shikar	22,740	169.52	134.1
Imazujen	31,878	221.96	143.6
Total	114,741	1036.13	110.6

Source: Anuario Estadistico 1940.

The population density in Iqar'ayen territory was among the highest of Spanish Morocco.[29] Between 1955 and 1982 the population of the entire eastern Rif (the Kart or Nador province) more than doubled once again, in spite of heavy emigration.[30] While in 1955 there were 276,000 people living in the Kart (14,000 Spanish residents included), by 1982 this number had risen to almost 600,000 inhabitants, of whom 20 percent lived in urban centres. Nador city had become by far the largest centre with an official population of 62,000.[31]

The demographic explosion was not matched by any substantial improvement of the agrarian infrastructure.[32] The growing of wheat and barley on poor mini-plots and livestock continued to be the mainstay of Rifian agriculture. Peddling, contraband, service in the Protectorate army, and labour mobility, were the population's chief means of supplementing the meagre income derived from agriculture. While in the pre-Protectorate period ownership of land and access to labour had been intimately tied to membership in a local community and lineage, this link was considerably undermined by Spanish colonial policy. Labour and land became commodities to be sold and bought in the market.

This transformation, among other factors, led to an erosion of the authority of the communal council and traditional leadership, for it increased the autonomy of the individual and the nuclear family at the expense of the agnatic line. At the same time, relatively independent tribal units were incorporated into a state structure and local positions of power and authority became bureaucratised. Finally, the Spanish reshaped Rifian space by creating small grid-patterned urban nuclei around *suq*-s, administrative and military posts, several of which were relocated. Contiguous territorial divisions became much more important than they had been in the pre-Protectorate era.

Chapter 4

Taming Rifian Society

Apart from commercial and military penetration, the Spaniards also intruded on Rifian society by classifying and re-ordering it according to Western views. This chapter deals with the Spanish representations of Moroccan and Rifian society as embodied in proto-ethnographic works. I will indicate how these perceptions and representations carried over into colonial policy, and compare early texts on the Rif with subsequent academic ethnographies.[1]

Pre-Colonial Images of the Rif

Before 1900 the Rif remained a virtual *terra incognita* to the Spanish. Despite the urgings of the *Africanismo* movement to conduct rational explorations of the African territories and tribes, little or nothing was achieved in this respect, not even in the territory closest to the Spanish sphere of interest, until the occupation of Melilla's hinterland during the campaign of 1909–11.[2]

The French, on the other hand, who were much more enterprising in their colonisation, devoted considerable resources to the cultural mapping of Morocco. This intellectual offensive was based on two fundamental assumptions of colonial policy. First, the French planned to preserve the cultural heritage of the Moroccan population, and second, they held that systematic ethnographic study would serve the implantation of rational colonial rule (Eickelman 1981: 26). Large-scale investigation of Morocco began in 1904 when the *Mission Scientifique au Maroc* was founded in Tangier. This institute produced numerous studies on history, administration, law, commerce and native crafts, tribal organisation, Muslim instruction, Arabic texts and dialects, and translations of important religious, legal and political documents, which were published in *Archives Marocaines* and *Villes et Tribus du Maroc*. In fact, these constituted the most important body of early ethnographic knowledge of the entire Muslim world.

It had been generally known in Melilla since the sixteenth century that the lands surrounding the enclave belonged to a confederacy of five Berber tribes, called the Guelaya. These tribes were first named individually in late eighteenth-century documents,[3] although even at the close of last century the authorities of Melilla had only a vague idea of the population size and number of warriors in each tribe. Judging from Spanish sources, military intelligence was rather ineffective, in spite of the fact that the authorities employed native informants (*confidentes*). The army attributed its lack of knowledge to the character of these informants: 'The Rifian lies for fun — pretending indifference — for ignorance and for mistrust' (Llanos y Alcaraz 1894: 330). Their image of Morocco consisted of two contrasting poles: a stagnant, archaic, closed Morocco under the control of a cruel and despotic Sultan, which mainly covered the central plains (the Gharb) and Atlantic fringe, as opposed to the primitive tribal backwaters of the *fronterizos*, anarchistic and outside the control of the Sultan.[4]

One of the first studies on the Rif to appear prior to 1900 was written by a French Arabist who lived in Algiers but had never visited northern Morocco (Mouliéras 1895). His main source of information was an Algerian *shaikh* of a religious brotherhood who travelled through northern Morocco between 1872 and 1893. This account is replete with errors, misconceptions and the biases of both the author and the Arab informant *vis-à-vis* the Berbers, which makes it of little ethnographic value. To cite just one example of misrepresentation: Mouliéras presents the Iqar'ayen (named Galiya) as one single tribe consisting of seven fractions, systematically confuses local communities with fractions, and grossly overestimates the total population at 110,000 inhabitants (Idem, 141–67). The image of Rifians which the author evokes is more interesting:

> Rude, still barbarians, the Galiyens nevertheless pass as slightly advanced compared to the rest of the Rif in matters of religious tolerance and civilization (p. 141).

The author is quick to attribute this assumed slight edge the

Iqar'ayen had over other Rifians in refinement of manners to their dealings with the *colons* of Western Algeria. Later on in the book he contradicts this rather benign image with tales of Rifian cruelty. There is, for instance, an account of what happened to a married man caught in the act of adultery with a married woman. The adulteress was killed on the spot, while the adulterer's arms and legs were amputated, his penis cut off and stuffed into his mouth before he was killed (pp. 159–62).[5] Spanish sources, the daily newspaper included, provide endless variations of this stereotype of fierceness, barbarism and cruelty. It was widely believed by the Spanish colonisers that any contact they may have with the Rifians would have a civilising effect on the natives, as in the following instance:

> Frontiersmen are people without any instruction or *cultura* other than what they have been able to acquire during their frequent contacts with the inhabitants of Melilla or during the brief periods they spend on the harvest in Algeria (Fernández de Castro y Pedrera 1911: 115).

Another proto-ethnographic work, this time based on first-hand observations and therefore more accurate than *Le Maroc inconnu*, was also written by a Frenchman (Delbrel, 1911). This explorer first came to the Rif in 1891 as a French spy, but later became an advisor to Bu Hmara, and finally an informant to the Spanish authorities in Melilla. His book contains useful information on trade, religion and geography, but is of very little value with regard to socio-political organisation. His long and extensive contacts with Rifians notwithstanding, the author bluntly reproduced European stereotypes about the 'Rifian character':

> The native of Guelaia is generally false and quarrelsome (heritage of the Semite and Carthaginian) and revengeful like the Roman; his bad faith is legendary, and his untrustworthiness and fickleness make normal social intercourse with him impossible (Delbrel 1911: 81).

The Germans who had become increasingly involved in Morocco by the turn of the century, also produced some proto-ethnographic works on the Rif. Of these Artbauer (1911) is by far the best, and his work stands out in its attention to ethnographic detail. This self-conscious ethnologist, who spent more than ten years in North Africa and the Middle East, travelled throughout the Rif with an Arab servant and interpreter for fifteen months. This is one of the first studies that contains valuable ethnographic photographs. His observations on material culture are most useful. On the other hand, he equally fails to come to grips with tribal organisation, although he clearly gives a more balanced view of the Rifians. Whereas the other works stress the cruelty of the natives, Artbauer stresses the noble side of their 'warlike', 'freedom-loving' and 'courageous' nature. He is one of the first European observers who displays a romantic stance that leads him to detect a sort of pristine purity in the Berber population, the quality of the 'rough diamond' as he calls it, praising their hospitality, their industriousness (which he contrasts with the 'laziness' and 'unreliableness' of Spaniards!) and thrift (1911: 10–13). He denied that the Rif Berbers were religious fanatics as was the received opinion of his time:

> That they mistrust Christians and show hostility towards them, has nothing to do with their religion, but rather stems from their negative experiences with the Europeans (1911: 148).

He wisely refrains from taking a stand in the current debate about the racial origin of the Rifians. The frequent occurrence of light complexion, fair hair and blue eyes led several scholars to believe that they were the descendants of Germanic tribes, which was one way in which Europeans tried to familiarise their apparent strangeness. The other strategy was to overemphasise their otherness and wildness, which then had to be tamed and domesticated by civilising instruction, coercion, and 'setting an example'. As we have seen, various authors believed that contact in itself had a beneficial effect upon the uncivilised Berbers.

The first Spanish author who displayed a rudimentary notion of the nature of tribal social structure was Cándido Lobera Girela, one of the architects of Spanish colonial policy in the first two decades of this century. In his interesting booklet on the problem of Melilla (1911) he gave a rough outline of tribal organisation. Each tribal unit consisted of four to five fractions (*farkas*), which were divided into a varying number of territorial communities (*dchur*), a grouping of houses, which had a communal council (*yemáa*), or sometimes two if the community was an extended one.[6] However, he failed to mention the two lowest levels of tribal organisation, the localised patrilineage (*dshar* or *dharfiqt*) and the household (*washun*). He then correctly observed that despite all the differences among fractions, Rifians always mentioned the tribe (*dhaqbitsh*) and not the fraction as their place of birth. The communal council which was the basic political unit consisted of all men who could handle a rifle and thus had a vote, although they could not always pass an opinion since this was the prerogative of the older and more respected members of the group.

The council appointed or elected a leader (*amghar*), usually the most learned, prestigious or wealthy man, who could count upon a large number of rifles coming to his service. The appointment was valid for one year and could be extended if he proved satisfactory. If he abused his power he could be fined, and in serious cases his house would be destroyed, or he would simply be killed. The leaders of the fractions constituted the tribal council, which in its turn elected a chief. When a tribe had submitted to the central government, it was the Sultan who appointed the *qaid*, which often provoked violent conflicts as we have seen in the preceding chapter.

The meetings of the tribal council were public and were held in the vicinity of the cemetery. If serious matters had to be discussed private gatherings were held in the *qaid*'s house. The tribal council dealt with taxes, with inter-tribal feuding, conflicts between fractions, extraordinary taxes, external politics, and the like. Normally, the *qaid* could not directly intervene in the communal council which was 'sovereign'. Lobera noted that if a *qaid* had been appointed by the Sultan or if his followers had imposed his dominance by force, the opposing fractions would suffer under his rule. Each tribe also had a *qadi*, religious judge. According to Lobera, tribal institutions were democratic in principle, although in practice chiefs often turned into tyrants until a bullet finished them off.

This is a rough outline of the Spanish view of tribal socio-political organisation when the Protectorate was established (Lobera Girela 1912: 77–80). As a result of Bu Hmara's rebellion the communal councils were completely disorganised. Lobera proposed reorganisations along the following lines. First, the communal councils were to be rehabilitated and 'become a kind of small municipality, of which all men above twenty would become a member'; their power, however, was to be reduced to a mere advisory level. The chiefs must be absolutely loyal to the Spanish cause and would receive a fixed salary. Since there were usually two or three powerful notables in each tribe, the appointment of one of them would of course offend the others. In order to avoid this problem, Lobera devised the following strategy:

Table 4.1 Levels of colonial administration

Spanish officials	Native counterparts
High Commissioner (representative of the government in Madrid)	Khalifa (representative of the Sultan)
territorial commissioner	. . .
district commissioner	. . .
local commissioner	–*qaid*
. . .	–*shaikh*
. . .	–*moqaddem*

each of these notables would be appointed to leadership positions in the local communities in which they had their largest following. They would be directly responsible to the local colonial officer and receive a good salary (idem, 81–6). Lobera's ideas were largely derived from the French Algerian administrative system and were put into practice when the Spanish occupied the eastern Rif.

With the establishment of the Protectorate the northern zone was divided into five administrative regions (*territorios*). The hierarchy of power and command was designed as shown in table 4.1.

The Khalifa was a mere ceremonial puppet in the hands of the Spanish. The native positions at the local level remained under the strict control of the *interventor local*, the basic cell in the colonial structure, who was generally an army officer. Tribal fractions came under the jurisdiction of a *shaikh*, while the *moqaddem* was in charge of the communal council, which was transformed into a purely advisory body. The *qaid* who represented the tribal unit to the Spanish wielded most power.

There was considerable confusion from the beginning over the question of whether patrilineal descent or territoriality should be the decisive criterion for the inclusion of people in administrative units. The Spanish favoured an unambiguous link between residence and membership in the group (*jma'a*), a link that was buttressed by the privatisation of land ownership. However, the notion of the tribe as a distinctive unit with its fractions and sub-fractions persisted, in spite of the precedence of territoriality as the principle of social organisation, and the incorporation and fixation of previously rather fluid levels of tribal segmentation into a state structure. The principle of agnatic descent was also used as a base for recruitment into a named *jma'a* (cf. Seddon 1981: 145). This administrative structure only became fully operative after the imposition of the *pax hispanica* in 1927.

The Spanish began their 'protective and civilising mission' ill-prepared and ill-informed. They had only a vague notion of the society and culture which they despised and planned to reform. It is not surprising, then, that they were completely taken by surprise when the central Rifian tribes, led into revolt by 'Abd al-Krim, managed to win almost total support among the tribes of the eastern region through the old channels of inter-tribal communication and mobilisation. With the exception of the Ait Shikar, the Iqar'ayen, who had been under Spanish control since 1909, joined the Rifian cause and inflicted heavy losses upon their masters. Fifteen years of the Protectorate had elapsed before the Spanish began to survey all the tribes under their control.

Military Ethnography

Before going into the details of the military ethnographies produced on the Iqar'ayen during the 1920s, let me first reconstruct the general images of Moroccan culture and society which prevailed among the Spanish *literati* in the preceding decade. I use as an exemplar a guide on North Africa and southern Spain, printed and published in Madrid in 1917.[7] The images it evokes are largely consistent with those divulged piecemeal through the *Telegrama del Rif*. After a brief folklorising description of 'the' Moorish wedding, baptism, funeral, bath-house, meal of couscous and tea ceremony, a short treatise follows on 'Moorish customs,' from which I quote *in extenso* (1917: 30–5):

> They take off their shoes before entering the mosque and cover their hair while praying; they evoke the name of God when they begin an activity; they write from right to left; they think that sentiments spring from the activity of the heart and that the passions strengthen its power. They are stubborn in their decisions; they venerate the old and possess a high sense of personality. They love justice and obey those who rule over them. They wash their hands before and after eating; while eating, they pay no attention to their table companions, shoving with their fingers the best pieces to their closest commensal. By law they can own up to four wives under the same roof. They stock up the products of the land in dry underground storage places,

Europeans erroneously believing that they hide their wealth. They love warfare, music, women, horses, hunting, flowers, birds, and practice charity. They approach death with serenity and do not weep over their deceased. They do not drink alcoholic beverages nor do they eat the products of the pig, and they spice their meals excessively. They remove the stones they find in the path of other pedestrians and collect the pieces of bread that could be treaded on. They hide their haircuts and remove the hair of the arm-pits and the hairy parts of the body; they shave off the moustache between the upper lip and the nose, and inter on the fourth day the part removed in the act of circumcision. They count with their hands in the reverse fashion of the Europeans by moving their fingers toward the palm of their hand; they mount a horse by the flank opposite to the one that is used in the Christian fashion. They wear clothes peculiar to their guild, the way of wrapping their turban, the colour of the *yilaba* or the inclination of the hood indicating the profession of a person. They never swear by the name of God; they are tolerant towards other religions and observe the Mohammedan cult with respect; the major feasts are: Aid Qebir (feast of the sheep, eight days), Aid Seguir (eight days following Ramadan), Mulud (birthday of the Prophet, eight days), and el Achur, the day of the alms. They attach amulets to their animals in order to protect them from evil and tame their harmful instincts; they hang relics to the door of the mosque and around the necks of their children; in every home there is a horseshoe or painting nailed to the door, the latter symbolizing Divinity; they consider several birds sacred, such as the martin and the stork; they believe in the existence of demons and evil spirits, holding many superstitious beliefs.They venerate the Virgin Mary and Jesus Christ, calling him Sidna Aisa and believe in his immortality.

This is a complex text which communicates images in a number of different ways. It is as revealing through what it does not mention as what it does mention, through the sequence and style of the enumeration, through the choice of words, and through the contrast it draws between Islam and Christianity. The following points strike me as being particularly relevant. The summing-up of cultural items in a matter-of-fact way is apparently intended to convey authority and factuality and mask dilettantism and prejudice. The use of the pronoun 'they' suggests a level of generality which immediately collapses upon scrutiny. The urban, male, well-to-do Arab obviously served as the model for 'they' ('they love justice and obey those who rule over them,' references to the mounting of horses, the length of festive days, guilds, religious tolerance, etc.), to the exclusion of the vast majority of the Moroccan population, i.e. Berber peasants, pastoralists and women.

Most of the statements contain in themselves a core of truth. However, they are transformed into stereotypes by the way in which they are summed up. They are presented as being of equal importance; for instance religious rites alongside the style of mounting a horse, which trivialises major cultural traits while over-magnifying minor cultural details. Cultural facts, completely removed from their context, are turned into arbitrary curiosa without meaning (for instance, the passage that refers to the removal of stones and pieces of bread from paths, the use of amulets to ward off the evil eye). The implicit blurring of precepts and values with praxis also nurtures the tendency towards clichés. The suggestive reference to the custom of polygamy is a clear case in point. The Western obsession with the harem is projected onto marriage practices among which polygamy is rather an exception than a statistical rule.

Another distorted statement is the assertion that Moroccans do not weep over their deceased. Without further specifications this so-called custom is turned into a stereotype. In fact, there are professional weepers who are paid to express the grief of the bereaved. Women are expected to express their emotions more openly than men and do indeed weep at funerals. Grief will be more difficult to control in the case of a deceased father or mother than at the death of young children; and so on. The condemnation of weeping in public in itself does not tell us anything of relevance about Moroccan culture. A striking feature of the text is that it pays undue attention to religion; it starts and ends with it. The so-called religious customs tell us more about Western preoccupations with Islam than about the religious practice and experience of Moroccans. It is interesting to observe that the text is largely constructed on the basis of mostly implicit and sometimes explicit contrasts between Islam and Christendom, a technique that established the alien nature of the society described. Only in the case of the Virgin Mary and Jesus Christ does the text deal with an instance of correspondence, albeit superficial, between Christendom and Islam. Other resemblances are simply ignored, particularly those concerning the 'superstitious' beliefs in the evil eye, demons, and evil spirits, which at that time were widespread in rural Spain itself. Nor are these beliefs broached in the guide's section on southern Spain.

In sum, this text shows how Moroccan culture was first

turned into a compilation of assorted, disconnected, and exotic traits, which were then reduced through trivialisation to a string of clichés and caricatures. In this picture of Moroccan customs there was no place for the Rifian Berber, who was left to the military ethnographer after having been pacified by means of physical force.

Between 1927 and 1931 all the tribes of the northern zone were surveyed by anonymous local commissioners. The reports were sent to the *Dirección de Marruecos y Colonias* where they were filed unpublished and consigned to oblivion. When I was doing research in the municipal archive of Melilla, I discovered a dusty set of these reports on the tribes of the Iqar'ayen and Ishebda-nen (Guelaia and Kebdana). These 'Cuestionarios de Kábilas' are small monographs in carbon-copy typescript, unsigned and undated. They vary considerably in size, quality, and content and are generally inferior to the ethnographic reports produced by army officers in the French zone.

The local *interventores* who wrote these small monographs were the only colonial agents who maintained contact with the population on a daily basis. Some of them developed informal and enduring relationships with the Rifians and were widely respected by them. A few of these men, who were on the whole completely untrained in ethnology, had a talent and liking for Rifian history and ethnography, had mastered some Rifian, and produced useful reports on a wide number of topics (cf. Hart 1976: 416).

The Iqar'ayen who, with the exception of the Ait Shikar, had joined 'Abd al-Krim's rebellion against the Spanish in early 1921, had been re-subjected to Spanish colonial rule towards the end of that year. Between 1922 and 1926 they were the subjects of surveys by the local commissioners. The latter apparently did not receive concrete guidelines on how to proceed, which may be judged from the considerable variation in size, outline, and themes of the reports.[8] The five reports all deal to some extent with the following topics: geography and ecology; tribal bound-aries and internal divisions; house types, population statistics; agriculture, commerce and industry; markets; inventories of maraboutic shrines and their cults; Rifian ethos and customs; justice, medical care and instruction; and public works and taxes.

The reports, which are poorly organised, contain unsystem-atised miscellanies of social and cultural details interspersed with moral verdicts by the authors. Not surprisingly, they are

excessively pedantic in tone and orientation, marred by all sorts
of prejudices. Sweeping assessments are generally made with
no hard evidence to support them. But in spite of this, the
reports also contain valuable data; a discussion of some general
themes which recur in all five accounts now follows.

All the authors have problems in providing a description of
the sociopolitical organisation of the tribes. In the report on the
Ait Shikar, the author correctly identifies four fractions each
consisting of between ten and seventeen local communities. The
Spanish term *poblado* — village or town settlement — is used to
designate a local community, which is then wrongly equated
with *jemáa* or communal council, thus betraying the Spanish bias
towards territorial divisions. A conception of patrilineal descent
groups is lacking in all five reports, as is the notion of *liff*, an
alliance between political units at any level of social integration
which often cut across segmentary bonds.

The reports give absolute numbers of inhabitants per fraction
according to sex and age; these raw data are not analysed. One
of the most striking but apparently unnoticed facts is a systematic male surplus both of adults and children in most fractions
and in four out of five Iqar'ayen tribes. Are females simply
under-represented in the population return because of their
inferior status? Or did these Rifians practice some kind of female
infanticide? In any event, this imbalance can hardly be attributed to chance, given its systematic occurrence. The average
size of settlements fluctuated around 250 inhabitants. In the Ait
Shikar 'one very large family' stood out for its 'industriousness
and great amity towards Spain,' a friendship that antedated the
Protectorate. This patrilineage was part of the largest and politically dominant fraction, facts which remain unconnected in the
report. Ties with the Spanish constituted a crucial factor in the
intra- and inter-tribal politics before and during the Protectorate.

Discussions of religion, in particular maraboutism and religious orders, occupy disproportionately large sections of the
reports. Detailed inventories of maraboutic shrines, their cults
and, in one report, elaborate descriptions of oral traditions, are
included. One of the authors could not resist the temptation to
depict the 'barbarian' cults of the Hamadsha and 'Aisawa, such
as head slashing and the dismemberment of living animals,
although he finally asserts that these religious orders have no
followers among the Iqar'ayen (Ait Shikar, 26–7). This is contra-
dicted in the report on the Imazujen whose author counted a

total of 518 followers distributed over eleven religious orders of which the 'Aisawa was by far the largest with 150 adepts. The author includes a spicy story of how during one of the sessions a female adept 'killed her son and devoured him, because he was black and she refused to accept him as her son' (Imazujen, 37). The reason for inclusion of this sort of 'information' can only have been the desire to create an image of primitiveness. All authors agree that the Iqar'ayen were only superficially islamicised:

> The inhabitants do not practice pure Mohammedanism for various reasons. One of them is their way of life in small scattered settlements far removed from Islamic culture and education. In consequence, this religion has imperceptibly suffered transformations to the extent that it has largely become a series of superstitions. This is, of course, true of the mass of the population; only the literate natives are true Mohammedans. Another reason is the proximity of Beni Sicar to Melilla, and the permanent commercial ties of the natives with this city; in consequence they have taken over many of our bad habits . . . It is worth noting that the most religious natives are those who preserve their customs and comply most serenely with the promises and obligations imposed upon them by the Spanish Protectorate; they are our best assistants, because this very attitude gives them major prestige and authority among their fellow countrymen (Ait Shikar, 27).

> There are a great number of absurd superstitions among the Ait Bu Ifrur (28).

> The tribe is only superficially islamicised (Ait Sidar, 5).

All authors hold that maraboutism basically amounts to opportunism and deceit. One author gives a full description of the annual festival of Sidi Ali al Hassani in the Imazujen tribe in which all tribes of the eastern zone participated apart from the General Commander of Melilla and various European families. 'They constitute a picturesque sight, very similar to our *romerias*' (yearly collective pilgrimages to saintly shrines) (Imazujen, 41). One author, after a long reflection on the Qur'an, writes that he finds 'a confusion of concepts and indetermination in concrete cases' (Ait Bu Gafar, 31).

In the early years following pacification the Spanish spent considerable sums of money reconstructing shrines they had destroyed during the fighting. But this policy, which was aimed at pleasing the tribesmen, soon gave way to open and system-

atic support of the Islam of the Five Pillars by providing subsidies for the building of new mosques and for pilgrimages of
the elite to Mecca, as opposed to the Islam of maraboutism,
religious orders, magic and evil spirits.

Many customs are considered to have originated from the
Quran. One of the local commissioners asserts that the seclusion
of the domestic domain from the outer world, especially in the
larger and more differentiated dwellings of the well-to-do —
'the anxiety of the Moor to envelop the intimate life in mysteries
is generally known' — originates in the belief of the Rifian that
in doing so 'he loyally carries out the dictates of the Koran' (Ait
Shikar, 32).

All reports contain the standard lamentation about the 'sad
condition of the Moroccan females':

> Among these indigenes nothing at all of the special attention and
> consideration, which the woman receives as proof of male gallantry
> among the civilized peoples. On the contrary, the native male has
> precedence over the female in all respects of life. For instance, one
> can frequently observe how men ride the donkey or mule while the
> weary woman walks behind them. Men consider a woman only
> slightly above the donkey. She is an object of lust while she is young,
> and becomes a labourer as soon as she has lost her youthful charms;
> she is always subjected to the tyranny of her master (Ait Shikar, 33).

> The woman is a spouse during the night and a servant during the
> day (Ait Bu Gafar, 79–80).

> They regard a woman as a lust object and working animal and their
> daughters as a wholesale commodity (Imazujen, 33).

One of the local commissioners, admitting that he never entered
a Rifian house, nonetheless presumes to give a harsh verdict
about the 'condition' of Rifian women:

> The aboriginal woman enjoys relative felicity within her home, but
> her ferocity and backwardness at times make her intolerable both as a
> result of her fickleness and harshness of her heart (Ait Bu Gafar, 80).

Such images of wildness emerge *ad absurdum* in sections about
the blood-feud, in which the colonial ethnographers attempt to
capture the essence of the Rifian 'character':

> The natives of this tribe, like all others, already display great bellicose

aspirations during their most tender infancy, families always having been linked in alliances to defend themselves against plundering; however, we must note that this unity diminishes every day, since Spain now protects them if necessary, so that they no longer feel the need to retaliate (Ait Sidar, 6).

The tribesman is indolent and apathetic and consequently his intellectual enlightenment is very limited; the lack of culture under which he lives renders him devoid of scruples or conscience; distrustful and reserved in the extreme, especially towards those who do not profess his religion; it is his fanaticism which characterises him most; only rarely does he say what he feels and he could not care less if he fails to tell the truth, doing his utmost not to become a slave of his word. They are false and quarrelsome, although actually few cases of criminal nature have been registered recently. For fear of raids on their goods and chattels they always carry arms of which they are aficionados; as the land is mountainous, they are agile and indefatigable, sober, courageous and fearless. These qualities linked with their ability in handling arms and their aptitude for fighting make them great soldiers if inculcated with some instruction and military virtues, which is easy to achieve with those who have been in contact with us for some time . . . (Imazujen, 32).

Blood feuding has decreased considerably since 1909. This however, does not mean that the native has lost his love for weaponry . . . his interest in the rifle has diminished, while his liking for small arms has increased, mainly because of their fancy decoration and because they see them on the European miners who are also fond of hand guns. Weapons with a blade have disappeared almost completely (Ait Bu Ifrur, 49).

On the whole, the treatment of the 'barbarian custom' of blood-feuding (Ait Shikar, 40) is superficial and stereotypical. None of the authors points to the connection between the harsh ecological conditions, the scarcity of fertile land and of water, and the occurrence of blood-feuding at all levels of tribal segmentation. Like many other socioeconomic and political conditions, the use of physical force is simply attributed to the Rifian ethos.

During the first years of the Protectorate, the Spanish tried to settle current blood-feuds by acting as mediators between conflicting parties and by organising large-scale ceremonies at which peace was negotiated through the payment of blood-wealth and the slaughtering of bulls.[9] This policy largely failed, initially because until 1921 Rifians were allowed to keep their weapons.

Eventually, however, there was a great reduction in blood-feuding. This was due to many factors, among them the overall pacification of the Rif, the centralisation of force and justice, the incorporation of large numbers of tribesmen into the native police corps and Protectorate army, as well as the registration of privately and state-owned firearms, and the prohibition of owning or carrying arms (with an exception for prestigious leaders). The Spanish, however, never succeeded in stamping out this custom entirely.[10]

The backwardness of Rifian agriculture was also attributed to race, specifically to the 'indolence' of the tribesman (Ait Shikar, 41). As one of the local commissioners put it:

> Because of his indolent nature, the native limits himself to tilling the land closest to his hamlet merely for the most basic subsistence needs. Moreover, agricultural techniques are still the same as a thousand years ago (Ait Bu Gafar, 44).

At the same time the authors boast of the progress made as a result of the introduction by the Spanish of the iron plough and chemical fertilisers. One should remember that these were very recent innovations in Spain, where in most regions agriculture was as primitive as Rifian agriculture. One of the ways in which the colonial masters tried to increase agricultural output was by privatising communal lands. One of the commissioners pointed this out very concisely:

> Those tribesmen who behave best and who are most enthusiastic about Spain's endeavour in the protectorate are authorised to cultivate the collective lands, on the understanding that they keep all the products of their labour, which heightens the enthusiasm they feel towards the protecting nation (Ait Sidar, 3).

Favouritism towards a very select Rifian elite was also evident in the field of education and medical care, which were showpieces used to entice select Rifians into cooperation:

> This is one of the best initiatives put into practice in our Protectorate. . . . tomorrow Spain will be able to count on strong assistants in the colonisation of our area of influence by creating a generation, a great part of whom will speak Spanish, possess a knowledge of our civilisation, and find new horizons for the development of their activities (Ait Shikar, 50–1).

It should be made clear that towards the end of the Protectorate the illiteracy rate in the Rif still amounted to more than 95 percent of the population (Cammaert 1985: 21).

At the outset of the Protectorate, health centres were established for each tribe, mainly in order to 'gain Rifian loyalty' (Ait Bu Gafar, 87). The greatly exaggerated efforts in this area were represented by the authors as follows:

> In the Rif hygiene scarcely exists in any respect at all . . . cohabitation with domestic animals seems to be prized; abhorrence of water and all ablutions must be their ideal. We are still far removed, rare exceptions aside, from complete native trust in our efforts. This is caused by ignorance which keeps the native tied to his ancient beliefs, which, in their turn, are sustained with great skill by the holy men who control native medicine and whose aim is exploitation; they deceive and separate the tribesmen from us, erecting a religious barrier that prohibits any mutilation and transforms some verses of the Koran into true therapeutic panacea (Imazujen, 70–1).

Again and again the comparison of Rifian primitiveness with Spanish civilisation is rammed home. While many assessments are not entirely inaccurate, the strictures of the authors would apply equally to most of Spain's rural areas in the 1920s. As a general rule factual details are entirely overshadowed by hyperbole, over-generalisation, simplification and caricature with social, economic and political conditions attributed to the workings of a collective, stereotypical Rifian character.[11]

To be fair, the military ethnographic accounts also contain accurate and valuable descriptions. It is striking, however, that these mostly deal with relatively unsensational topics such as the etiquette of hospitality, celebrations of birth, marriage and death, and patronal festivals (cf. Ait Shikar, 35–40). On the other hand, these descriptions focus condescendingly on the differences between, rather than on the similarities with, Spanish customs, thus accentuating the 'alien' and 'exotic' nature of Rifian culture.

On the whole, the Spanish despised everything Rifian, probably because it uncomfortably reminded them of the rural Andalusian society which the majority of the colonists had come from. In this way they created social and cultural distance, which from an outsider's point of view would not have appeared to be so very great. The Spanish Protectorate generally supported the Arabic language as against Berber, classical Islamic as opposed to local architecture, formal Islam as against maraboutism and sufism, and the *shari'a* against customary law (cf. Valderama Martinez 1956). This policy was deeply rooted in the ancient stereotype of the early medieval civilisation of Al-Andalus and its noble urban Moor, as opposed to the equally ancient cliché of the Berbers of Barbary as a bloodthirsty and primitive lot.

The hostile, harsh, and negative view of the Rifians gradually gave way to a softened and more realistic image. Once the Rifians had been domesticated, and no longer threatened the colonisers, they were increasingly perceived as 'noble primitives' and 'brothers' though still minor and less developed ones. The turning point came in the mid-1930s when the Rifians *en masse* supported rightist and eventually Nationalist Spain. The colonial rhetoric of the Franco regime became replete with slogans of 'Moroccan-Spanish fraternity'.[12] The instruction of military colonial agents at the *Academia de Interventores* became more scientific. Courses and conferences for and by local military commissioners were often devoted to ethnographic subjects. In the course of the 1940s the best pieces of Spanish colonial ethnography were produced.[13]

Academic Ethnography and the Rif

Edward Westermarck, the Finnish anthropologist who taught in London for most of his career, may be considered a founder both of modern anthropology and of professional Moroccan ethnography.[14] Unlike other early anthropologists who relied on material collected by amateur ethnographers, Westermarck found it useful 'to acquire first-hand knowledge of some forms of culture which differ from our own' (1926: I, v). Using his villa in Tangier as a base, he travelled widely through Morocco between 1898 and 1926, gathering a huge mass of data on customs, beliefs and rituals. His three major works (1914, 1926, 1930) are largely descriptive and encyclopaedic. Unlike his contemporaries he performed almost no analysis on his data and paid little attention to social organisation. His most important book, the 1,200-page *Ritual and Belief in Morocco* (1926), is a collection of curiosities gathered during field trips and interviews at his villa with informants from all parts of the country. His material on the Rif, which he never actually visited, is derived from interviews with Ait Waryaghar and Ait Thimsaman at

Tetuan and Tangier. The stereotype of the bloodthirsty Rifian entered the profesional anthropological literature through Westermarck, who probably took for granted the verdict of an Arab *sharif* who acted as his guide, interpreter, and key informant:

> . . . a man who has not taken anybody's life before he is married is not considered a man (1926: II, 12).

On the whole, however, such unqualified statements are rare in Westermarck's work. As a professional outsider, his view of Morocco was much more detached than that of the military ethnographers who were deeply involved in pacifying and subjecting the Rifian population. Even though most of Westermarck's ideas, methods, and interpretations are now outmoded, much of his material, notably on *baraka* and *jnun*, remains valuable today from an ethnohistorical point of view.

Carleton Coon, an American anthropologist, was the first trained fieldworker to conduct extended research in the Rif in the late 1920s. His fieldwork would have been impossible without the establishment of the *pax hiberica* and the support and services of the Spanish military authorities, a fact he acknowledged in the preface of his monograph (1931: vii). The stated aim of his research was to capture the essence of Rifian society before the commencement of the Protectorate — in his own words — 'Rifian life still led according to the old style' (vii). His general characterisation of the Rifian people sharply contrasts with the harsh and outright negative judgements which we have pointed out above:

> Their keen comprehension, ready acceptance of the purpose of our inquiries, high degree of cooperation, and generous hospitality never failed to astonish us (vii).

He found the Rifians 'brave, honorable men, and most pleasant companions' (410). Such expressions of warm sympathy for 'our people' became a convention of anthropological writing in the opening and concluding lines of monographs. Less rosy feelings towards informants and their society remained hidden in the personal diaries which were not intended for publication.[15]

The pacified condition of the Rif thus created room for the emergence of a romantic view of the 'noble savages'. In the case of Coon this view was fully expressed in his ethnographic novels (1932, 1934), in which he gave free rein to his imagination, which had to be restrained in the earlier scientific monograph (1931). Coon also conformed to the genre conventions of the anthropological monograph of his day by the almost complete suppression of the colonial context. Only in his preface did he allude to it, although it was in distorted and euphemistic terms:

> Its wealth of manpower, the intelligence of its people, and the natural resources of the country will in time repay her [Spain] amply for the deservedly considerate and friendly attitude which, so soon after the end of the fighting, she has already begun to show in the administration of this conquered people, whose virile spirit of independence has for the first time in history been effectively curbed (vii–viii).

Note that Coon simply considered it natural that the Rifians should be subjected by a more powerful nation, that they were forced to abstain from all sorts of violent behaviour and reshape their way of life in terms of Western, that is 'civilised', modes of conduct. Perhaps he also paid tribute in this passage for the support he got from the Spanish military authorities.

On the whole, Coon succeeded in containing contemporary preconceptions about 'primitive society', although now and then they come to the surface, as in a revealing footnote to a section in which he discussed the boys market in the Jebala where kidnapped boys were sold 'for the purpose of sodomy':

> The whole Jebalan area is permeated with this type of sexual depravity . . . which is accompanied by a low esteem for women. . . . Bride purchase, a trait common to all Moroccans but the Jews, is in the Jebala literally applied, since here the wife becomes a definite chattel of her husband, not usually the case elsewhere. The atmosphere created by this combination of cultural factors is in striking contrast to that of the Rif, which, *although primitive is wholesome and vigorous* (111, fn. 1; my italics).

Coon clearly hints at the pure and undepraved state of the central Rifian tribes, which he attributed to the relative isolation of this mountainous heartland. In his time, peoples studied by anthropologists were by definition 'primitive peoples'. In fact, the unreflected use of this term in implicit opposition to 'civilised' was common coin among anthropologists as well as in the wider society. The connotations of the concept are clear: original, wild and inferior on the one hand, and pristine and pure or para-disiacal on the other hand. These notions constituted a power resource for the dominant Western society and, in fact, served as a legitimisation of colonial hegemony. Thus in the eyes of the colonists the Rifians occupied the transitional realm between wild and human, a highly ambivalent position. The Western perception of them was likewise ambiguous: they inspired both fear and repugnance and, at the same time, admiration.[16] Given the condition of *pax hiberica*, positive but nevertheless patronis-ing admiration could gain the upper hand. In Coon's work an awareness of the intimate link between the identity of anthro-pology, the identity of the research object, and notions of Western civilisation and superiority played out in the colonial context, is still absent.

It is worth taking a closer look at the structure of Coon's monograph. It consists of two parts; the first describes Rifian culture, the second, which is more substantial deals with race. The author uses a holistic approach to culture. He successively deals with: physical geography, oral tradition, documented history, material culture (the *pièce de résistance* of the first part), social organisation, government and warfare, markets, public buildings and public instruction, law, rites of passage, religion, magic, and an analysis of the distribution of cultural traits. It is striking that the chapter on social organisation is so meagre and superficial (only six pages long, scarcely a tenth of the chapter devoted to material culture). In the last chapter of the first part, the aim of his study is revealed in its clearest formulation:

> A compilation of the traits of material and social culture which are characteristically Riffian shows that these traits are definitely concen-trated in what may be called the Central Riffian Nuclear Culture Area . . . This area may be regarded as the stronghold of *archaic culture* in northern Morocco (Coon 1931: 174, italics mine).

The second part on race serves to prove the existence of such an 'archaic culture'. Of course, Coon's theoretical approach and methods have long since been untenable.[17]

In what respects does the work of a professional anthropolo-gist (and outsider) like Coon differ from that of the military ethnographer working in the same period? First, there is an obvious difference in scope and substance which is not only a reflection of differential access to time, and research resources, but above all of training. The work of the former is superior in systematics, coherence and analysis and has the advantage of a more objective concept of culture. The term culture (or civilisation) as used by the amateur, military ethnographer is basically the Spanish ideology of culture with its preoccupation with the nature of dominance. Professional ethnography is driven by ideas about the connection between a variety of cultural factors, although the question of dominance is not altogether absent, as I have tried to indicate.

Until Morocco's independence in 1956, Spain, for obvious reasons, dominated Rifian ethnography. The Franco regime, however, constituted a formidable obstacle to the development of an academic ethnography, in contrast with French Morocco where Berber ethnography flourished throughout the 1940s and 1950s.[18] In the Spanish zone ethnography remained very much a hobby for a small, devoted group of military commissioners. The ethnography of the Rif finally came of age thanks to the talent and long-lasting efforts of David Montgomery Hart who wrote an exhaustive monograph on the Ait Waryaghar, the largest, most important and renowned Rifian tribe.

A student of Coon, Hart first came to the Rif in 1952. He spent eleven years in Morocco, four full years of which were devoted to fieldwork in the central Rif. He was the forerunner of a host of American anthropologists who flooded the country in the 1960s. This growing interest in the area was linked to the ascendance of the United States, which superseded France as the main politico-military and economic ally of Morocco. Hart received substantial financial backing from the Ford Foundation and the American Museum of Natural History, which enabled him to live up to the image of the American as generous spender and provider of small presents (cf. Hart 1976: xx), an image that was firmly established in Morocco by the US army during the Second World War.

The voluminous monograph is ethnography in the traditional sense, that is, largely descriptive and holistic with thorough attention to detail. Although a clear problem and argument is lacking, the author puts analytic emphasis on blood-feuding in the context of the native's model of segmentary descent, and their territorial ties cross-cutting the system of alliances. The book bears a strong imprint of British functionalism, and shows the influence of *Saints of the Atlas* (Gellner 1969). Given the fact that the ethnographic present is the period prior to the imposition of the *pax hiberica*, a large part of the book consists of historical reconstruction through interviewing old men. The first eleven chapters of the book provide us with a very detailed account of the society and culture of the Ait Waryaghar. The remaining five chapters deal with the social and political history of the Rif within the Moroccan context.

The *Aith Waryaghar of the Moroccan Rif* is conventional ethnography in two other respects. There is a very strong male bias in the study, which cannot simply be attributed to the male dominance and sexual segregation of Rifian society. Hart's data on women are meagre, scattered and often contradictory.[19] A second drawback of the functionalist perspective is the relegation of recent changes to a few final pages. 'The winds of change' (pp. 445–449) have affected Waryaghar society in two fundamental respects. First, there has been a rapid erosion of patrilineage, clan, and tribe, paralelled by the equally rapid rise of the individual and his or her nuclear family. This transformation is intimately connected with the second major change, the progressive proletarianisation and labour nomadism of the former tribesmen. The Rif has become Morocco's most underdeveloped region. Due to the great impact of Melilla, these processes set in earlier among the Iqar'ayen and affected them more profoundly than the Ait Waryaghar.

These profound changes are the focus of David Seddon's *Moroccan Peasants* (1981) on the Arabic-speaking Ulad Settut to the east of Melilla. Seddon's study in a sense complements Hart's monograph both in subject matter and in theoretical perspective, which is strongly influenced by Marxism. The line of research set out by Hart is further pursued by Raymond Jamous in his book *Honneur et Baraka* (1981) on the Ait Bu Ifrur. This monograph on tribal sociopolitical organisation and blood-feuding prior to the establishment of the Spanish Protectorate is informed by a more explicit structural-functionalist perspective.

In conclusion, it is worth stressing that Rifian (and Moroccan) ethnography, both amateur and professional, has been marked by a near-obsessive concern with agnatic descent elaborated into segmentation, with tribe, egalitarianism, and, more recently, with the negation or rejection of these presumed realities. The controversy which these issues have sparked hinges on the question of whether segmentation should be regarded as native (one could add, elite) ideology, ordinary behaviour, or both. Extreme positions are taken by Hart and Gellner on one side and by Geertz, Rosen, Rabinow and Eickelman on the other.

Since the debate has been recapitulated several times,[20] I confine myself to the basic question: why has this at times heated debate been going on now for almost two decades? No satisfactory answer can be given by simply pointing out differences in theoretical perspective and research stance.[21] The debate also implicitly addresses the identity of anthropology itself and the nature of the society that has engendered this discipline. In other words, at a deeper level lies the fundamental question of differences and resemblances between 'us' and 'them'.

The studies of Hart and Gellner are prompted by a search for essential differences between Berbers and Europeans. Hence, their preoccupation with the reconstruction of the 'authentic' or 'original' state of Berber society, still untouched by Western influences. Their 'ethnographic present' refers to the pre-Protectorate period which they then tend to extend into the historical present. Given their search for differences, it is not surprising that they stress those features of Berber society which are alien to Western society, i.e. agnatic descent and its articulation in segmentary tribal organisation, as well as a host of 'exotic' customs. What they try to prove is that Berbers are really different, and as such, a legitimate subject for anthropological inquiry.

In the opposing camp Geertz and his followers have developed an action-oriented model of Moroccan society that bears more resemblance to Western society. Hence their stress on 'the negotiation of reality', on dyadic contacts, and the fluidity of interaction. Their studies reveal that Moroccans are in many respects like 'us'. It is not surprising, then, that Clifford Geertz is one of the few anthropologists who is praised in Said's study of Orientalism:

> An excellent recent instance is the anthropology of Clifford Geertz, whose interest in Islam is discrete and concrete enough to be animated by the specific societies and problems he studies and not by the rituals, preconceptions, and doctrines of Orientalism (1978: 326).

To be fair, Geertz neither succeeds in escaping the fallacy of overgeneralising his Sefrou data and of projecting his voluntaristic model of Moroccan society back into the past without providing adequate documentation.

One of the positive effects of the segmentation debate is a growing awareness of the ideological preconceptions and political realities which inform ethnographic research. A testimony to this trend is the growing number of studies which critically reflect on earlier ethnographies, on the relationships between anthropologists and informants, and on the impact of North-South relationships upon the shaping of ethnographic texts (cf. Rabinow 1977, Crapanzano 1980, Dwyer 1982, Wolf 1982, Barley 1983, Fabian 1983, and Herzfeld 1987).

Chapter 5

The Making of a Jewish Community

Forty years ago Moroccan Jews constituted the largest Jewish community in the Muslim world, but by 1975 only 20,000 were left, fewer than 10 percent of the Jews who had lived in Morocco prior to its independence (Tessler & Hawkins 1980: 64). Anthropologists who have worked in Morocco have remained remarkably silent about the Jewish minority. Their work contains at best a few marginal notes on the Jews who in the recent past lived in the Muslim and Berber communities they studied.[1] This neglect is puzzling, considering the important role Jews have played over the centuries both in pre-colonial and colonial economies, and as negative referents of the Muslim identity.

Jews are of particular relevance to this study as they have been specialists in trans-frontier communication. Moreover their role in the transformation of the Hispano-African frontier was crucial. This chapter deals with a forgotten Jewish community, the 1,100 Jews of Melilla who constitute the third largest community of Spain (Chouraqui 1985: 466). Their history represents a small part of the saga of North African Jews, of their struggle to begin a new life within a Catholic enclave, and how their presence brought about several changes in the host society.

Legends of Origin

In spite of cultural differences, Maghribian Jews shared the so-called legend of al-Kahina. This epic-historical narrative, which also became part of the Muslim tradition, refers to a Berber woman of the Djeraua tribe in the Aurès (Algeria) who adopted Judaism and led the Berbers in resisting the first Arab advance in the year 688. She is said to have reigned over the

Maghreb until 693 when she was killed during the second Muslim penetration into Berber land (cf. Chouraqui 1985: 84–6). Her name connotes both priest and saint in Hebrew. The legend, among other things, underlines the potential political power of a Jewish holy man, albeit in the shape of a doubly marginal figure, that is a Berber woman (cf. Goldberg 1987: fn. 15).

The Jews of Melilla have adapted and appropriated this legend to fit their particular circumstances. There was, according to oral tradition, a firmly established Jewish colony in the town of Melilla at the end of the seventh century when the Arabs began to penetrate Morocco. The deeds of the legendary hero al-Kahina, who in the Melilla version is depicted as a male, are set in this colony. The local account traces his descent back to the members of a priestly caste who fled Jerusalem in the sixth century before Christ.[2] This hero courageously led the town's defence against the Arab invaders. The account does not relate what happened to the Jewish colony after the Arabs had conquered the town, although according to another legend, given below, the Jewish colony was still in existence in the 1480s just before the town was destroyed and abandoned by its inhabitants after being caught up in a war between the rulers of Fez and Tlemcen.[3] The Spaniards eventually occupied the deserted town in 1497.

This legend of origin, in which the hero al-Kahina figures as a mythical forebear, not only establishes the antiquity of the Jewish presence in this corner of the Maghreb — 'we were here before the Arabs and Spaniards' — but also provides a link between the Melilla colony and the Holy Land.

The second legend belongs to the lore of those Jews whose parents and grandparents were born in the small Jewish communities of the eastern Rif. It refers to 1492, a key year in the history of Judaism when Sephardic Jews were expelled from the Iberian Peninsula, many of them crossing the Mediterranean to settle in Morocco. This legend narrates how in this year a learned and pious rabbi, Saadia ed-Dati, together with six other rabbis and their families, fled from Spain by boat. They were shipwrecked in sight of the Rifian coast but managed to get ashore. Roaming the countryside in search of a place to settle, they stopped at a Berber hamlet called Farkat, in the vicinity of present-day Nador. Rabbi Saadia went to the Jews of Melilla to offer his spiritual services, which, however were declined because of internal strife. The rabbi returned to Farkat where he and the other rabbis became the victims of an epidemic. After having taken a ritual bath (*tbila*), rabbi Saadia wrapped himself in a funeral shroud and lay down in a tomb. He told the Berber and Jewish villagers that there would soon be a tempest and that a big rock would cover him as soon as he passed away. This happened during one of the nocturnal vigils of the villagers. Those present could not explain how the mysterious rock had fallen upon the rabbi's tomb. Some of them began to claim that it had been sent from Heaven. The rabbi has been venerated as a holy man since that time and has become the spiritual patron of the eastern Rif Jews.[4]

Several Jews of urban Moroccan origin rejected this story as the product of superstition on the part of their illiterate rural brothers. As one of them told me: 'Some of those fanatical Berber Jews believe that the rock was sent by God. I believe it must have rolled down from a nearby mountain during an earth-tremor'. However, he did not question the other details.

Elderly Rifians claimed that they also considered the shrine of Rabbi Saadia to be a sacred place, which they, however, called Sidi Yusef, after a Muslim saint. In fact, at the beginning of the twentieth century both Muslims and Jews were visiting the shrine (Fernández de Castro y Pedrera 1911: 16). For generations the shrine has been guarded by a Rifian family who are paid for their services by the Jewish community of Melilla, which also financed the building of the road that leads up to the shrine (at the hamlet of Messamer). Until the 1950s Rabbi Saadia was very popular among the working-class Jews of Melilla and Nador. His fame for healing barrenness also attracted Jewish women from Orania. Each year at the beginning of May, Jews from Melilla and the Eastern Rif gathered at his shrine to celebrate the anniversary of the rabbi's death (*hillula*). They camped nearby with relatives and friends, reciting prayers, eating commemorative meals and celebrating the rabbi's supernatural powers. However, the Moroccan government has suppressed collective pilgrimages from Melilla since the Arab-Israeli war of June 1967.[5] This has served only to accelerate the decline of the cult, which was already going through a crisis because of the large-scale emigration of local Jews to Israel, Latin America and France.

While the cult of rabbi Saadia has now largely disappeared, the legend remains alive and continues to be transmitted to younger generations. The legend establishes a link between the Jews of Rifian origin and the Jewish civilisation of Spain, a connection that has always been denied by the Jews of urban Moroccan origin. It also validated the claim of rural Jews to membership in a holy lineage founded by the rabbi through divine intervention. Finally, both the legend and cult point to the co-existence and interdependence of Jews and Berbers, and to the similarities in their beliefs and practices.

The Beginning of a New Jewish Colony

The size and composition of the enclave's population was strictly controlled by the military authorities until the mid-1860s. The only non-Hispanic residents were Berber slaves and renegades. When Melilla was opened up to international trade, a Royal Decree of 1864 allowed Spanish citizens and 'aliens' to take up free residence in the enclave. However, the local authorities remained ambivalent with regard to foreign residents for the remainder of the century.

Jewish contacts with the *presidio* must have dated back for many centuries, although there is little documentary evidence for this. However, an ancient Jewish cemetery in the Alcazaba, which was an outer precinct during the nineteenth century, still testifies to the historical presence of Jews in Melilla.

Oral tradition claims that in 1862 an Algerian Jew and his wife settled in Melilla in order to trade with the Rif. When sustained trade relations proved difficult because of political turmoil in the hinterland this Jewish merchant returned to Algeria.

As a result of the Hispano-Moroccan war of 1859–60 the Spanish army occupied Tetuan between February 1860 and May 1862. Although the Spaniards pillaged the Jewish quarter, the large community of Jews nevertheless welcomed the victors. When the Spanish troops withdrew, many Jews fled to Gibraltar, Oran, Ceuta and Tangier (Cohn 1927: 8; Leibovici 1984). The Royal Decree that abrogated all dispositions against foreign residence in the enclaves must also have encouraged Jews to come to Melilla. The third event of importance was the new constitution of 1869, which, for the first time in Spanish history, guaranteed some tolerance of religions other than Catholicism and restricted public worship.

The first Jews who appear in the documents of the municipal archive are Judah, Ysaac and Mesod Obadia who sought the mediation of the military governor in their conflict with two

'Moors' over the possession of a skiff and its cargo. The case was settled in June 1861 in the presence of the governor, an interpreter and the parties involved.[6] Three years later several members of the Obadia family who lived among the Ait Sidar moved to the enclave. The first Jews who were granted Spanish nationality were four merchants from Tetuan who traded with the Rif.

Several documents contain the declarations on the civil status of the first Jews, statements sworn before the notary in the presence of Spanish and Jewish witnesses. One of them reads as follows:

> I, José Bensaquen Levi, declare that no registers of birth, marriage and death were kept in the city of Tetuan; I testify the truth of the fact that Samuel Bensaquen Izrad and Ledicia Levi Abudarha [his parents] were both born in Tetuan on March the 4th of 1846 and have resided in Melilla since 1868, of which five years have been devoted to commerce in an establishment open to the public; that I have always been of good conduct (signed by José Salama, Sentob Benchimol and two Catholic witnesses).[7]

The census of 1880 yields interesting data on the young Jewish community of Melilla.[8] The civilian population amounted to 690 inhabitants, of whom sixty were classified as foreigners. Fifty-five of these were Jews who lived scattered over five streets in the old town with a concentration of twenty-three in the San Miguel street. There were only nineteen women among these first Jewish residents. Adult Jewish males first set up business in Melilla before bringing the rest of their families over. While in the Catholic households children were listed according to age, male children systematically preceded female children in the Jewish households.

When they came to Melilla all Jews, of both sexes, spoke Spanish, and the males were also literate in Arabic. These urban Jews, the majority of whom were descendants of the Sephardic Jews expelled from Spain in 1492, had retained an archaic version of Spanish with some Hebrew and Arabic words (*Haketia*) for use in the home (cf. Cohn 1927: 5). Married women were named after the first family name of their husband and father, which indicates a strong patriarchal tradition. The majority of the first Jewish residents maintained dual residence, a situation that could last as long as ten years. They set up business partnerships with Jews in Oran, Gibraltar, Tangier, and Tetuan, towns they frequently visited and which were part of the marriage circuit. This fact points to an intimate interlocking of family and business interests. Men from the urban merchant class married late, often in their early thirties and only when they were economically independent of their fathers, while women married ten to fifteen years earlier.

All Jews with a permanent residence in Melilla were merchants from Tetuan except for one who came from Gibraltar. There was only one female head of household. This widow, who was born in Tetuan in 1844, came from Oran to Melilla at the age of twenty and started to work as a laundress. She had four daughters between nineteen and fourteen, the oldest of whom had married at the age of sixteen. The largest household was that of José Salama Grofé, one of the Jews who had acquired Spanish nationality in 1863. Born in Tetuan in 1840, he came to Melilla at the age of twenty-three. He married a daughter of the first rabbi of Melilla, who was also an important merchant. In 1879 he brought his wife over from Tetuan. At that time they had four children, Samuel, Jacob, Meri and Simi, respectively eighteen, thirteen, seventeen and fourteen years old. At the age of sixteen Meri was married to a son of the brother of her father. José's son-in-law and his first grandchild became part of the household, which also included his widowed mother and sister.

Descendants of these first residents told me stories about the problems facing the first generation of Melilla Jews. There was considerable discrimination against them. For instance, when applying for residence permits they had to produce certificates of good conduct. At first the military governors prohibited the import of kosher meat and wine, and obstructed Jewish worship. Jews who had adopted Spanish nationality were not allowed to trade with the Rif, and there were numerous possible minor offences and humiliations in daily interaction. José Salama, the most powerful merchant who acted as an informal community leader, wrote several letters to the government in Madrid in which he denounced such harassment.

The Arrival of Rural Jews

That there were two different Jewish communities in Morocco became apparent with the arrival in Melilla of the first Jews from the tribal hinterland. In order to understand the nature of this cleavage a short digression into the history of the Moroccan Jews is necessary.[9] When the exiled Jews from Spain (*megorashim*) arrived in the coastal cities of western Morocco, they were often ill-received by the native Jews (*toshavim*). The latter feared the technical, educational and commercial superiority of the Sephardim who, moreover, brought their own customs and ideas that differed considerably from those of the native Jews. The newcomers almost immediately assumed the leadership of the Jewish quarters. The descendants of the Sephardic Jews assimilated completely in the long run with the native Jews of Tetuan and Tangier. The urban Jews referred to the rural Jews of the interior disdainfully as *berberiscos*, Berbers.

The majority of the city Jews were craftsmen, small traders and at times moneylenders. The small stratum of elite merchants constituted an almost closed group within the Jewish communities. They controlled Morocco's maritime trade, and acted as court bankers and middlemen between the European powers and the Sultan. Consular representation became the virtual monopoly of this mercantile elite (cf. Bowie 1976). They were inclined to mysticism and the study of the Zohar, maintained close bonds of kinship and commerce abroad, spoke Spanish and French, and were oriented to European culture. Several of the first Jewish residents of Melilla belonged to this class of comfortably-off brokers, and quickly adopted Spanish customs.

The first rural Jews, who had lived among the Iqar'ayen for centuries, settled in Melilla in the early 1880s. Between 1881 and 1884 eighty-five of them, constituting fifteen households, moved to Melilla, where they all settled in the new barrio of Mantelete opposite to the port.[10] The composition of households reveals that there was a high degree of local endogamy among them. Of the eighteen married couples eleven were born in the Ait Sidar and one in the Ait Bu Gafar. The remainder were from mixed origin. Two marriages involved Iqar'ayen men with Timsaman women. That there were indeed contacts between rural and urban Jews is revealed by the fact that three tribal Jews married women from Tetuan and Oran. The pattern of marriage residence was unmistakably patrilocal. Two of the eighteen married men had remarried at least once.

Marriage customs among the rural Jews differed considerably from those of the urban Jews. Women married at an early age, usually between twelve and fifteen. Five women gave birth to at least one child before they had reached the age of fifteen. Rural Jewish men married around twenty. The average number of children per married couple was 3.5, which may be considered high, given the high rate of infant mortality. There were four extended households, one including a husband's sister, the second a wife's sister, the third a son-in-law and two grandchildren, and the fourth two daughters-in-law with two children. The rest were nuclear families. In contrast to urban Jews, divorce did occur among the rural Jews.

Their naming pattern was also different. The majority of patronyms were Berber-Arabic, such as Benmusi, Benaid, and Benamu, but there was also an incidental Levi or Serfati, which were typical Sephardic patronyms. All first names given to men were biblical ones, except for an occasional Mimum or Dudu, which contrasts with female first names which were rarely biblical.[11] This naming pattern suggests an opposition between a Great Tradition of men and a local female tradition. It is also interesting to note that the popularity of the female names suggesting the idea of supremacy, such as Sultana, Reina and Luna, conveys a positive female self-image, emphasising the crucial role of women in the perpetuation of Judaism. This female self-image contrasts with the picture of female inferiority in the literature.[12] These data on the rural Jewish family are born out by the census of 1887 in which the immigrant families from the Imazujen and Ait Shikar are implied.

Nearly all men from the tribal hinterland gave trade as their occupation, while, in fact, peddling wares and handicrafts were combined activities. There was one rabbi who served the Iqar'ayen Jews, and one man gave his occupation as silversmith, which was a Jewish monopoly in Morocco. Tribal Jews spoke Rifi as their first language, but most men also knew some Spanish and Moroccan Arabic. The vast majority was illiterate.

Little is known about the conditions under which these Jews lived before they emigrated to Melilla. We do have some scattered observations in the (proto-)ethnographical literature which however are contradictory in several respects. According to Mouliéras (1895: 155):

The Jews are extremely numerous in the tribe of Galiya [Iqar'ayen]. They live in hamlets and work as cobblers, rope-makers, jewellery-makers and tinkers; none of them are peasants. They rent their houses, for they are not allowed to own property. Each Jew has a

[Berber] protector. They travel to Tangier, Oran and Spain on business; they talk Rifian and are well treated by the Rifians.

Llanos y Alcaraz (1894: 300) arrived at a different conclusion:

> The Jews who live in the countryside are the victims of much abuse,
> injustice and lamentable humiliations. They are obliged to wear a
> handkerchief on their heads, to ride a mule in the female fashion,
> and to pay protection money whenever they pass with their wares.

Artbauer (1911: 150–1) is one of the few Western observers who
reported that there were also Jews who leased land, which they
themselves farmed. He pointed at the deep-rooted mistrust of
Jews in the Rif, and held that urban Jews enjoyed much more
freedom than their rural counterparts. Like other writers, he
stressed the vital role Jews played in the regional network of
weekly markets and in foreign trade and smuggling. Finally, he
observed that Jews were obliged to follow certain regulations of
dress, such as the wearing of black gowns and skull-caps.

Carleton Coon (1931: 95) is the most explicit author on the
social position of the Jews in the Rif, writing:

> The Jews, while living in the places settled by them, such as Galiya
> and Beni Bu Frah, form distinct colonies which in the past were not
> often molested. Jews going into other regions could formerly do so
> only under the protection of some important man in that region. The
> patron of the Jew considered him as his bondsman or slave, while the
> Jews regarded the contract as merely a commercial one. The Jew was
> allowed to work at some trade, but must turn in his receipts to his
> patron, who gave him food and lodging and a certain amount of
> money besides. The patron was responsible for the Jew's safety and
> protected him against aggressors. . . . The Riffians, in common with
> other Mohammedans, consider it a desecration of gunpowder to
> shoot Jews, killing them only with stones and knives. Since the
> Spanish and French occupations the role of the Jew has of course
> changed. He is at present allowed to go to markets to trade, and is
> ordinarily not molested.

He further noted that the Jews who lived in the vicinity of
Melilla specialised in metalwork, a despised occupation among
Rifians. Their specialties included brass trays, sugar-hammers,
silver and pewter brooches, silver rings, and bracelets. 'Abd al
Krim set them to work making hand grenades (1931: 65–6). Hart
(1976: 155) added that among the Ait Waryaghar Jews were at

the bottom of society, beyond the pale and without political importance. Nevertheless, for a powerful man to 'have his own Jew' was considered a sign of respect and the killing of a Jew was 'an infinitely worse offense than to kill a fellow tribesman' (ibid. 280).[13] In contrast to Coon, Hart asserts that, despite the restrictions inherent in their social position, the Jews enjoyed considerable freedom to travel in tribal areas.

Only three informants whose parents lived among the Rifians were able, or willing, to talk at length about their parents' past. The three accounts given to me are consistent in their emphasis that conditions differed according to time and place. They, for instance, agreed that conditions were worse for Jews in the central Rif, and that they were considerably better in the immediate hinterland of Melilla. They also agreed that 'on the whole living among the Berbers was not really bad in normal times.' Two of my informants cited cases of Jews who were obliged to fight in the *harcas* of their patrons, though normally they were not allowed to carry weapons nor to ride horses, which were the mark of men of honour. They all affirmed the obligation to wear distinctive clothing, that is a black skull-cap or a kerchief to cover their head. They had to remove their footwear when passing a mosque, and were frequently harassed by children. None of my informants mentioned the obligation to ride a mule or donkey in the female fashion. Regarding patronage and freedom of movement I noted down the following statements:

> Certain leaders of tribal communities took us under their protection. They recognised our problems and helped us, while we, in our turn, supported them. In other words, we made common cause. I have heard of cases of Jews who were invited to live as neighbours to tribal leaders.
> When I was a child my grandfather, who lived among the Ait Bu Gafar told me that at harvest time he went to the threshing-floors to sell mats and baskets and to repair saddles and harnesses, in exchange for which he received grain and straw. We held a monopoly over the sugar-trade, which we exchanged for barley and wheat.
> At the beginning of this century my father made tours along the hamlets to buy up goatskins which he then sold here [in Melilla]. He also went on his donkey to the markets of Dar Quebdani and Tafersit [important pre-colonial trade centres].

Opinions differed on the payment of the so-called *djazzat* or protection money given to powerful men for safe conduct. One informant held that they had to pay protection money whenever they travelled, another informant denied this.

As to Jewish occupations the informants were unanimous. All Jews were hawkers and a minority had specialised in the making of packsaddles and harnesses, metalworking, silversmithing, tailoring and as shoemakers of traditional footwear. One informant knew of a case of a Jewish family who owned land in the area of the Ulad Settut, an Arabic-speaking tribe to the east of Melilla. Another informant summarised the condition of the rural Jews as follows:

> On the whole, the life of our forebears was one of poverty, humiliation and humility. The safest conduct was to adopt an attitude of docility. In those days, Jews had to work hard for little reward.

From the timing of the tribal Jewish emigration to Melilla, it can be deduced that Jews suffered from political instability in the Rif. The first wave of immigrants coincided with drought and a plague of locusts in the early 1880s, which was also a period of increased feuding. The short war of the Iqar'ayen with Melilla in 1893 was preceded by a second wave of Jewish immigrants. The third and largest came during the Moroccan civil war of 1902–1907.

But in times of peace the outcast status of the Jews also carried some economic benefits. They could maintain a monopoly over a number of vital occupations shunned by both Catholics and Muslims and they could derive some leverage from switching between Berber protectors. That they were excluded from the game of honour and power implied that they were sought out as brokers. Although considered cunning by the Rifians, they were trusted more than fellow Rifians and urban Arabs. As marginal and ambiguous people the Jews were cast in the role of economic mediators, though this position also carried the risk of becoming scapegoats in difficult times.

Consolidation of the Jewish Community

The immigration of urban Jews from Tetuan, Gibraltar, Tangier, Oran and Nemours in Algeria continued throughout the 1880s and 1890s. In fact, these immigrants provided much of the capital needed for urban development. When from 1888

onwards the new barrio of Poligono was constructed in the
outer territory of Melilla, many Jews moved from the ancient
town and Manelete to the better houses in the new quarter,
which fast became the most lively trading barrio of the enclave.
The prestigious new quarter of Reina Victoria, which is today
the heart of modern Melilla, was largely constructed with
money invested by Jews who came from Tetuan, and the first
affluent Jews moved there in 1909. It came to be popularly
known as 'el barrio de Sion'. A Spanish writer on life in Melilla
during the 1890s commented on the Jews as follows:

> The rich merchants sincerely love Spain . . . almost all of them wear
> European clothes. . . . They stand out for their affability, good man-
> ners, and gentleness of customs. . . . They live mainly in the Mante-
> lete and Poligono. . . . In their traffic with the Moors, they treat them
> disdainfully and call them pirates. They have to throw them out of
> their shops frequently and mostly for good reason. On the other
> hand, the Jews appreciate Moors [urban Arabs], who, though they
> are no better than the local ones, create a better impression (Llanos y
> Alcaraz 1894: 344 ff.).

At that time there were already two synagogues and a Jewish
cemetery in Melilla. In 1893 thirteen prominent businessmen
took the initiative in founding a 'Circulo de Amistad' promoting
good relations between civilians and the garrison. Among them
figured four leading Jewish merchants, including José Salama.[14]

A list of the seventeen most important Jewish traders published in Llanos y Alcaraz (1894: 350), indicates the predominance of Jews of Tetuan origin. The only rural Jew among them
was a merchant who came to Melilla in 1882 from the Ait Sidar.
By that time Salama & Sons had already established itself as a
commercial stronghold; this wholesaler and banker represented
the French shipping holding company 'Compagnie Générale
Transatlantique', acted as a local agent for Crédit Lyonnais and
maintained links with banks in London, Manchester, Paris,
Marseille, Gibraltar, Málaga, Oran, Tetuan and Tangier. The
second most powerful businessman operated on a regional
scale. This man owned trading offices in Fez, Casablanca, Moga-
dor, Tangier and Tetuan.

The major attraction of Melilla as a place of residence for these
merchants was that as a free port it had become a major entrepôt. French sugar, Spanish olive oil, English cotton, candles,
soap, tea and ironware were traded through Melilla to Morocco

and Algeria, while fish, skins, almonds, wool and later iron ore moved in the opposite direction. The Jews acted as intermediaries in this trade. Prior to the pacification of the Rif they profited enormously from the tense relations between the Spanish and the Rifians. Given their trading experience, the networks they brought with them, their linguistic skills and mobility, they fitted perfectly into the role of brokers. Leading Spanish *africanistas* resented the success of the Jewish traders. Lobera, the mouthpiece of Spanish interests in Melilla, sourly called them *'acaparadores* of the trade with the tribes' (1912: 122). The term *acaparador* is unmistakably pejorative, referring to a person who is involved in black market operations, especially in time of war. In fact, during the brief war of 1893 between Melilla and the Iqar'ayen the military commander expelled several Jewish and Muslim traders 'for trading in contraband with the enemy'.[15]

In the first decade of the twentieth century, the Jewish colony of Melilla grew enormously. Destitute Jewish refugees from the tribal hinterland and the important colonies of Taza and Debdu poured into Melilla to seek refuge from the civil war that ravaged eastern Morocco. Most of them had been stripped of all their possessions. These hundreds of Jews were lodged in improvised camps under canvas and fed by the Jewish charity foundation. By 1910 the tents had been replaced by wooden shacks. These new immigrants were frequently harassed by Spanish soldiers who came to the camp in order to insult, molest and steal. Jewish community leaders sent letters of protest to the Commandant General with the final result that the quarter was placed under permanent surveillance by the military police.[16] The Salama family were the main financiers behind the replacement of the tents and wooden shacks by brick houses. By 1920 a new exclusively Jewish working-class neighbourhood had emerged, which was simply called 'el barrio hebreo'.

In 1900 there were 950 Jews living in Melilla, some 16 percent of the civil population.[17] By 1910 the Jewish population had almost doubled (cf. de Morales 1909: 598), and in 1917 the ethnic composition of the population according to barrio was as indicated in table 5.1.

Apart from Jews and Muslims, who were almost all Moroccan citizens, there were 254 other foreigners listed in the census. These represented twelve different nationalities, among which French and Cubans predominated.

The Jewish inhabitants were concentrated in seven of the

Table 5.1 Composition of the population in 1917

Barrio	Spaniards		Jews		Muslims	
	Male	Female	Male	Female	Male	Female
Pueblo	673	835	10	17	1	2
Alcazaba	351	379	–	–	–	–
Mantelete	180	198	13	15	48	39
Reina Victoria	1,155	1,455	333	280	28	10
Carmen	2,432	2,701	191	228	4	–
Poligono/Hebreo	897	1,120	909	858	19	1
Cabrerizas	199	233	–	–	–	–
Bateria J.	468	450	–	–	–	–
Reina Regente	178	177	–	–	–	–
Asturias	314	316	–	–	–	–
Jordana	737	925	24	25	–	–
San Lorenzo	1,140	1,283	–	–	10	10
Arizón	2,051	2,078	–	–	21	7
Industrial	1,010	1,138	–	–	2	–
Alfonso XIII	46	50	–	–	–	–
Zoco	80	94	–	–	–	–
Hipódromo	1,022	1,111	–	–	5	–
Real	2,964	3,185	–	–	15	12
Total	15,897	17,728	1,480	1,423	153	81

Source: Junta de Arbitrios. Su gestión durante los años 1917–1918, A.M.M.

eighteen barrios. The remaining neighbourhoods were Catholic working-class and lumpenproletarian barrios. The most central quarter of Melilla, Reina Victoria, had a fair representation of Jews, who belonged to the upper and middle classes of local society. Jewish artisans and small traders lived in the Carmen and Poligono barrios, while the Hebrew barrio was overwhelmingly proletarian. Further scrutiny of individual barrios of a mixed ethnic nature reveals a strong tendency towards ethnic segregation, with the exception of the city centre. The Poligono, for instance, was a popular market neighbourhood where Jews were heavily concentrated in four streets. While the Jewish population had increased considerably since 1910, its proportion in the overall population had dropped to less than 8 percent.

The Jewish community continued to grow slightly during the 1920s. In 1928 Jews numbered 3,283, which amounted to 6 percent of the total population. Throughout the 1930s and early

1940s the number of Jewish residents fluctuated between 3,000 and 3,500. By the end of the Second World War there were still 3,059 Jews living in Melilla. Shortly after the foundation of the new Jewish state, hundreds of working-class Jews emigrated to Israel on government subsidies. The second wave of emigration took place after Morocco gained its independence. By 1965 the number of Jewish residents in Melilla had dropped to 1,200.[18]

The boom brought about by the Spanish army's occupation of Melilla's hinterland from 1909–1911 gave a strong impetus to the Jewish community. Jewish traders played a prominent role in the provisioning of the Spanish army of occupation.[19] The twenty-odd merchant families who settled down in Melilla in the last three decades of the nineteenth century were all able to consolidate and reinforce their family businesses. They availed themselves of the economic opportunities created by Spanish colonial expansion and associated themselves firmly with the Spanish Protectorate. They embraced Spanish culture, however, without abandoning their own religious traditions. They also profited from the savings which Rifian seasonal workers returning from the Oranie largely spent in Jewish shops.

These big merchants were the vital links between Melilla, Algeria, French Morocco and the Rif. The most powerful among them acted as agents of Western European trading and banking houses. By 1915 four Jews sat in the council of the local Chamber of Commerce. Of the eight shipowners, five were Jews, and of a total number of seventy-nine wholesale traders twenty-seven were Jews. The textile trade was a virtual Jewish monopoly, nineteen of the twenty-seven textile merchants being Jews. The largest local entrepreneur in the retail food trade was a Jew who had married into the Salama family. The Cohen brothers operated a vast commercial network in jewellery — the production and distribution of jewellery was another Jewish monopoly — that covered most of Morocco, with offices in Oujda, Tetuan, Fez, Casablanca, and Tangier. The Garzon trading company, which specialised in confectionery, shoes, perfume and travel goods, had offices in both Gibraltar and Manchester. Abraham Levy was a typical middle-range merchant whose commercial activities ranged from the port of Málaga from where he imported groceries and olive oil, to the immediate hinterland of Melilla where he bought up hides and distributed his imported products through client Jewish ambulant traders. He had offices in Melilla, Nador and Seghanghan.[20]

The popular Spanish stereotype of Jewish commercial conservatism may have been largely true for the small and middle traders; it certainly does not apply to the largest entrepreneurs who were true innovators. These pioneers began as individual merchants who expanded their business through their sons and partnerships with other members of the extended family. The most powerful trading families, such as the Salama and Benarroch, succeeded in holding the family capital together through the second and third generations by transforming the inherited wealth into diversified limited liability companies. This corporate form of business, which became prominent in Spain in the 1920s, ensured continuance of familial control while at the same time protecting individual partners through limited liability. The Benarroch, for instance, made this transition in the third generation when in 1928 the oldest grandson of Moises Benarroch, the founder of the family firm, started a flour-mill in Nador with a nominal capital of one million pesetas (Morales Lezcano 1984: 191). This 'Harinera Española Benarroch S.A.' became one of the largest companies of the eastern Rif.

The extra-local marriage patterns of the Jewish entrepreneurial elite ensured that every merchant had relatives and thus potential business partners in the major cities of Morocco and Algeria, sometimes in Spain, and even in France and England. Family ties reinforced confidence and mutual interests. The associates were, so to speak, born into the enterprise and had a vested interest in maintaining and expanding it. The most powerful trading houses, whose owners had adopted Spanish citizenship in the founding generation, were able to invest their capital in property, both in Melilla and the Peninsula. For instance, the Salama family provided much of the capital needed for the construction of the Hebrew barrio, while a son of Moises Benarroch was one of the biggest financiers of the barrio Reina Victoria. The high level of formal education and linguistic expertise in the second and third generations, the extent of personal and familial networks along ethnic lines, together with positions of authority and patronage in local society, constituted the cultural power of this entrepreneurial elite.

These prominent merchants played a leading role in building a Jewish community. As the pace of immigration accelerated, an increasing number of destitute Jews poured into Melilla. The strong feelings of communal obligation to help fellow Jews in trouble — a religious duty for which the benefactors received spiritual blessing — resulted in the foundation of the Jewish benevolent society 'Ozer Dalim' (after one of the many names for God, 'He who helps the poor'). An elementary Hebrew school was founded in 1905, which was gradually expanded into a Hispano-Israeli college for boys. When a prestigious secondary school for girls run by nuns refused entry to Jewish girls on the grounds of their religion, José Salama took up the matter with the bishop of Málaga. The Catholic prelate intervened on behalf of the Jews and Salama is said to have become one of the major benefactors of this college. In 1924 a new large synagogue, named 'Or Zaruch' ('Descending Light'), was inaugurated. This impressive building, located on a central street running parallel to the main avenue, was a gift by Yamin Benarroch to all the Jews of Melilla, 'regardless of origin, nationality and class,' as the memorial plaque in the main entrance hall testifies.

The wealthy merchants who dominated the Jewish Community Council used charity — housing, clothing and food — to monitor the religious and moral behaviour of working-class Jews. During the first three decades of this century a class divide developed within the Jewish colony, which largely coincided with the gap between immigrants of urban and rural origin. The small mercantile elite was able to move into the upper class, associating itself firmly with the protectorate and adopting the Spanish culture. However, its members remained devoutly Jewish and did not abandon their religious tradition and identity, as is shown by the fact that in the first half of the century propertied Jews remained an endogamous connubium.

The privileged Jews found themselves increasingly opposed by a restive mass of Jewish casual labourers, a number of whom had turned away from Judaism. Their poverty was partly due to the problems they encountered in adapting to the harsh conditions of a frontier society. Melilla offered few new economic opportunities to this reservoir of cheap labour. Male unemployment, under-employment and job insecurity were great. Married Jewish women had to earn a living as domestic servants or worked at home as seamstresses. Close attention to the local daily newspaper yields numerous illustrations of the tensions and sometimes violent confrontations among Jews. There was fierce competition both for the scarce job opportunities and for housing. Wife-battering, alcoholism, gambling and disturbances among neighbours were the most current manifestations of this social misery.

Nevertheless, only a small minority of working-class Jews became militants in the socialist movement, and these were mainly dock-workers. In 1931, at the advent of the Second Republic, two Jewish labourers were elected to the municipal council for the Spanish Socialist Labour Party. After much hesitation, informants revealed some of the atrocities committed by Falangists and Muslim servicemen against the Jewish community at the outbreak of the Civil War. Six militant Jews were shot by order of a drumhead court martial and many Jewish women were raped in the Hebrew barrio by Muslim soldiers in the service of the Protectorate Army. The hair of several Jews was shaved in the shape of a cross. Synagogues were closed down. Dozens of Jews were imprisoned in forced labour camps in Morocco, or drafted into the Nationalist army.

Jewish commerce, however, was left untouched, which indicates the importance of the role of Jews in the colonial economy. Excesses against Jews occurred mainly during the first weeks of the Civil War. Although Synagogues were soon reopened, various forms of humiliation and harassment continued until well into the late 1940s. On Easter Sunday, for instance, bands of young Catholics paraded in front of Jewish houses making rough music and molesting Jews who dared to appear in the streets. Effigies of Jews were ostentatiously burnt. These rites of humiliation, mainly directed against working-class Jews, became a custom which continued for more than fifteen years.[21] Large numbers of workers, peddlars and small artisans emigrated to Israel in the late 1940s, so leaving their problems behind them.

On the other side of the class divide, the Jewish merchant families not only dominated the Jewish community but also began to play an increasingly prominent role in the society at large.[22] When the Second Republic began José Salama's son Jacobo was president of the 'Israelite Community of Melilla' which by this time had been officially recognised. (Henceforth the term Community with a capital as opposed to a small 'c' refers to the formal organisation.) A brother-in-law acted as vice-president. Jacobo Salama also sat on the municipal council and acted as vice-president of the Chamber of Urban Property until his death in 1933. The spiritual leader of the Community, Grand Rabbi Reby David Cohen was assisted by three Cohens, all prominent merchants, who sat on the Community Council.

Other members of the Salama family held posts in the College of Commercial Agents, the Mercantile Club and the Red Cross. The local section of WIZO, the Women's International Zionist Organisation, was presided over by the widows of three former Jewish leaders, Reby Abraham Cohen, Isaac Benarroch and Samuel Salama. Of the 199 major property owners, thirty-two were Jews, and eight Muslims. The Salama dynasty which, in the 1920s, had also become a family corporation continued as the most powerful trading house. Its nominal head was José Salama's widow, but in practice the business was run by their three sons Jacobo, Moises and José. On the occasion of the municipal elections of 1931, the chief editor of the local daily newspaper wrote the following editorial in which he explicitly referred to the Jewish community:

> The Sephardic Jews of Melilla and Ceuta have contributed spiritually and materially to the organisation of our democratic parties, and put their faith in the idea that with the advent of the Republic, they will probably be fully reintegrated into their fatherland of origin and liberally profess their religion in our city. Someone correctly defined the Sephardic Jews as 'Spaniards without a fatherland'. Today, many have indeed adopted Spanish citizenship, although more, many more, wish to become Spaniards. They are discouraged by the barriers, long-winded procedures and difficulties they have to face.[23]

The editor probably alluded to the obvious class bias in granting Spanish citizenship. However, when I discussed this issue of nationality with informants, they pointed out that many Jews preferred to keep their Moroccan nationality, because of the commercial advantages this carried and in order to evade Spanish military service. Only after Morocco gained independence did the overwhelming majority of Melilla Jews opt for Spanish nationality.

An Ambiguous Minority

Though most of the Jews who now live in Melilla are Spaniards, they remain the ambivalent minority which they have always been since they first settled in the enclave. They are a small, well-established and in some respects well-integrated community within the local society. The leading members of the community define themselves as the custodians of Jewish tradition in Spain. As the president of the Community Council put it: 'We are proud to be the oldest and most devout Jewish community in Spain.'[24]

The inner core, that is the most active members of the Community, see themselves as conservatives in faith and ritual. Indeed, I observed a high level of religious observance compared with the Catholic and Muslim segments of the enclave. Whereas the great majority of the Muslim shops are open on Friday afternoons and festive days, the shops of Jewish merchants remain closed on the Sabbath (*shabbat*) and on the numerous festive days of the ceremonial calender. While churches and mosques are little used for daily services, the synagogues are frequented by young and old men, particularly for evening prayer (*ma'ariv*). A typical street scene is of small groups of Jewish men of different ages, wearing skull-caps and chattering at the doors of houses along the perimeter of the city centre, between nine and ten in the evening. Apart from the main synagogue there are ten private houses where men may congregate for the three daily prayers if ten adult Jews, the minimum required for worship (*minyan*) have come together. Devout Jews always refer to these houses as synagogues, proudly stating that their community boasts eleven houses of worship.

There is, however, a growing minority who think of themselves as liberal and secular Jews. These people are peripheral to the Community and synagogues, and participate at most only in the major religious festivals. The contrast between urban and rural, propertied and unpropertied has been replaced by the division between conservatives and liberals, devout and secular.

Frequency and intimacy of contacts between Jews and other ethnic groups is closely connected with the Jewish self-image and sense of identity. The following two propositions can be put forward. Jews who identify themselves strongly with Judaism and Zionism tend to maintain a high level of intra-ethnic interaction and an active stance in communal affairs, while their ties with Catholic Spaniards tend to be minimal and single-stranded. On the other hand, Jews who mainly derive their identity from the family and not primarily from religious observance, identification with Zionism or participation in the Community, tend to have frequent and many-stranded contacts with Catholic Spaniards. The dozen or so mixed marriages, that is Jewish-Catholic couples, belong to this category.

Thus on the basic question of Jewish identity conservatives

and liberals hold opposing views. Conservatives assert that a Jewish person must be the son or daughter of a Jewish mother, have gone through the prescribed rites of passage, know the Law, perform the ritual obligations, and maintain a level of regular participation in Community life. Leon Serfati represents this type. He is a self-confident and cheerful man in his mid-thirties, who finished secondary school, is literate in Spanish, Hebrew, Arabic, English and French, and speaks some *Rifi*. His grandfather was a merchant from Tetuan who was among the first Jews who settled in Melilla. Leon is married and has two children. His wife took a bachelor's degree in English and helps her husband in his store. Leon calls himself a conservative Jew. He sits in the Community Council and is a cantor in the main synagogue. He maintains that the Jews of Melilla are tolerant of and open to other religions:

> All the peoples of Holy Book believe in the same God, it is custom that makes them different. We respect Catholicism and Islam. You, for instance, are welcome to our religious services. When Pope John XXIII died, our rabbis held a service in honour of his memory because of what he did for advancing ecumenical tolerance.

Abraham Levi represents the liberal point of view. He is a small, thickset, nervous man in his early sixties, whose parents came to Melilla from the neighbouring tribe of Ait Sidar at the beginning of this century. He grew up in poverty, attended elementary school for three years, and began to assist his father, an itinerant trader, at the age of ten. Through hardwork and self-education he succeeded in finishing school and entered training college. As a student he became involved in politics, was arrested when the Civil War broke out, and spent sixteen months of forced labour in an internment camp. After the war he became an agent for Swiss clocks and watches, finished training college, and worked as a part-time teacher in the Hispano-Hebrew college. He is one of the founder members of the local Lions Club and was voted onto the municipal council as an independent candidate within the socialist bloc. He defines himself as a freethinker. On the question of Jewish identity he passed the following opinion:

> A Jew is a person who feels himself a Jew. Although I consider myself an atheist, I privately respect religious rites and festivities because of my mother.

He openly sympathises with the Zionist cause and has visited
Israel several times.

Another informant expressed an intermediate position:
'When a person says he is a Jew, he should either identify
himself with Judaism or Zionism. If not, he cannot be considered a Jew.' These differences in self-perception, identity,
and styles of life are not apparent to Catholics or Muslims. Jews
are the same in the eyes of all other ethnic groups, forming one
closed community of their own. The following statements about
Jews are common coin among Catholics and Muslims:

> Although there is some contact between Jewish and Catholic stu-
> dents, Jews remain typically Jews. They stick to their own lot, their
> traditions, and community. [a Catholic teacher] There is much in-
> breeding among Jews, you know, which results in a denigration of
> their lineage. As traders they are all conservatives. [a Catholic shop-
> keeper]

> Hebrews discriminate against us more than Catholics do. They
> separate themselves from us. Our Jewish neighbours do not even
> greet us. [a Muslim trader]

> They are really a breed apart. You must have noticed that they are
> always celebrating. I simply do not understand how they earn so
> much money while their bazaars are closed most of the time. [a
> Muslim waiter at the time of Passover]

It is not surprising that the Jews themselves are highly ambivalent on the matter of their national identity. Formally, they are
all Spaniards, except for a dozen or so who hold Moroccan,
English, French or Venezuelan nationality. I noted down the
following statements made by Jewish informants with regard to
their national identity:

> My home is Melilla and since this city belongs to Spain I am a
> Spaniard.
> We have set down roots here, we feel part of the city. We feel
> Spanish in every respect.

However, most acknowledge a special tie with Israel, as one
informant put it in the presence of a Catholic Spaniard:

> Our bond with the state of Israel is purely spiritual.

Yet, later, when the Catholic had gone, the same man asserted:

> Of course, it is only natural that we would like finally to return to our land.

Older informants especially expressed their wish to emigrate to Israel after retirement, and others would like to be buried in Eretz Israel. In fact, most of the Jews of Melilla have relatives and friends there and many have visited the Holy Land on more than one occasion.

The same ambivalence can be detected in the views of Catholic Spaniards when they talk about the status of Jewish co-residents. They agree that Jews have been living in Melilla for generations and that as a consequence they are *melillenses*. Yet, they never refer to them as Spaniards, and consistently label them 'Hebrews' (*hebreos*), indicating that they continue to be considered as foreigners.

Most Jews belong to the middle class and are relatively prosperous, though they tend to play down their status both in verbal and non-verbal behaviour. As one of them phrased it: 'Today, there are no big fortunes among us. To be sure, there are some really propertied men, but the majority is of rather modest economic status.' This may be a way in which Jews defend themselves against the popular stereotype that all Jews are rich and to be envied. However, ironically enough, their non-conspicuous behaviour — in which they differ from Catholics, Muslims and Hindus who tend to show off their wealth — reinforces another stereotype, that Jews are greedy. This is obvious in the following anecdote about the only Jew who sits on the municipal council:

> Last night, as usual, we [a group of councillors] went to the bodega Madrid after the meeting to have some drinks and *tapas*. To our great surprise Abraham Levy joined us. But we were even more surprised when he paid for a round, which never happened before.

This statement simply implies that Jews do not wish to socialise with Catholics and that they abstain from participating in exchange circuits, which is often taken as an indication of their presumed stinginess. The same inclination towards inconspicuousness is displayed in local politics, from which they generally remain aloof. In public they present themselves as apolitical.

In spite of popular stereotypes and self-representation, several Jews have acquired social prominence because of material success. They are members of the 'Maritime Club', the 'Casino' and 'Hippic Society' (a horseriding club), which are elite bastions of Spanishness. José Anselem, for instance, who has been president of the Jewish Community Council since 1980, holds the post of secretary of the Chamber of Commerce and is a member of two of the three associations mentioned above. Although Jews constitute less than 2 percent of the total population, one fifth (some thirty merchants) of all the wholesalers in Melilla — who hold import and export licenses — are Jews.[25] The remaining 130 Jewish traders operate in the retail trade. Since Morocco's independence, the role of these merchants as intermediaries in long-distance trade has been gradually taken over by Hindu entrepreneurs who have begun to monopolise the increasingly important trade with the Far East. This change of roles is a result of shifts in the world economic system, in particular the rise of Japan, Singapore, Hong Kong and Korea as producers of cheap luxury commodities. On the other hand, there is still a remarkable Jewish presence in the branches of jewellery and textiles, two traditional Jewish niches.

The younger generations tend to move away from commerce into the more prestigious professions, while trade guarantees personal autonomy — a warmly cherished value — for the older generations. It has to be noted that historical conditions forced Jews into trade and that before 1950 most academic careers were closed to them. There are now three Jewish doctors, three pharmacists, one dentist, one optician, two professors, four secondary school teachers, three electricians, one building contractor, three employees in the Spanish Airlines, one bookbinder, one engineer, one garage-owner, a dozen civil servants, eleven bar-owners, and a dozen or so skilled labourers.[26] The president of the Community Council proudly claimed that there are no unemployed Jews in Melilla: 'We possess an enterprising spirit, we are always busy earning a living.'

However, there is one Jew who is a thorn in the side of the Community Council, an old tramp who has been roaming the streets for several decades in spite of persistent efforts to dissuade him from such vagabondage. This man, who is popularly known as 'el Tarzan', was drafted into Franco's army at the outbreak of the Civil War. He returned home mentally ill and never recovered. However much the Community Council tries to give him shelter and food, Tarzan prefers to live on the streets where he eats, sleeps, and collects garbage. Once in a while he is picked from the street by members of the Community Council who then take him to the public bath-house for a thorough scrubbing. Having been re-clothed and fed, he is set free again, but always resumes his nomadic way of life.

The Jews of Melilla are a proud community. They boast a high educational level, the Community Council providing scholarships to promising young men to study theology in both London and Jerusalem. They claim that there are rabbis of Melillan origin in England, France, Denmark, Guatemala, Venezuela, Zimbabwe, Hong Kong and Singapore. The community maintains its own elementary school and provides teachers of Talmud, Hebrew and Jewish history for pupils in secondary education. The president claimed that delinquency is non-existent among Jews who according to him, display a high level of moral conduct and are law-abiding citizens.

The Community Council acts as a channel for all internal and external relations and exerts control over its members. It is part of an umbrella organisation of Hispano-Jewish communities which unites the Jews of Madrid, Barcelona, Valencia, Málaga, Sevilla, Ceuta and the Canary Islands. One of its activities is the annual organisation of summer camps for young people which are intended to promote inter-community cohesion. The Council's headquarters is in one of the largest buildings it owns, and it also houses the Hispano-Hebrew school, the ritual public bath, a medical office, and a hall where communal festive ceremonies are celebrated. Since religious law prohibits internment in niches and exhumation, which are practiced among Catholic Spaniards, the Community has its own cemetery and its own gravedigger. It employs a rabbi and a kosher butcher and imports wine from Israel which is used in the ceremony of blessing on Sabbath and festive days.

The major division within the Jewish community is between the sexes. Male dominance and segregation of the sexes are marked among them. Women attend public religious services infrequently and when they do attend, as on the festival of Yom Kippur, 'the shabbat of the shabbats', they are set apart from the men on a special balcony. Men legitimise sexual inequality as follows:

> Our women are exempted from religious duties in order to enable them to devote all their time and energy to our children and households. The mother is the priestess of the home.

On the other hand, according to religious law a Jew is the son of a Jewish mother, the basic criterion on which membership in the community rests. The family is the matrix of Judaism and the guardian of Jewish identity. The female role in the transmission of Jewish tradition is thus crucial.

Nevertheless, gender inequality is expressed in a number of important rites. First, there is a rite that communicates the relevance of male primogeniture. When a first son is born a special ceremony called *rescate*, literally ransom or ransom money, is performed by a Cohen. The latter takes the baby away from his parents and returns him to the father in exchange for a little ransom money, which goes into the treasury of the Community Council. According to my informants, this ceremony commemorates that all first fruits go to God. This is a feast of great joy in which the family, community, and the spiritual realm are linked together through the baby and the ritual specialist. This interlocking of the private, public and spiritual domains is repeated at the circumcision (*brit milah*), which is performed on the eighth day after birth in the main synagogue. A woman, who is either a close relative or friend of the parents, takes the baby from the mother's arms and passes him to a man, an equally close relative or friend, who sits in a ceremonial seat ('Elijah's chair') and comforts the baby while the operation is performed. The ceremony is concluded with a banquet.

In both rites which bear a strong resemblance with Catholic baptism, especially with regard to the vital role of the godparents, the passage of the baby from a non-person to a member of the Jewish community has to be effected by special mediators who substitute the biological parents. This passage is sealed by the *barmitzvah* in which thirteen-year-old boys become full members of the religious community. There are no parallel rites for girls, which indicates their subordinate status. For them, the first full-fledged public rite of passage is marriage, which consists of two parts. The first is the legal rite according to Spanish civil law which is performed in the town hall. The second part involves the signing of the marriage contract before the rabbi. The contract stipulates among other things the dowry which is transferred from the bride's father to the groom. This contract is then kept by the bride's mother, which indicates the importance of the mother-daughter tie.

Of the dozen or so non-endogamous marriages all but two are between a Jewish man and a Catholic woman. If the couple have decided to bring up their offspring in the Jewish tradition, the brides have to swear so in the marriage contract, but even then the rabbi must formally recognise the offspring as Jewish. I know of only two cases in Melilla of Jewish women who are married to Catholic men. Both relinquished their Jewish identity. Intermarriage between Catholics and Jews is, in fact, a recent phenomenon. The first case I heard of involved a teacher who married a Catholic woman in the early 1950s. He had to sign a declaration that he would have his offspring baptised. In retrospect he summarised this difficult phase of his life as follows:

> My determination to marry Isabel raised hell in both families. We had to go through many official barriers as well. You know, at that time Jews and Christians were not yet equal before the law of Spain [he interjects a story about a friend who wished to enter the military academy but was refused because of his Jewish background]. We have only one child, a daughter. In a sense I was both disappointed and relieved that our baby was a girl, for the birth of a boy would have entangled me in a great moral dilemma.

Since the passing of the new democratic constitution, the obstructions to mixed marriages have been removed. Today, Christians and Jews are equal before the law, and civil and church marriage have been separated. Yet marriages between Jews and Catholics remain exceptional. The family continues to be surrounded by high ethnic barriers.

There was only one ceremonial occasion in which both Catholics and Muslims played an important ritual role. Jewish immigrants brought the *mimuna*, a feast which marked the end of *Pesach* (Passover) and was celebrated by Jewish communities throughout North Africa, to Melilla and retained the tradition.[27] Elderly informants of Jewish, Catholic and Muslim background still vividly recall how it was celebrated in the 1920s and 1930s when they were children. They all called the feast by its Spanish designations, *fiesta de la galleta*, the 'festival of the biscuit' or *fiesta de las mesas* ('festival of the tables'), names that are still in use today. Many Jewish families continue to celebrate this ceremony, albeit on a modest scale and with a less pronounced inter-ethnic participation.

On the seventh day of Passover Catholics and Muslims brought greenery to the threshold of Jewish houses which was used to decorate the front door and living room. A variety of sweets, snacks and drinks adorned the tables. At twilight the Jews opened up their houses to relatives, friends and neighbours, including their Muslim and Catholic acquaintances and neighbours, who all feasted on the delicacies laid out on the tables. The mood was one of joy, abundance, joking and singing, all informants mentioning the free and easy nature of the gatherings. On the following morning Jewish families went on a picnic. No mention has been made of Jews dressing up as Muslims and men as women, a theme that has been noted in other Jewish communities in Morocco, Algeria and Tunisia.

The first striking fact about the 'festival of the biscuit' is that it lacks a basis in Great Hebrew Tradition (the literary as opposed to oral tradition). The Talmud even recommends semi-mourning instead of joy on this last day of Passover, which commemorates the passage through the Red Sea — redemption through exile — and the drowning of the Egyptians, who were, after all, also the children of God (cf. Chouraqui 1985: 217). This feast may also be seen as a double rite of passage. It both celebrates the arrival of spring and the re-incorporation of the Jewish community into local society after six days of seclusion, withdrawal and inward-orientation. The symbolism of fertility and renewal is striking. The Jews open their doors to blessing and good fortune from the outside. The front door, which is the *limen* between the private and public domain, is decorated with greenery. Homes are opened up to friends and neighbours where an abundance of food and drinks are offered. The picnic in the pine wood stresses the bond with nature and marks the beginning of a new annual cycle as well as a return to normal life. Thirdly, the 'festival of the biscuit' celebrates the interdependence of Jews, Christians and Muslims through commensality — a powerful performance of bondedness — and informal sociability, which are rare as inter-ethnic occasions in daily life.

This temporary acting out of belonging together is characteristically attended by structural reversals. The bosom of Jewish identity, the home, is bared for one evening, intimate family space being turned into a public domain. Catholics and Muslims who provide the Jews with greenery assume the role of servants, a role they normally ascribe to the Jews. In the evening Jews act as hosts to Catholics and Muslims. In doing so, they assume a structurally superior position, whereas in normal times they are considered and treated as guests, a structurally inferior status.

The erosion of the inter-ethnic character of this celebratory event in recent times, has been fuelled by important shifts in

Jewish-Muslim-Catholic relationships, in particular by the legal, cultural and political emancipation of the Jews. As Spanish citizens, the Jews are, in theory if not in practice, the equals of the Spanish Catholics and superior to the vast majority of Muslims. The emigration of the working-class Jews has resulted in a homogenisation of the Jewish community which, on the whole, has become economically stronger in comparison with the Muslim and Catholic communities. With regard to education, the Jews have attained a great deal when compared to large sections of the Catholic and Muslim population.

Whereas the 'festival of the biscuit' in the past linked the structurally subjugated Jewish minority to the dominant majority, it now expresses the force of Jewish cultural identity. The transformation of the feast from an open ethnic event into an increasingly exclusive Jewish celebration paradoxically highlights both the integration of the Jewish community within the enclave through more balanced economic, legal and political ties with the majority, and the separateness of the Jews as an ethnic minority. In other words, it expresses their basically ambivalent position in this society. They are both the permanent strangers or guests who remain conscious of a distant and sacred homeland and the influential and well-established insiders who have succeeded in carving out a relatively prosperous and worthy position in a secular fatherland. But the secular fatherland they have chosen is itself between Europe and Africa, a transitional space. The saga of the Jews of Melilla not only reveals how an ethnic minority has managed to capitalise on its structurally ambiguous position, but also how it has at times suffered from it.

Part 2

Ritual, Power and Ethnicity

6 Melilla's main mosque with public bath and tea-house (1984)

7 Cemetery of Melilla. Below to the left Jewish burial ground (1984)

8   Partial view of Cañada de la Muerte (1984)

9   Muslim cemetery and shrine of Sidi Wariach in no man's land between
the enclave and Morocco (1984)

10 Legionnaires carrying their spiritual patron Christ of the Good Death to a dais at the entrance of the town hall on the occasion of the presentation of a new national flag to the Foreign Legion (1984)

11 Spanish soldiers interested in Moroccan craft commodities (1984)

12 Shop window of photographer specialising in pictures for soldiers to send home to their fiancées and mothers. They are often dressed up to represent Arabs (1984)

Chapter 6

A Ceremony of the National Flag

In Melilla the Spanish flag is seen everywhere. The omnipresence of this symbol is, of course, linked to the city's status as a garrison and seat of numerous government offices. More important still is the basic fact that Melilla remains disputed territory, an enclave in an alien setting, cut off from the motherland by the sea. This invests the national colours with special importance and meaning. Apart from the daily display of the national flag on official and military buildings, it figures prominently in almost every ceremony and ritual. Moreover, there are occasional celebrations in which the flag plays a focal part. This chapter will deal with one special occasion of extraordinary emotive resonance, the blessing and presentation of a new national flag. I will discuss the specific meanings and structure of this event within a local context, and also address the general question of the relationships between ceremony and power.

Symbolism of the Flag

All nation-states hold ceremonies in which the national colours are the focus of attention. National flags are saluted, blessed, kissed, honoured, waved, paraded, hoisted and lowered on special occasions. But they are also trampled upon, burned, besmirched or displayed in improper contexts. In all these circumstances strong emotions are directed at, and vested in, a coloured piece of cloth. It is perhaps the most powerful symbol of the nation-state, assuming sacred qualities, and focal in what has been called civil religion. Following Ortner (1973), the national flag may be called a 'key symbol of the summarising type'. It synthesises complex ideas and experiences. It converts intricate notions about the nation-state into relatively undifferentiated sentiments and commitment, as in the case of patriotism. It may

111

also be called a 'dominant symbol' following Victor Turner (1974: 134), since it occupies a central position in a broad gamut of ritual performances.

The symbolism of the national flag rests primarily in its ceremonial display. It is employed as a rallying point for identification by a collectivity and for concerted action. The national flag is the repository of legitimate state power. It is no accident that it is so conspicuously displayed by the institutions which represent the strong arm of the state or that it is the main target of those who contest the legitimacy of state power. But why should flags have such strong emotional appeal and have attained such symbolic and ritual prominence? Raymond Firth, one of the few anthropologists who has devoted systematic attention to the symbolism of flags, points out some preliminary answers:

> . . . the special qualities of flags which make them a prime choice for symbolic use are availability and variability . . . The adaptability of flags in display means that their symbolic value can appear over a great range of ritual occasions. Again, their basic characteristics can be recognized at a distance, and they are as effective among illiterate as among literate populations. Finally, simple actions with a flag can implicate complex themes . . . it is a prime vehicle for conveying attitudes towards a social unit of which one is a member, or expressing other sentiments (1975: 342).

The special characteristics of national flags are dramatically highlighted by the reactions provoked by violations of the flag as, for instance, when they are approached without due respect, misused, defiled or destroyed. These and other points will be illustrated in the case to which we now turn.

Celebrating Ethnic Hegemony

Spanish-Catholic Melilla is a fragmented community. The main divisions are between established and immigrant status, social class, political creed and region of ancestral origin. One recent strategy for counteracting these divisive forces has been to revive collective rituals: the Holy Week celebrations with their brotherhoods, the festival of the Virgin of Rocio with its picnic, processions relating to the town's patron saint, the carnival and several other secular celebrations. Another reaction has been the rise of political activism of a nationalistic kind with its hate campaigns against Muslims.

In the summer of 1983 the municipal council took a unanimous decision to present a national flag with the new constitutional emblem to the regiment of the Foreign Legion based in Melilla. It is significant that this decision coincided with a period of serious labour and ethnic unrest. A strike of municipal gas, water and electricity workers almost brought the city to a standstill. The inhabitants of a depressed Muslim ghetto rose in protest against the miserable conditions in their barrio and staged a demonstration in the city centre, the first collective action of the Muslim population in more than fifty years. Serious riots erupted when some of the demonstrators began to attack cars with knives, sticks and stones, crying slogans against Melilla and Spain. A national flag was ripped from its staff and burnt in the main square in front of the town hall. The police reacted furiously and the Muslim acts provoked great outrage among the Catholic inhabitants. Some days later the Mayor made the following statement in the local newspaper:

> The anti-constitutional acts against the symbol representing the unity of all Spaniards, and the other isolated and irresponsible deeds of recent days, force the people (*pueblo*) of Melilla, through its town council, to voice its most indignant protest and to react against these breaches of peace, liberty and unity with a ceremony of redress . . . Melilla cannot, and must not remain silent in the face of the insults to the flag of all Spaniards . . . The town council, having sounded the views of all *melillenses*, summons the people of Melilla to render homage to the flag next Saturday at 1.00 p.m. in the Plaza de España. Long live Melilla, long live the Constitution, long live the King, long live Spain![1]

On the prearranged day, more than 1,000 inhabitants waving the national colours gathered in the main square for a ceremony of 'indemnification' of the national banner. In his address to the crowd the Mayor evoked the key concepts of manliness, honour and pride:

> He who contemplates this flag and does not feel pride, if he is a man he is not a Spaniard, and if he is a Spaniard he is not a man.[2]

This is the backdrop against which the presentation of the national flag to the Foreign Legion on 19 March 1984 has to be considered. The timing of the flag ceremony was agreed between the commander-in-chief, the commander of the Foreign Legion and the mayor of Melilla. In order to add importance to the celebration, the date chosen was the feast day of Saint Joseph, and this, moreover, coincided with the annual commemoration of the raising of the siege of 1774–5 by the Moroccan sultan Mulay Muhammad Abdallah, the most critical years in Spanish Melilla's existence.

The first public announcement of the flag ceremony appeared in the local newspaper — which played an important role in the creation of an emotional ambience — on 8 March. It was described as 'a ceremony of extraordinary importance for the relationship between our city and the garrison.'[3] Some days later similar statements were published along with an official invitation from the mayor for the whole *pueblo* to participate 'as a just homage to the city's garrison with its deep-rooted military traditions.' Actual preparations began one week before the event took place. The centre of the city had been decorated with thousands of small flags. By then the flag ceremony had become the major topic of conversation in the streets and bars.

An article in the 16 March edition of the newspaper anticipated the emotional atmosphere by recalling similar ceremonies in the past. The author reflected on the ceremony's deeper meaning as follows:

> . . . a flag kissed with profound emotion and sacred unction by all those who swear an oath of allegiance, testifying with this act that they will defend it, if necessary, by shedding their blood to the last drop.

Violent historical episodes were evoked in which the Foreign Legion rescued Melilla from occupation by Rifian rebels. The act to which the author referred is in fact the so-called *jura de bandera*, a very emotive experience common to most Spanish men. This traditional rite of initiation into the army is of extreme importance in the life-cycle of Spaniards. It ritually marks the end of basic training of conscripts and volunteers and is in fact a rite of initiation into manhood and citizenship attended by the families of the novices, a rite that creates long-lasting bonds of comradeship between those initiated on the same day.

Five days before the ceremony the new flag arrived in Melilla to be displayed to the public in a glass case in the town hall. This national treasure was constantly guarded by two soldiers, while numerous citizens came to view the expensive and valuable national symbol. Two days before the celebration the mayor once again urged the people of Melilla to attend the ceremony, while there was a great deal of public discussion between people about whether they would attend or stay at home. Only one man, a civil servant, openly stated that he would not attend:

> I won't go, that kind of show doesn't mean anything to me. I don't like such unnatural events at all [he makes a burlesque of the legionnaire's way of marching].

The day of the celebration dawned cloudy and chilly. It was an official holiday for the Catholic inhabitants, but just a normal working day for the Muslim population. Local Muslim and Moroccan street traders, money-exchangers, beggars, lottery-sellers, drug-dealers, shoe-shine boys, car washers and pick-pockets flocked to the city centre and prepared to secure their share of the festival that was about to begin.

The ceremony officially began at 10.30 a.m. with a solemn mass in the church of the old town where all the civil and military authorities were gathered. Only a handful of citizens attended the mass. One of my informants commented: 'if they are not made to, people here do not go to church.' The Jewish councillor waited in the porch of the church until the mass was finished. Then those in authority proceeded to the military parade-ground of ancient Melilla where a wreath of flowers was placed at the monument of the 'heroic defenders' of Melilla, a rather bleak performance watched by a small crowd of citizens. A former mayor who had instigated the resumption of this ceremonial act in the early 1960s complained to me about the lack of pageantry and poor turnout of the public: 'A people which does not respect its traditions is not a worthy people,' he concluded.

Descending from the old walled town to the main square (the *Plaza de España*), the ambience changed completely. A huge crowd had gathered in front of a *tableau vivant* of all local army units whose soldiers were in full-dress uniform. Civilians had also dressed up for the occasion. Thousands of inhabitants eagerly waited for the spectacle to begin. Next day the news-paper wrote: 'this ceremony drew the largest crowd of any in recent years', estimating the crowd at 20,000.

The ceremony then proceeded as follows.

11.20 a.m.: bugle calls signalled the army units to their assigned places in front of the monumental, neoclassical town hall. Meanwhile episodes from Melilla's history, emphasising the role played by the Foreign Legion, were recounted to the crowd using a public address system.

11.45 a.m.: the old national flag of the Foreign Legion that was to be replaced was carried to the dais as a military band played the national anthem.

11.50 a.m.: the mayor and his spouse arrived, followed by the Civil Governor; both received a ceremonial salute and were welcomed by the commander of the Legion.

12.00: the Commander-in-Chief of Melilla reviewed the troops, while the highest civil and military authorities took position in the place of honour. Then the major part of the performance began with salutes. The old national flag was solemnly and slowly carried to a dais at the entrance of the town hall while the national anthem was played again; it was followed by the new banner flanked by the mayor's wife, who acted as godmother to the flag, and the commander of the Legion who was both godfather and the recipient. The latter then began to recite an oration in which he implored God to sanctify the flag and

> make sure that triumph will always accompany our passage through history and that one day we will arrive at the final victory of eternal salvation. May the benediction of God Almighty, Father, Son, and Holy Ghost descend upon this flag and always remain with it and may the angel of God guard it forever . . .

whereupon the priest consecrated the flag with holy water. After this solemn act, the mayor's wife, as godmother, confessed that

> . . . as a Spanish mother I am proud that this glorious flag, to which our fathers, the fathers of our sons have sworn and to which their sons will swear their allegiance, is in your magnanimous custody; and I feel proud as a woman of Melilla, that is to say doubly Spanish, of carrying this flag in the name of this *pueblo* . . .

Her speech over, she handed the consecrated flag over to the Legion's commander, who accepted it, kissed it and addressed the godmother as follows: 'My dearest lady, I want you to know that you represent to us the ideal Spanish mother . . . My fellow legionnaires, this flag is the sacred symbol of our immortal nation. We hereby pledge our obligation to defend it with our lives.' His final words were punctuated by the loud cheers of his men, by the firing of salutes, and by the shouts of 'Long Live Spain' from the crowd.

The next part of the ceremony involved the so-called enthronement of 'Christ of the Good Death', the Foreign Legion's spiritual patron. Six legionnaires carried a large crucifix in horizontal position to a second dais where it was placed in an upright position between the two flags; this highly emotive act, accompanied by the rolling of drums and sounding of bugles, was followed by a minute of complete silence. In fact, this rite is performed every Saturday on the parade ground of the Legion's barracks in honour of those who have died in battle, a ceremony that is generally known as 'the Legionnaires' Saturday' (*Sábado Legionario*).

The mayor and the commander of the Legion then placed a crown of flowers with the national colours at the foot of the crucifix. The flags were finally carried from the platform to their places of honour between the ranks of legionnaires while the military band played the national anthem for the third time.

The concluding part of the ceremony consisted of a grand military parade along the main avenue where the troops were cheered by thousands of enthusiastic spectators, who reserved their loudest applause for the Foreign Legion and the Civil Guard, the toughest units in the Spanish army. The Legion is quite spectacular as it marches with its black rams as mascots. The soldiers' fierce, brusque and perfectly attuned movements, their wide-open shirts exposing sun-tanned chests and tattooed biceps only add to the excitement.

In the audience I could observe the transfixion, the profound way people were seized and almost hypnotised by the pageantry. Several informants told me that shivers were running up their spines and that they came out in goose pimples. There were also Muslim onlookers in the background of the *plaza*, while others were simply making their living by selling all kinds of refreshments, sweets and trinkets. After the parade, bars, taverns and restaurants quickly filled up with people who spent the rest of the day eating and drinking and basking in the communal feeling. There were also a few critical comments on the ceremonial event. One of the socialist councillors, a passionate opponent of the mayor, strongly criticised the occasion: 'the mayor must have gone mad to give such an expensive flag to that fascist Legion.'

Several workers agreed with him and added that the money would have been better spent on unemployment projects.

Structure and Meaning of the Flag Ceremony

The ceremony represents a complex pattern of acts, sentiments and notions. It opens up a whole spectrum of meaning for the Catholic inhabitants of Melilla. The blessing and offering of the flag is a grand spectacle consisting of clearly differentiated parts and a broad gamut of dramatic techniques, and is attended by a huge crowd. Although there is considerable reference to religious notions and use of sacred symbols, the role of the army is much more important than that of the Church. The role of the priest is limited to the formal blessing of the flag, while it is the commander of the Legion who actually invokes the favour and assistance of God.

A special time and place is created in order to lift the participants and audience out of everyday existence. The setting is the main *plaza*, the theatre of public life, which is transformed into a stage by the erection of platforms and decorations. The time is also special. The day is a holiday and the ceremony starts at noon, a turning point in the day, which is accentuated by the ritual noise of bugle calls, salutes, and music.

All actions are explicitly staged, performed, and stylised both in image and sounds, gestures and words, according to a preconceived scheme and a rigidly prescribed protocol. The sequence of actions is also clear-cut — there is no room for improvisation. There is a clear beginning, a building up towards a climax, and an end. The passage through these stages is stressed by audiovisual means.

The presentation is plainly evocative. A wide variety of dramatic strategies and powerful symbols is used in order to capture the crowd's attention and arouse primordial sentiments of belonging to the collectivity, feelings of superiority and uniqueness. Such sentiments are contagious. The themes of collective honour and moral unity are dominant and the flag both represents and evokes these qualities. The dramaturgical techniques for working up strong emotions involve music (the playing of the national anthem), percussion, special dress, grand rhetoric and splendour. The purpose of this audiovisual over-stimulation is to create excitement and induce a trance-like state

in both performers and spectators. This emotional impact re-
quires, in its turn, theatricality.[4]

There is also a strong element of repetition in the celebration,
both of internal elements (bugle calls, salutes, the playing of the
national anthem) and of the ceremony as a whole, which has
been performed in the past and will be performed again in the
future. It is part of the ritual repertoire of the Spanish nation-
state. It is flexible enough to accommodate local peculiarities,
such as specific timing, a different stress on various parts of the
ceremony, and the use of particular symbols, in this case 'Christ
of the Good Death.'[5] The presence of the main pillars — state,
nation, Church and army — and the themes of power and
solidarity are unchanging elements and together constitute the
overt structure of the ceremony.

Particularly important is the incorporation and expansion into
this ceremony of rites which are usually more circumscribed in
their ambit such as the *jura de bandera* rite and the rites of
baptism and marriage. The relation between the institution of
godparenthood, normally part of the domestic scene, and the
blessing and presentation of a flag, is not obvious; this is yet
another dramaturgical strategy. The blessing of the flag is put on
a par with baptism and marriage through the metaphorical use
of godparenthood. The flag with the new constitutional emblem
is not only blessed, it is baptised, a rite of incorporation, in
which godparents are the intermediaries. The new flag, therefore, is a metaphor of rebirth, in the image of the family, of
Spain as a democratic nation and of Melilla as a Spanish city. It is
an action through which the bond of Melilla with the motherland is renewed.

The vocabulary of the marriage ceremony connects the flag
with the *pueblo*; in other words, through the flag the people of
Melilla are married to the Spanish state. The Legion, as godfather to the flag, becomes the protector of the boundaries of the
family and the nation. The part played in this ceremony by the
institution of godparenthood is thus a crucial one. The extension
of a domestic ritual to, and its elaboration in, the public domain
add to the compelling force of the flag ritual.[6] The flag as the
focal symbol of nationhood is thereby transformed by the intervention of 'Christ of the Good Death,' into a symbol of life
and fertility. The allusions in the speeches to the spilling of
blood for the sake of perpetuating the symbol are also notable in
this regard.

In sum, the meaning communicated through the ceremony to the audience arises from the complex pattern composed of elevated speeches, patriotic slogans, salutes, gestures, colours, ritual noises, images, symbols and the carefully structured sequence of actions. It also derives from the context in which the ceremony is performed. There is a background of ethnic conflict behind the flag ceremony. Prior to the 1983 celebration, Muslims had challenged the legitimacy of Catholic dominance by destroying the Spanish flag, which immediately called for rituals of redress. While the ceremony was primarily inward-focused, intended for the Catholic sector of Melilla, it simultaneously addressed the 3,000 or so naturalised Muslim inhabitants, whose presence in the background was meaningful in that they were witness to a show of ethnic hegemony. The flag ceremony thus took the shape of a ritual of inclusion and exclusion. It was a renewal of Catholic solidarity and a regeneration of Catholic power that was being enacted. The message may be summarised as follows: 'We belong to this place which we have defended with our blood and we shall never be separated from Spain. We are in complete control of this city.' The vocabulary of the speeches focused on ancestry and consanguinity.[7] The flag ceremony simultaneously aimed at overriding internal divisions within the Catholic community simply by denying them, stressing *esprit de corps* in the face of a common enemy that threatened national honour and integrity, and by employing symbols that alluded to a higher order — the divine realm and the Spanish nation-state.

What does this case tell us about the links between ceremony and power? We have suggested what the flag ceremony *expressed*. It is, however, more difficult to isolate the power of the ceremony and establish how efficacious it was. It could be observed that the drama did indeed take hold of the actors and spectators alike, that it dramatically invoked a strong feeling of Spanishness. But are there also effects which last beyond the limited period of time in which the actual event took place? In order to deal with this problem a diachronic perspective is needed that sets the ceremony back into the flow of socio-political life. Even then only a speculative answer is possible.

The flag ceremony seems to have served political power in at least three related respects. First, it evoked and inculcated national honour and pride and a belief in ethnic superiority. Second, it restored a sense of community by making visible the strength of the Catholic entity, and the state that in daily life remains invisible. It generated primordial sentiments of belonging to those collectivities. And, finally, it legitimised the dominance of the Catholic segment of Melilla by evoking divine patronage. The symbolism and ritual of the flag is effective, then, in the sense that it clothes the claim to dominance in notions and associations that have moral force going beyond the particular occasion. It channels and stylises emotions, which constitute the raw fuel of political power.[8]

I believe that the flag ceremony also had the unintended and indirect effect of further alienating a minority of Muslims with Spanish nationality, a group which disposes of considerable tactical strength in education, finance and commercial networks. One of their informal leaders told me that they had experienced the ceremony — from which they had been excluded — as a serious affront and an open challenge. It was precisely this group that two years later initiated and led a Muslim rebellion in which the flag of Islam came to play an important role.

Chapter 7

The Cult of the Cemetery

'If you want to study our history, go to the cemetery,' I was told by a man to whom I had explained my reason for coming to Melilla. Barely a week had passed since my arrival in the enclave. 'Our history is the total sum of our deceased', was the almost stereotypical statement of informants when I asked questions about the city's past. After many talks with Catholics and several visits to their graveyard, I began to suspect that in this society the burial ground occupied a more central place in the concerns of the inhabitants than in any other part of the Western Mediterranean area I had visited. This was more true of the Catholic community than of the Muslims, Jews or Hindus. So came about the beginning of a small ethnography of the cemetery, which I came to see as part of the cult of Spanishness.

In an excellent article on rites of passage, Barbara Myerhoff (1982a: 109) suggests that 'the interplay of biology and culture is the subtext of all rites of passage'. In the case of death ritual this means that the corpse (nature) is transformed into a properly deceased person, which in many cultures is a person who embarks on a *new* life in the hereafter. It is not surprising then that in many societies mortuary ritual is replete with symbols of sexuality, fertility and rebirth (cf. Huntington & Metcalf 1979, Bloch & Parry 1982).[1]

Death is a highly dramatic event that triggers off great anxiety and tension. It interrupts the normal flow of social life and exposes the vulnerability of the social order by questioning its assumed eternal quality. It highlights the transitoriness of life. Each individual death calls forth a re-adjustment of social relationships and a re-definition of roles and statuses. The community needs to recover from the crisis provoked by death, and mortuary ritual serves this vital function. Through symbolism and ceremonial acts, faith is restored in the eternal nature of society and the persistence of individuals. Many characteristics of a society thus reveal themselves against the background of death (Huntington & Metcalf 1979: 2). Death rituals not only mirror but also shape social values (Geertz 1973: 94 ff.). Through their mortuary rites people re-create their society (Bloch & Parry 1982: 6). This explains the pronounced symbolism of fertility and rebirth in funeral rituals, particularly in tribal and peasant societies. As I will show, the notion of death bringing forth life is also present in the cult of the cemetery in Catholic Melilla.

One would not expect to find a strong emphasis on life symbolism in the cult of the dead in a place like Melilla. This is a pre-eminently urban mercantile society that places high value on the nuclear family, personal achievement and autonomy, and consumerism. Moreover, the enclave is marked by a high degree of transience and a large floating population. In this context one would not expect the death of an individual to be felt as a threat to the continuity of society, nor would one expect the image of death as regeneration of life to be prominent. Indeed, one would anticipate that dying, and the disposal of the dead had been pushed to the backstage of public life, to an enclosed domain of specialists, a sphere that is almost entirely separated from ordinary social life.[2] In Melilla the reverse holds true, particularly in the Catholic community of the enclave, which more than other segments takes its example from the ethos and lifestyle of western metropolitan society. This peculiar fact not only contradicts general Western European trends but also the basic pattern of funerary and post-funerary practices in Spain where we find the greatest intensity of mortuary ritual in the agrarian communities of the north, while the area of lowest intensity is that of the Mediterranean littoral from Barcelona south to Andalusia (Foster 1960: 155). How can we account for these apparent contradictions?

The simplest and least satisfactory answer would be that the relative isolation and enclave character of Melilla facilitates the retention of attitudes and rites which have disappeared elsewhere. Nor will the problem be solved by restricting our analysis to the representational dimension or the symbolism of the death ritual. Many ethnographies of death deal with the social order in a highly abstract and ephemeral manner. Mortuary ritual is too often detached from the configuration of people and their activities of which ritual is a part.[3] One has to know the matter-of-fact preoccupations of the living in order to understand the specific shape of mortuary practices. In the case of Melilla, this means taking into account the demographic and social structure of the enclave within its geopolitical context. What follows is not a systematic comparison of mortuary rituals among Catholics, Jews, Muslims and Hindus, but rather an analysis of the characteristics of the cult of the dead among the Catholic inhabitants of Melilla against the background of inter-ethnic relations.

The Catholic Ancestors

Until well into the nineteenth century high-ranking families and members of the Religious Confraternity of the Souls in Purgatory were buried in the crypt of the church. The rest of the deceased were interred in the *atrium* (an open court) or outside the church in a yard (de Morales 1909: 546–7).

When in 1892 a new Catholic cemetery was inaugurated outside the walls of the ancient town, the dead of the old churchyard were exhumed, carried in a funeral procession to the new burial ground where they were interred with great religious pomp after the new burial space had been blessed and consecrated with holy water. This ritual marked a major transition in the town's history: the beginning of an era of rapid demographic, territorial and economic expansion. It is highly significant that the forebears were part of this ritual. Their second burial in new territory marked the dawn of urban growth.

The old town consisted of three fortified precincts. Until the 1880s almost all the inhabitants lived in the compact and overcrowded inner precinct because of the endemic hostility of the surrounding Berber tribes.[4] In 1880 there were 689 civilians living in the *presidio*, of whom 629 were classified as 'nationals' and the rest as 'foreigners', predominantly Jews. The first Jews settled in Melilla in the late 1860s. One of their first demands had been for permission to construct a Jewish graveyard. The military governor allotted them a small parcel of land outside the third precinct. This plot was walled and inaugurated as a resting place for the dead by the rabbi who had come to Melilla with the first merchants from Tetuan. That they were allowed to inter their dead in local territory can be viewed as a token of goodwill and acceptance of the Jews into local society. In fact it was a tacit recognition by the authorities of the vital role Jewish capital and commercial networks played in the economic development of the enclave. In local Catholic terms the granting of a burial ground to 'foreigners' meant that they were to be allowed to put down roots.

The construction of a port as well as a war with the Berber tribes of the hinterland provided great economic impetus at the end of the nineteenth century. Significantly enough, the *casus belli* of the Spanish-Berber war of 1893 had been the profanation of a Muslim graveyard on the Melilla-Moroccan border by some Spanish soldiers who urinated against the tomb of the most important marabout of the region.[5] This serious violation of Muslim honour provoked fierce reaction by Rifian fighters who killed hundreds of Spanish soldiers within the space of a week and ritually mutilated their corpses.[6]

By 1900 the civil population had increased eightfold. Almost 5,000 Christians, 950 Jews, 95 'Moors' and two Hindus were recorded in the census of the year.[7] Massive immigration created a new division in the community of 'nationals': the established families of Melilla and the newcomers. The *familias de arraigo*, as the former were called, played a central role in local society, not only in commerce and politics but also in the cult of the cemetery.

Today, the old families, such as the Bernales, Bejares and Orelles, are still widely known as the 'rooted ones'. They came to the enclave as artisans and shopkeepers (*tenderos*) and invested their savings in property. In 1886, three extended families of shop and canteen-keepers owned twenty-five of the thirty-six private houses, while the Bejares were by far the largest landowners, controlling 4,400 square meters of *huerta* (garden) land which amounted to 66 percent of the total 'rural' area.[8] These families grew rich when the demand for housing and building plots rocketed towards the end of the century.

Today, there is hardly any suitable land left for cultivation within Melilla's twelve square kilometres. There are some dozens of mini-gardens around so-called *chalets* or small villas to which only a few people have access. These plots and houses represent an important symbolic value for the owners as marks of rootedness and distinction.

Juan Bejar owns one of these mini-estates. His great-great-grandfather came from Mallorca to the enclave in 1861, opened a tavern and within five years owned five houses in the ancient town. Juan Bejar inherited the plot of land on which he built a villa. As an engineer he works part of the year at the American military base of Morón de la Frontera in Spain. He is the leader of a small political party of about 300 ultra-nationalists who strive for an independent Melilla freed from the 'Moors'.

Bejar's party represents the values of the comfortably-off Catholic middle-class families whose parents and grandparents were born in Melilla and who consider themselves the true *melillenses*. These families are the *pieds noirs* of Melilla. They are mainly professional military men, state functionaries and merchants. They constitute the backbone of colonial society and project their hopes and anxieties onto their *patria chica*, their mini-country. Their patriotism is locally known as *melillismo*, which, because of the small territory, has converted itself into a fierce, inflated nationalism. They are also the main participants in the cult of the dead.

Death in Melilla

There are basically four ways of dealing with the dead in the enclave. Ethnic apartheid in daily life is reflected in the segregation of mortuaries, burial and cremation grounds, and in the sharp ethnic demarcation of dying and mortuary practices. In other words, death is an intimate sacred domain with clear-cut ethnic boundaries, and apart from a few rare exceptions, outsiders are jealously excluded from participation in mortuary ritual. Funerals and post-funerary rites are thus the most guarded of rituals which emphasise the marking and maintenance of ethnic boundaries. While outsiders are sometimes invited to celebrations of joy and prosperity such as birth and marriage ceremonies, they are barred from witnessing occasions of anxiety and grief.

Death may also become an extremely important issue in inter-ethnic politics, as is aptly demonstrated by the fact that one of the main and most persistent demands of the Muslim minority for many years has been the right to bury their dead in Melilla territory. The Catholic authorities have consistently rebuffed this demand, which may be seen as a statement that Muslims do not belong to local society. Consequently, Muslims are forced to inter their dead — many of whom were born in the enclave — across the border in Morocco, or in a zone of no man's land between the enclave and Morocco. Recently, some of the Muslim funeral processions have turned into political rituals of rebellion.[9] But death may also become a major issue in *intra*-ethnic strife. An example of this occurred in the early 1980s when the struggle for leadership in the Muslim Community aggravated a conflict over the use and control of the communal hearse. That the Catholic cult of the cemetery should be viewed in a geopolitical context was brought home to me by frequent references to the dead in discussions with Catholic informants about the future of the enclave:

> I'll stay where my deceased kin are resting. Let them not touch my dead!

But before going into the political dimension of the cult to the dead, let me first briefly outline Catholic funerary practices in Melilla.[10]

The ideal is for a person to die at his or her home having been cared for by the closest female relatives. The basic strategies for coping with death derive from general Catholic ritual and are roughly threefold: the wake at night in the house of the deceased, burial on the next day at noon or mid-afternoon, and prayers and masses for the welfare of the deceased's soul, especially on the anniversary of the death, and on the days of All Saints and All Souls. The traditional *novena* or prayer session at the home of the dead on nine following evenings has become obsolete, along with the Religious Confraternity of the Souls in Purgatory. The *novena* has been replaced by a mass on the Sunday following the burial.

The preparation for the wake — the washing and clothing of the corpse and the decoration of the coffin — is now generally carried out at the undertaker's funeral parlour. The wake involves kin and close friends, whereas the funeral is a more communal rite in which a larger number of people participate. The size, quality and importance of the funeral depends upon the social status of the deceased and his or her family. Generally the corpse is taken by hearse to the church for the Requiem Mass. The priest and two acolytes accompany the coffin to the cemetery in a motorised procession. Here the final rite is simple. Male relatives carry the coffin from the entrance of the cemetery to the grave or niche where the priest chants a brief prayer of blessing and splashes the coffin with holy water. The audience is almost exclusively male. Then the coffin is lowered into the grave or placed in the niche, and then there follow brief formal condolences with the family. Finally, part of the cortege returns to the house of the deceased where a funeral meal and drinks are offered to the guests. Among the well-to-do these meals are elaborate and are increasingly provided in restaurants.

Mourning basically includes the wearing of black and abstention from ostentatious behaviour. The length and intensity of mourning depends upon the degree of kinship with the deceased and on the sex of the relations. As in most parts of the Mediterranean, mourning procedures in Melilla are much stricter for women than for men. While in recent decades mourning has become less rigorous and visible for most categories of people, this has not been the case for elderly women, particularly widows. There appear to be few differences in mourning practices between Melilla and cities of similar size in the Peninsula, but more are found in post-funerary rites.

The City of the Dead

Melilla's *campo santo*, literally 'holy land', is a true necropolis. It is a peaceful and somnolent miniature city, with its gardens, paved streets, squares and avenues. Located on a bluff that juts out high above the Mediterranean, it borders on the old town. It is an immured and ordered world separated from the adjacent Jewish cemetery (opened in 1893 when the ancient one of San Carlos closed down) and Hindu cremation ground by high walls. At the rear of the graveyard are the enclosed sections holding the memorial monuments of the various army units. Among them stands out a huge pyramid-like monument-cum-chapel which is devoted to soldiers and officers who died in the notorious battles in the war for the pacification of the Rif.

Separated from the military graves are several enclosed courtyard-like civilian sections. The main entrance gate allows access to the first court that is closest to the city itself. It boasts carefully tended flower beds and groups of trees. This is the most richly decorated, most frequently visited and best tended part of the cemetery. It is also the oldest and most prestigious section. The outer walls and some of the inner walls contain rows of burial niches four to six layers high. The first court, which is the heart of the cemetery, also houses the impressive family pantheons of the wealthy, which resemble mansions. In this part, most graves and niches are privately and permanently owned by the most established segment of the Catholic population. The second court is of more heterogeneous composition and a less impressive and less decorated replica of the first section, with few pantheons. The niches and graves here are simpler, and there are fewer flower-beds, although it contains some coppices. Here only some of the graves and niches are privately owned, the remainder being rented.

Finally, between the second court and the military terraces is a rather untidy and unadorned zone containing niches and graves of lesser quality. The majority of these are rented from the municipality for a limited period. This zone also contains the plot of unconsecrated earth where the suicides, atheists and foetuses are interred. Working-class people and leftists who died fighting for the Popular Front during the Spanish Civil War (1936–9), or who were executed after the uprising in July 1936, were buried here in an unmarked mass grave. Until recently, this plot was separated from the rest of the graveyard by a wall. One of the first actions of the democratically elected Town Council in which the socialists held the majority was to demolish this wall and erect a modest commemorative monument.

One of the graves in this section clearly stands out from the others. It is a tomb that is permanently covered with fresh red and white flowers. Attached to the big marble cross is a smaller beautifully carved crucifix and on top of it stands a small silver crucifix. A bust of Christ and a small statue of the Virgin and Child stand on a small platform that has been placed on the grave. This tomb is visited daily and tended by elderly working-class women who venerate the soldier who rests here as a saint. The origin of this cult is shrouded in mystery. All I could discover about the soldier was that he committed suicide after killing a policeman. The motives and circumstances of these bloody events are unclear. The marble cross carries a small plaque with the following epitaph beneath a photograph of the deceased: 'Here rests: Benito López Franco of Cetina, Zaragoza (Spain). He died on January 17, 1950 at the age of twenty-two. May he rest in peace.' The women who tend the grave were unable or unwilling to give more detailed information about the soldier. Neither were they prepared to discuss the unofficial cult, in spite of the fact that its existence is a matter of common knowledge.

The necropolis is of a blazing and sparkling white, which contrasts with the city centre where few whitewashed buildings can be found. On the other hand, in many respects the cemetery and the city are mirror images, the former symbolically replicating the structure of the latter (cf. Gilmore 1977: 445–6). The first court of the graveyard roughly corresponds to the inner city where the wealthy and rooted families live. The second resembles the *barrios* adjacent to the centre where the social strata of smaller merchants, civil servants and skilled workers are concentrated. The third zone roughly represents the outlying working class districts and, finally, the military sections are situated at the back and periphery of the cemetery. This location expresses the largely segregated and temporary existence of the troops in local society. Soldiers were clearly outsiders who lacked close associations with the city, which is evident by the decay of this section.

As with the society of the living, the necropolis is a very compact and overcrowded space. From its inauguration in 1892 until the end of 1980, 66,335 civilians were buried there as well as 3,689 foetuses, which are listed and interred separately. These figures do not include the remains from the ancient graveyard which were transported to the new resting place, nor do they include those of the soldiers and civil servants transferred from several cemeteries in Morocco after its independence in 1956. The municipal cemetery is run by the following personnel: one administrator-surveyor, one master grave-digger and six subordinates, a bricklayer, a carpenter, a cleaning woman, a night-watchman, and about six workers who have been assigned to the cemetery by the Social Security Council.[11]

With the exception of the military and parts of the working-class sections, graves and niches are carefully tended, overwhelmingly by female relatives of the deceased. A large banner at the entrance of the cemetery reads as follows:

> La cultura y buenos sentimientos de los pueblos quedan reflejados en el cariño y cuido que prestan a sus difuntos/The refinement and good feeling of towns [or nations — H.D.] are reflected in the affection and care they pay to their deceased.

Indeed, the Catholics make an explicit connection between the degree of civilisation (*cultura*) and the attention paid to the deceased. The appearance of the cemetery, especially of its first court, clearly expresses this notion.

Visiting and Tending the Graves

There is a close link between social status, in particular 'rootedness', location of the graves, tombs and niches, and the intensity of the cult of the dead. Families with several generations of forebears in the graveyard consider it to be the *fons et origo* of Melilla.

The worlds of the living and the dead are tied to one another by the string of people who visit the necropolis on a daily basis in order to pray and tend the graves of their deceased kin. According to the gatekeeper of the cemetery, approximately one thousand people pay a visit to the city of the dead on Fridays, Sundays and festive days. On other days of the week the mean fluctuates around five hundred. Tombs, niches, pantheons are the most sacred of all private property. A man may sell his house or shop but he would never even consider selling the family grave. 'We belong to where our ancestors are buried,' is a standard expression, a ritual formula that expresses an intense feeling of belonging and continuity. Leaving the dead behind is to lose them, and one's roots, forever.

For the larger part of the Catholic population the deceased are thus roots which nourish the living. The cemetery is aptly named 'La Purísima Concepción', the Immaculate Conception. In the Catholic tradition the Virgin is the pre-eminent model of sexual, bodily and moral purity. She went straight to Heaven in corporeal form. As the antithesis of Eve, the Virgin is the master symbol of uncorrupt fertility, a source of divine life.[12] She is the patron of a limbo where the sins of the flesh have to be removed through putrefaction of the corpse, a precondition for entering eternal life. Her image, together with that of Christ on the Cross, whose Passion purified the human race of its original sin, most frequently adorn the graves and niches.

Another striking feature is the predominance of red and white flowers at and on the graves. Red represents the Resurrection and white the Transfiguration. Both colours symbolise the joy of eternal life, which the Resurrection promises to every believer.[13] More generally, red and white represent blood, life, purity and vitality. Their counterparts, representing death and mourning, are black and purple. The symbolism of life and rebirth is particularly pronounced at the celebration of All Souls' Day, which is the highlight of the cult of the cemetery. Red and white chrysanthemums are used in abundance as ornamental flowers. They are not only prized for their beauty but for the fact that they bloom in November, an otherwise 'dead' season, so they are very appropriate symbols of life. Throughout the night and day people burn candles and olive oil lamps at the graves and niches of their deceased kin, taking turns in keeping vigil and making sure the flames do not go out. On this day thousands of people flock to the cemetery, many with snacks and drinks to be consumed at the graveside, to pay homage to the dead and celebrate being with them in spirit.

On All Souls' Day the entire municipal corporation pays its traditional visit to the cemetery in order to place garlands of flowers at the graves of the functionaries who have died 'in [the act of] public service'. The General Military Headquarters also pays homage to the dead by celebrating a solemn mass at the monument to 'the heroes of Monte Arruit' (in commemoration of the Spanish defeat of 1921 at the hands of 'Abd-al Krim). And, finally, many emigrants who live in Spain return to their native city to pay a visit to those left behind in the burial ground.[14]

There is a striking analogy between the tending of domestic gardens and the graves and this holds particularly true for the 'rooted families'. Both the garden and the grave are extensions of the domestic domain. Both are the object of intense attention. Many graves are in fact miniature gardens planted with flower-beds and perennial plants. Apart from houses, the grave and garden are the only pieces of the scarce land which can be privately owned in Melilla. They are vinculations with the *patria chica*. Given the extreme scarcity of land, people treat their gardens with much care and devotion, not unlike peasants who have an emotional and spiritual tie with their land. Many Catholics maintain a similar relationship with the graves of their kin, which then become a substitute for the garden. The life-giving force of the earth around the grave is tapped like that of a garden. Both are to a large extent female domains.

Middle-aged, elderly and widowed women predominate among the visitors to the cemetery. These women, dressed in black, stand out against the sparkling white of the graves, walls and monuments. The omnipresence of women beyond a certain age, approximately forty-five, at the cemetery is a general Mediterranean phenomenon.[15] Ageing or menopausal women are specialists in mediation between the family and the supernatural, between the living and the dead. When a woman has young children and a husband she has little time to devote to spiritual matters. But when her children grow older, and especially when her husband dies, she has more than enough time to spare. More important still, elderly women are supposed to be unattractive and sexually inactive. In most cultures the menopause entails some kind of de-sexualisation and de-feminisation (Hastrup 1978: 59). In a society where sexual activity and menstruation are regarded as polluting agents, post-menopausal women are less impure than their menstruating, sexually active sisters. The misogynist tendencies in the Catholic tradition, in which Eve and the Virgin Mother are the two dominant models of femininity, inculcate a much stronger sense of impurity and guilt in women than in men. Women's greater involvement in religion and stronger preoccupation with death should be seen in the light of Catholic dogmas, which are reinforced by local beliefs about the 'natural' inferiority of women. Women in consequence devote much more time and energy to purification and redemption than do men. An additional factor is that women live longer than men and that at marriage they are usually considerably younger than their husbands, which means that widows far outnumber widowers.

For this reason older women spend much time praying for the deceased as they face and prepare for their own death. As women grow older their role as mediators between the domestic and supernatural domains, between the living and the dead, becomes more important. This role is part of the general sexual division of tasks in which women bear more responsibility for the spiritual well-being of the family than men. As the vital links in the networks of kin and neighbours, and as guardians of tradition, they act as pivots in the chain of mediation between the human and the supernatural worlds. They pray for the welfare of the dead and ask them favours for the living in return. Like the Virgin Mary, the souls in Purgatory are intermediaries between human beings and a distant God.

The elderly women who frequent the cemetery are invariably dressed in black. They cover their heads with a black shawl or *mantilla* when they leave the house. Black, which is initially a sign of mourning, assumes a new meaning in the context of the graveyard. According to Leach (1976: 19, 27), the white of the bride as opposed to the black of the widow not only expresses opposed life stages but also the contrasting pairs of good and bad, happy and sad, pure and contaminated. However, I doubt whether this view is correct. The black of the menopausal or widowed women and their frequent visits to the cemetery should rather be seen as expression of complete humbleness vis-à-vis God, a sign of renunciation of earthly pleasures, a statement of purity. To be sure, this purity is of a different kind than the inherent purity of the virgin or bride. It is 'intentional' rather than 'intrinsic' (cf. Christian 1972: 153).

For these women, then, the cemetery (like the church) is a place of spiritual refreshment where the ritual of tending the grave and praying to and for the deceased washes away the sins accumulated during earlier stages of life. The graveyard is a place removed from the confusion, strife and backbiting of daily city life. It is an enclosed space where elderly people, in particular women, may experience a sense of purity.[16] Approaching death themselves, they come to communicate with their beloved ones who have gone before them, to relive the past, and to brace themselves for their own death. The rites they perform contain a strong element of purification and should be seen as a prelude to dying.[17]

Whereas on normal days elderly women predominate, on Sundays and feast days the public is more heterogeneous as to age and sex. Entire families pay a visit to the cemetery. The customary evening stroll along the main avenue and *plaza* of the city centre, the *paseo*,[18] is then partly transferred to the grave-yard. Apart from brief moments of contemplation and prayer at the family tombs or niches, and the placing of flowers, the main activity is strolling, viewing other graves and visitors, and exchanging greetings. The most crowded parts of the cemetery are the first and second courts, the sections where the ancestors of the established families are resting. At these early evening hours, roughly between seven and nine o'clock, the worlds of the dead and living merge and the deceased are reincorporated into the world of the living. For the *melillenses* the presence of the dead in a way legitimises the existence of this small colonial society. The sociability at the cemetery provides them with a sense of continuity of the past in the present and into the future. Or, as an informant cogently put it: 'as long as there is one dead Catholic in this city, it is difficult not to imagine a living one'.

This significant sociopolitical function of the cemetery becomes manifest on the eve of All Souls and the following day and night, when the domain of the dead is invaded by the living, and large parts of the city are left deserted. There are other inversions as well. The night, normally a time of silence, rest, withdrawal and darkness, then becomes a time of noise, activity, expansion and light. In fact the night is the highlight of the All Souls celebration. The reversals in the structure of time and space (and corresponding activities) create a special mood, an *esprit de corps* through the dead, and a sense of perpetuity of community.

Similarly dramatic evocations of a lasting Catholic rule over

Melilla also occurred in the wake of an unexpected incident. One morning in the early autumn of 1983 the Catholic community of Melilla was shocked by the news that their cemetery had been desecrated overnight by 'libertines' (*gamberros*). People were quick to insinuate that the authors must have been Muslims, who five years earlier had carried out a similar violation of the cemetery. The local newspaper report read as follows:

> Yesterday morning the assault on the *campo santo* was the major conversational topic in virtually all Catholic social circles. Expressions of repugnance and consternation filled the air. Yesterday afternoon — like today, Friday, as happens every Friday and weekend — a multitude of *melillenses* flocked to the precinct in order to find out whether the resting-places of their loved ones had suffered from the vandalism of those who penetrated the enclosure, surreptitiously or not.[19]

Next day the mayor, councillors and chief of police paid a visit to the cemetery in order to express public indignation over this offence. The police launched a thorough investigation but did not catch the perpetrators of this act. Repairs began on the very day of the official visit, which is exceptional in a society where the implementation of public works usually takes a long time. With the celebration of All Saints and All Souls in the offing, the traces of what was considered a most serious attack on the integrity of the Catholic community had to be effaced as soon as possible. The heat of the reactions and the heightened activity at the cemetery were intended to restore the challenged moral and political supremacy of the Catholics. Six months later several of my informants spontaneously brought up the incident when we visited the cemetery. All tried to convince me that this act of vandalism must have been carried out by 'Moors'.

Let us finally consider a particular instance of the cult of the dead in Melilla, the celebration of death by the Spanish Foreign Legion, the sole unit in the army that explicitly glorifies death. The official motto of the Legion says:

> To die is the major honour. A man only dies once. Death comes quickly and is painless. The most horrible thing for a man is to live as a coward.[20]

'Long live Death!' is its battle cry. The death's-head is one of the favourite tattoos of the legionnaire, along with a crucifix, the

Legion's spiritual emblem. Its anthem, 'The Betrothed of Death', phrases the relationship between the legionnaire and death in barely veiled erotic terms. The message is that the betrothal on the battlefield of the legionnaire with Death, represented as female, contributes to the reproduction of the Nation.

This theme is also prominent in one of the Legion's rituals, the so-called *Sábado Legionario* (Legionnaires' Saturday). This rite is performed on Saturdays in the parade ground of the Legion's quarters in honour of those who died in combat. The ceremony is brief and simple. The entire regiment stands in line at the back of the plaza. Six legionnaires, flanked by four guards of honour, come forward holding up a large crucifix in a horizontal position. Marching brusquely, the soldiers carry the statue to a platform on which it is put in an upright position between the Legion's banner and the national flag. This ceremonial act is accompanied by the beating of drums and bugle-calls. Then the highest ranking officers salute before the statue. After a minute of silence the soldiers sing their anthem at the top of their voices; this is followed by a short parade. The function and symbolism of this ritual are unequivocal. 'Christ of the Good Death' sacrificed himself for the redemption of mankind. By reference to this act of divine self-sacrifice, death in battle is elevated to an act of self-immolation for 'God and the Nation', the greatest honour a legionnaire can achieve. The rite then inculcates a contempt of death into the participants. The commemoration of those who fell on the battlefield serves to reinforce fellowship in arms in the face of death. It has to be stressed that once every month this rite is open to the general public and that it is incorporated into several of the city's major pageants.[21] The legion's sacrifices are thus linked to the perpetuation of this Spanish corner of Morocco.

Death Cult and Ethnicity

In recent years much has been written on death and mortuary ritual. In these studies relatively little attention has been devoted to the proxemics of the cemetery.[22]

The nature of the rituals performed in the necropolis of Melilla differs little from those enacted in the cemeteries of Spain and indeed of Latin Europe generally. What sets Melilla apart is the intensity of the cult of the cemetery and the communal sentiments expressed by it. In Melilla the cemetery is located near the city centre, while elsewhere graveyards are transitional zones, almost invariably situated towards the fringe of the town area or between town and countryside. The attention and resources which the Catholics of Melilla devote to the dead also contrasts sharply with the austerity of Jewish and Muslim commemorations of the deceased. Jewish and Muslim burial grounds are decorated simply and much less frequently visited.

The geopolitical condition of Melilla, i.e. the tensions and anxieties this status generates in the Catholic population, go a long way to explain the specific shape the cult of the cemetery has taken in this colonial enclave. They realise that their society is isolated from the motherland. They never cease complaining about the problem of what they call *incomunicación con la Peninsula*, that is problems in communication with Spain. They live in an alien and hostile environment and know that the perpetuation of their society is problematic and precarious. This condition enhances their awareness of distinctiveness and heightens their search for meaning and legitimation in the past. Hence the strong link with their ancestors and the inclusion of tens of thousands of dead into the dwindling community of the living. And hence the importance of ancestry buried in the soil of Melilla for the definition of a true *melillense*.

The sense of isolation and insecurity which is exemplified by the cult of the cemetery has increased steadily over the last three decades. From 1950 to 1975 more than 25,000 Spanish inhabitants emigrated to the motherland both for economic and political reasons.[23] Since 1961, Morocco has incessantly claimed the enclave. Many politicians in Madrid consider Melilla a colony which should be abandoned. The Catholic inhabitants were shocked and demoralised by the rapid Spanish withdrawal from the Western Sahara after the 'Green March' of hundreds of thousands of Moroccans into the disputed territory in the Autumn of 1975. They fear a similar fate will befall their city. Their reaction is either emigration or a clinging to the past. The cult of the cemetery not only reflects the problems and preoccupations of the living but also helps to alleviate them.

Chapter 8

Ritualisation in Inter-Ethnic Encounters

In situations where there are blatantly uneven distributions of power resources among ethnic groups, social intercourse across ethnic boundaries tends to become tense and delicate. This is evident in the situation under discussion because the dominant group feels threatened by a hostile Moroccan state that emphatically rejects the legitimacy of Spanish presence. It is not surprising then that the Iberian sector of local society regards the growing number of immigrants from the Moroccan hinterland as a sort of fifth column. Yet at the same time Spanish dominance is dependent upon the regular flow of goods and people across the border and on the unskilled labour and consumer requirements of Rifian immigrants.

How do the dominant and subordinate groups deal with this paradoxical and conflicting situation? Several modes of behaviour have developed ranging from avoidance to many-stranded involvements.[1] It will be argued that ritualism operates to varying degrees in the problematic and competitive relations between people of different ethnic backgrounds. I will focus mainly on Iberian-Muslim relations since these are dominant in the statistical and sociological sense. But let me first make a general statement about inter-ethnic encounters in Melilla.

Catholics, Muslims, Jews and Hindus are constantly thrown together in daily life. Yet, however frequent such contact is, social encounters mainly take place in the economic domain which — just as in many other societies where ethnic affiliations are powerful dividing zones — is a relatively 'safe' area where the maintenance of ethnic boundaries is little endangered.[2] In Melilla the Chamber of Commerce is the only formal institution in which members of all ethnic groups participate in a fairly representative way. Instrumental and balanced exchanges of the single-stranded kind, such as occur between shopkeeper and client, employer and employee, constitute the predominant mode of inter-ethnic interaction. The degree of mutual involvement in these transactions is usually reduced to a minimum. There are, however, exceptions to this general pattern.

Accommodation among Ethnic Elites

Money is an indispensable expedient for crossing ethnic barriers. Older informants frequently pointed out to me that today there is much more ethnic 'mixing' than there was. This is certainly true of upper-class young people. Even though they remain a small minority, there are now several Jewish, Hindu and Muslim students in the two most prestigious private Catholic colleges. Most Jewish businessmen are now members of the *Casino Español*, once a bastion of Iberian identity and Catholic commercial interests. Rich Muslims, Jews and Hindus have been accepted in the *Club Marítimo*, an exclusive recreation place for the elite. The public library is now dominated by a Muslim clientèle and most of the fashionable discothèques and pubs enjoy a mixed audience. Some Hindus, Jews and Muslims have managed to acquire summer homes in a small recreational park near the beach. However, physical proximity, shared membership in associations, and common elements of lifestyle may — and in fact do — go together with the maintenance of ethnic boundaries and ethnic distance. Indeed, in Melilla sustained amicable relationships across ethnic barriers remain rare.

On the other hand, there are some occasions on which the ethnic segments of the upper class meet and socialise and these are strongly ritualised. The occasional *gran galas* (exclusive music festivals in formal dress and with stylised social intercourse) and the *cenas-bailes* (full dress supper dances) are cases in point. Another such occasion at which the initiative was taken by two dozen men from the four ethnic groups was the founding of a local section of the Lion's Club, an exclusively upper-class male association. Its secretary, the only Jewish and non-Catholic member of the municipal council, told me that the specific aims of the Club include 'eradicating envy and the lack of vision, and fighting the abuse of drugs.' There is a strong taboo on the discussion of religious and political topics during their meetings. Anyone of a 'sound moral condition' may become a member of the Club, which means that it will remain an exclusive association.

A more regular form of ritualised inter-ethnic interaction is the *agasajo*. In standard Castilian this concept refers to a buffet-supper invitation, token of esteem and kindness. *Agasajar* means to give a banquet and to ply guests with attention and respect. In Spain these words are rarely used in a colloquial form. In Melilla, however, they are quite common and have acquired special meaning. In this setting *agasajo* means an informally organised yet highly formal gathering where members of the various ethnic segments of the upper class meet, socialise and pay their respects to each other.

This cultural institution is rooted in pre-colonial modes of communication between the enclave, the tribal hinterland, and representatives of the Moroccan Sultanate. There are several documents in the local archive which refer to infrequent dealings between these parties in terms of *agasajo*, the etiquette of hospitality and of fêting guests. *Agasajar* is a curious mixture of the Moroccan tea ceremony and the Spanish banquet, an expression of hospitality of a reciprocal kind. An example of this took place in 1905 when two important Arab traders had opened an office in Melilla and invited their Catholic counterparts and potential associates to a gathering that began with a tea ceremony but at which liquor and mixed Moroccan-Spanish snacks were also served.[3] By organising this party the hosts had entered the local circuit of hospitality.

The *agasajo* became fully institutionalised when the authorities of Melilla began to seek out leaders from the tribes in the hinterland (*hombres de prestigio*) whom they bribed into becoming 'friends of Spain' by offering them all kinds of privileges. These men were used as symbols of 'Spanish-Moroccan fraternity' and modelled into examplars of 'noble Moors.' They were invited to Spanish ceremonies, while they in turn invited the top echelons of Melilla to attend major Berber celebrations.[4] These occasions invariably consisted of elaborate banquets, speeches and mutual shows of homage. The host paid homage to the guests by his invitation and by showering them with food, drinks, gifts and special attention, while the guests, in their turn, honoured the host by accepting the invitation to attend.

Apart from the larger ceremonies, individuals frequently took the initiative to offer a banquet to selected members of their social network who came from different ethnic backgrounds, 'fraternising once again the adepts of the three religions which in our city live together in delicate harmony.'[5] Sometimes there were special reasons for celebrating an occasion with a banquet, as in March 1921 when:

> last night the very Spanish Muslim Sidi Mehidi Ben Chocrón offered a banquet in honour of the learned Sidi Dris Ben Said, Arab secretary of the High Commissioner. On the menu figured the most typical and delicious dishes of Moroccan cuisine.[6]

The following contextualised examples will illustrate that the *agasajo* is a well-tried form of ceremony used by the elite in the politics of ethnicity.

In the early 1980s a new leader emerged in the Muslim community of Melilla. Ahmed Moh, born in the enclave of Rifian parents, won a Moroccan scholarship to study in Spain and became one of the first Rifian men in Melilla to hold a western university degree. After working a couple of years as an economist for the Moroccan government in nearby Nador, he returned to Melilla and opened a bureau specialising in giving advice to illiterate Muslims on how to handle bureaucratic affairs. At the same time he managed to obtain a job as an administrator in the town hall. He soon began to show political ambitions. Through bribery and by putting pressure on his clients he succeeded in amassing enough support to oust a rival for the presidency of the Muslim Community Council, a semi-official religious association that acts as a mouthpiece for Muslim interests. His next step was to enlist in the Spanish Socialist Workers Party (PSOE), which had recently gained a majority in the municipal council. As a naturalised Muslim he was admitted to the rank-and-file. It was then that he started to organise buffets at his home to which he invited prominent local politicians and civil servants along with the highest representatives of the Jewish and Hindu Community Councils.

After several attempts he managed to break into the circuit of *agasajos*, although only as a peripheral member who participated infrequently. In March 1984 he gave a buffet in his spacious house. Apart from several prominent members of the Muslim Community, there were representatives of the Hindu and Jewish Communities, of the Socialist Trade Union (UGT) and the PSOE. The highest-ranking government officials, however, were conspicuously absent as were the most powerful Hindu and Catholic businessmen. Apart from the host's wife, the only women present were Spanish Catholics who had come with their husbands.

The fifty guests or so were all in formal dress. The host and some of the other Muslims wore the ceremonial white *jellaba*. A lavish Moroccan meal was served, consisting of pastry, roast mutton with almonds, fried chicken with almonds and raisins, couscous, fruits, and sweets. The minted tea was prepared and poured by the religious leader of the Muslim Community, who was the most distinguished Muslim guest. After the dinner this man recited a *sura* from the Quran, followed by formal speeches by the host, the president of the Jewish Community and the secretary-general of the PSOE. They all stressed inter-ethnic fraternity, coexistence and cooperation. Drinks were then served and the party split up into small groups that discussed current economic and political affairs, or gossiped about absent and present invitees.

I heard the host make a remark to the secretary general of the PSOE about the recent replacement in the party of lawyers by economists in the highest echelons of national politics. An economist himself, the host made a thinly disguised application for a post in the executive committee of the local party. The *agasajo* was officially concluded with a recital by Berber musicians who also played some flamenco songs for the pleasure of the Spanish guests. Toward midnight the first and most prominent guests began to leave. A small number remained behind until the early hours of the morning and the atmosphere grew increasingly informal.

The overall ambience had been rather formal and sober. People talked in low voices and held back, while normally sociability in these parts of the Mediterranean is loud and flamboyant. Social relaxation did not appear to have been the prime purpose of the gathering. The host had done his best to create an atmosphere of exclusiveness, in which he only partly succeeded since the president of the Hindu Community Association, the most powerful local businessman, and some prominent government officers had politely declined the invitation.

Later I began to understand, by listening to several comments made by men who had attended this gathering, that Moh had infringed the code of *agasajar* in several respects. As a parvenu he had pressed too hard his claim for core membership in the *agasajo* network. Moreover, it was considered rude that he had overtly displayed his ambition for a place among the leadership of the PSOE, insulting several of the guests by his show of rivalry. More seriously, he had broken one of the basic rules of the *agasajo*, namely that ethnic differences should be played down. Moh had achieved the opposite by staging a display of Muslim identity. Several of the non-Muslim guests were particularly shocked by the recitation of the *sura*, which the host had apparently built into the occasion in order to please the religious leader and gain his support. The all-Moroccan meal was also considered inappropriate. Finally, Moh's interpretation of his role as host had been too domineering. This maladroit performance sealed his fate. He was ostracised from the elite circuit. In hindsight this case was instructive, for it revealed the basic principles of the *agasajo* code.

Agasajos also serve as part of most official types of meetings which take place between representatives of the dominant and subordinate ethnic groups. The following case is illustrative. At the beginning of 1984 the socialist mayor and some of his councillors paid an official visit to the *Cañada de la Muerte* ('The Ravine of Death'), a Muslim ghetto on the periphery of the enclave. It was a memorable event for it was the first time that a mayor had set foot in this poverty-stricken corner of the enclave. He went to see for himself the lack of infrastructural amenities. After a ceremonial welcome, the guests were taken on a tour through the ghetto by the informal community leaders. This was followed by an *agasajo* of pastries, snacks and tea. In his address to his hosts the mayor promised to have street-lighting installed within three months. Both the mayor's speech and the host's reply alluded to the *convivencia* of Christians and Muslims. Before the officials departed, the mayor offered his hosts tea and sweets in a local tea house at the entrance of the barrio.

This type of inter-ethnic encounter, the central part of which is also called *agasajo*, differs from the normal *agasajo* in three respects. First, the convocation, organisation and purpose of the gathering is official and formal, while the ordinary type has no official function and the guests are invited through personal networks. Second, it is an open event, taking place in a public place, in this case the tea house and an annexe of the mosque, while in the normal type the gathering takes place in someone's home, or in a public place hired by a particular individual. Finally, this type of *agasajo* is part of a larger event which only takes place occasionally, as opposed to the former type which is held at regular intervals. The mayor immediately reversed the roles of guest and host by inviting the communal leaders to tea before he left the ghetto. In the non-official type the act of reciprocity in hospitality is postponed until a later point in time when the roles of host and guest are reversed.

The event just described was followed up about four months later when the street-lighting was officially inaugurated by the mayor. On this occasion he brought a large retinue of party members — too large according to barrio dwellers — who were offered another *agasajo*. Money had been collected among the ghetto's heads of family in order to pay for the twenty-two kilos of best mutton, pastries, drinks and tea. One of the informal community leaders told me that the guests had abused Muslim hospitality by coming in such large numbers to feast upon a meal paid for by one of the lowest- income barrios of Melilla. By officially inaugurating the street-lighting and forcing the expenses of an *agasajo* upon the barrio's population, the Spanish transformed a normal public service into a special favour (in Catholic quarters public lighting is taken for granted and would never have been switched on with a ceremony of this kind). In other words the *agasajo* had degenerated into a Spanish show of superiority.

An *agasajo* should also be clearly differentiated from a related phenomenon, the so-called *tertulia*. This is a small group of male friends who regularly meet at a designated place to drink, talk and pursue common interests. This type of gathering is homogeneous and exclusive in the sense that it includes only upper and middle class men of the same ethnic group. It is primarily a social group that also serves economic and political ends. The *tertulia* is small, rarely comprising more than six men; it is informal, intimate, and meets at least once or twice a week. The number of people at an *agasajo* varies according to circumstances and may range from twenty to more than sixty people. Its membership is less stable and more differentiated. There are core members who meet frequently and others who participate less often.[7] *Agasajos* are less intimate than *tertulias* because they are held less frequently and are attended by a far greater number of people of heterogeneous ethnic backgrounds.[8]

By now it should be clear that we are dealing here with occasions of ritualised behavior. The *agasajo* in its various manifestations is a formalised event, repeated over time, and governed by a strict code of hospitality. Moreover, it carries a symbolic message that revolves around the key notion of *convivencia*, the peaceful co-existence of ethnic groups. This notion is not only stressed in formal speeches but is also salient in the act of drinking and eating together in the domestic domain. The symbolism of commensality is prominent and creates at least a temporary communal bond.[9] Apart from the exchange of food and drink, there is also an interchange of courtesies — basically statements of consideration and goodwill — and of practical information regarding business and politics.[10]

What we note in the *agasajo* is a peculiar mixture of what Goffman has called 'avoidance rituals' and 'presentational rituals.'[11] On the one hand, participants in the *agasajo*-circuit employ forms of deference which keep them at a distance from the sensibilities and tensions inherent in everyday inter-ethnic encounters. Hence the basic rule of playing down ethnic distinctiveness. On the other hand, specific statements are made about the way participants regard one another, that is as *gente fino*, urbane people, and how they should deal with each other, that is, as equals belonging to the same social class and of civilised breeding. In other words, the main criteria for membership are prominence, compatibility, and economic equality. The tone of the gatherings is one of reciprocity. When I stress the ritualised nature of these events this is not to say that they are devoid of instrumentality. Although the instrumental function of the gatherings is concealed in the performance, they offer one of the few opportunities for coordinating the political and commercial activities of the various segments of the upper class.

How then do the ritualism and symbolism of the *agasajos* relate to the power structure of the enclave? They play down religious and ethnic identity and affiliation and accentuate class solidarity. Ritual permits the construction of a temporary and artificial world. *Agasajos* create a temporary ambience of oneness, fraternity and equality that does not exist outside these occasions, denying that there is any ambiguity. Equality is stressed, yet the egalitarian balance is fragile.

In non-ritualised public life the Catholic-Spanish sector of the enclave does indeed exclude even the most powerful naturalised members of the other ethnic groups from sharing political power and full citizenship. This sector considers itself above Jews, Hindus and Muslims. So the solidarity and intimacy asserted in the gatherings sharply contrast with the avoidance behaviour prevalent in everyday life. Notwithstanding the pervasive rhetoric of *convivencia*, a subtle and benign condescension can be detected in the pantomime of the Catholic participants, who, in fact, dictate the terms of peaceful co-existence. The formal dress is European, the food is in part Moroccan, but the standard is European and it is eaten in the Spanish fashion. The Catholic Spanish set the standards of civilisation, of being gentlemen in public. Once one has acquired these Spanish habits, then ethnicity can be downgraded in importance and class accentuated. This emphasis on class is a way of defusing ethnic divisions and an acknowledgment of social mobility.

Instead of reflecting or otherwise fitting the enclave's power figuration, the ritualised behaviour displayed at these parties denies the tensions and imbalances which characterise inter-ethnic relations in Melilla. They reproduce the hierarchy of class, whose terms are Spanish. Because the Catholics set the standards, even though they are presented in terms of 'universal' standards, the *agasajo* indirectly also invokes the hierarchy of ethnicity and therefore serves to reproduce this hierarchy. Yet, it also reveals the participants' recognition that they are caught up in a web of interdependencies. However, some re-conciliation of interests of the various ethnic layers of the upper class is indeed effected through these ritualised events.

Non-Reciprocal 'Joking' and Avoidance

Ethnic jokes circulate throughout Melilla. These are based on stereotyped representations of physical appearance, clothing, language, character and customs. Stereotyped images of any particular ethnic group are remarkably uniform among the other groups. Common motifs include the pomposity, boorishness, uncleanliness, and arrogance of the Iberians; the stupidity, ineptness, ignorance, brutality, untrustworthiness, and excess-ive sexuality of the Muslims; the slyness, effeminacy and obesity of the Hindus; and the insipidity, avarice, and covetousness of the Jews. Ethnic jokes are expressions of deeply-rooted racial antagonism and fear of the 'other'. They are only told at intra-group meetings, though I once heard a Jewish entertainer capi-talise on the motifs mentioned above before a mixed Jewish-Catholic audience. I will not deal here with ethnic humour in general but rather with asymmetrical 'joking' in Catholic-Muslim relations.[12]

Non-reciprocal 'joking' is a mode employed fairly frequently by middle and working-class Catholics in their daily encounters with Muslims. Illiterate and poor Muslims are most at risk in this respect, being teased and ridiculed, sometimes mildly, more often in a cruel manner. The contacts of most Muslims with the other ethnic groups, in particular with Iberians, occur in humiliating circumstances. As dependents, inferiors or clients they frequently find themselves in situations in which they just cannot practice avoidance. They have to approach Spaniards for favours and services. For instance, as domestic servants Muslim women are often infantilised. They are addressed with *tu* or with their nickname, chided by their employers in the presence of third parties, talked about by their masters with others while they are present, and they are easy targets for jokes.

Since it is only one party, invariably the Catholic-Spanish one, which makes fun of the other, the 'joking' should be labelled asymmetrical. It takes many different forms and occurs in various situations. Let me give a series of examples to indicate the nature and range of this behaviour. During Ramadan, a period of intensification of Muslim identity, Muslims are frequently ridiculed:

A regular Spanish customer in a bar is watching a football match transmitted by the Moroccan TV. The match is frequently interrupted by short shots of religious celebrations, which increasingly irritates the customer. After several such intermezzos he shouts at the Muslim waiter, who practises Ramadan: 'I shit on your Ramadan, God damn it!' an insult provoking hilarious laughter among the other Catholic customers.

Early one morning in one of the most prestigious bars where only Catholic clients are present, a Muslim cleaning woman starts scrubbing the floor. One of the Catholic waiters calls her attention: 'Hé, *niña* (girl), how pale you look today and how slow you are. That's what comes of your Ramadan. Shall I make you a cup of coffee and some toast?' The elderly woman briefly interrupts her work and is unable to hide her irritation, whereupon the waiters and customers burst into laughter.

Isolated Muslims who find themselves in the presence of two or more Catholic-Spaniards are the most frequent targets:

Three Catholics who are having their customary evening stroll pass the doorway of a bank where a Moroccan vagabond is busy making preparations for spending the night there. The three take a brief halt, while one of them addresses the vagabond as follows: 'Hé, *morito* ('little moor') are you going to guard the savings you have in this bank?' His companions find it very amusing when the victim starts to swear in Rifian.

One afternoon I was strolling with a Catholic informant in the main public park. My companion started a conversation with a friend who was supervising a Muslim gardener, busy pulling weeds out of a flower-bed. My companion made some comments upon the quality of the gardener's work. After a while the boss called the Muslim in order to give him further instructions. The man approached, greeted us, and pulled out a packet of cigarettes which he offered around. When they were declined he lit one and began to smoke while listening to his boss. Then my companion made the following assertion: 'The only thing I really appreciate in Moors is their tidiness. For instance they shit in their couscous casserole and clean it very thoroughly afterwards (turning to the gardener). That's true, isn't it?' The man burst into laughter, while the Muslim shrugged his shoulders, threw away his cigarette, gave a salutation and walked away to resume his work.

A popular way of burlesquing Muslims involves an exaggerated imitation of the typical accent and tone they have developed in speaking Castilian. This often occurs in mixed bars. Some years ago a local centre-right politician showed bad taste by imitating the Rifian way of pronouncing Spanish on a national radio channel.

Particularly cruel are the puns made on expressions in Arabic or Rifian as in the following instance:

> A small group of Catholics were drinking in a pub when a young Moroccan peddler entered with a plate of roasted almonds. Approaching their table, he was greeted with an obscene pun on the Arab reciprocal greeting formula; 'sâlâmo 'alîkum, maricón eres,' which means: 'Good day, you're a fag.'

Equally cruel is the collective mocking of the Muslim praying posture, popular among children.

In sum, there is a whole range and repertoire of 'jokes' which Catholics use in order to deride, mock, caricature, make fun of, humiliate and insult Muslims. The usual reaction of the victims is to remain silent, pretending not to understand, or deliberately refusing to understand the 'joke'. Sometimes they play along with the game and join in the laughter, but they rarely show anger. They are not in a position to reciprocate the 'jokes' and insults, because of their dependent and inferior status.

The liberties taken by the Iberians vis-à-vis relatively power-less Muslims can be seen as non-reciprocal 'joking' behaviour.[13] Individual Muslims, who are temporarily isolated from their own group, are teased, mocked, humiliated and insulted not by virtue of peculiar personality traits but rather because of their ethnic background. In many of the situations described above, 'joking' is an almost prescribed or compulsive mode by which Catholic-Spaniards deal with Muslims. The topics, puns and imitations are highly standardised and stereotyped. Here we have another ritualised mode of behaviour that is particularly current in the middle and working class sections of the Iberian community.

The 'jokes' and puns are especially rough, obscene and insulting in those cases where the power differences between aggressors and victims are minimal. Catholic workers resent the growing number of naturalised Muslims who are now contracted for municipal labour, because they are cheaper, while they themselves remain unemployed. Ritual insults and insinuations about the integrity of Muslims are then employed to keep them at a distance, to establish and reinforce a dominance that has become vulnerable. The 'jokes' raise a barrier between 'us' and 'them'. The jocular, condescending, and insulting remarks directed at Muslims generate feelings of superiority among Christians. 'Jokes' and insults that cannot be reciprocated aim at undermining the morale of the victims, a strategy to force them to remain in an inferior position.

Among the very few occasions of ritualised reciprocal aggression in inter-ethnic encounters are the football competitions which were recently being held between Muslim, Catholic, Jewish and Gypsy teams. These matches are often heated confrontations during which the opponents inflict minor injuries upon each other. A match might occasionally degenerate into a massive fight among players and spectators in which the police are forced to intervene. During one of the matches I attended, a Muslim spectator stepped into the arena, raised up a picture of Jesus Christ which he then tore up demonstratively. Several Catholic spectators then jumped into the arena and chased after the man. Amidst growing chaos the referee had to call off the match.[14]

Starting with Radcliffe-Brown's famous essay on joking relationships (1952 [1940]) anthropologists have made a sharp distinction between avoidance and joking relations. The assumption is
that no joking relationship can be established with those towards
whom avoidance behaviour or respect is expected.[15] This may
be valid in kin-based societies but cannot be maintained in the
case of complex societies in which ethnicity is a dominant
principle of social organisation. In Melilla we see a peculiar combination and alternation of avoidance and 'joking' in Christian-
Muslim contacts. In general, avoidance is an institutionalised
mode of behaviour, a way of dealing with tension and conflict
by avoiding open confrontation. Mutual avoidance is usually
practised by Christians and Muslims outside the economic sphere.
This behaviour particularly occurs when solitary Catholics meet
two or more Muslims, or when a group of Catholics comes into
contact situations with a group of Muslims. However, there are
several types of avoidance as there are various forms of 'joking'.
For instance, strict avoidance should be distinguished from the
avoidance rituals in the *agasajo* in which avoidance is combined
with presentational rituals.

There are many different situations in daily life where people
from various ethnic backgrounds find themselves spatially very
close yet at the same time socially distant. Behaviour in the
micro-space of a tavern or bar offers an illustration. Open
discrimination is rarely practised in bars. Only in exceptional
cases are Muslims refused admittance to Catholic establish-
ments in an overt way. Most of the Iberian bars are patronised
by both Catholics and Muslims, though bars owned by Muslims
are avoided by Catholics. In mixed bars Muslims and Catholics
usually act as if they do not see each other. They do not
acknowledge each other, nor do they start conversations. Social
separation is reinforced by the fact that Muslims always talk *rifi*
among each other, a language which only a handful of Catholics
can understand.

Catholic bartenders and clients use indirect means to make
Muslims feel uncomfortable. They might, for instance, stare
them out if they stay longer than necessary, that is, if they are
not consuming some refreshment. Muslims are served more
slowly and indifferently, even if they are regular customers. In
many subtle ways they are made to realise that they are admitted purely for economic reasons, i.e. because they consume
goods on sale. They are not treated as individuals but as rep-

resentatives of the general category of *moro*. The structural position of Rifian immigrants in Melilla is rather like being a permanent stranger,[16] while those who perform vital functions for the Catholic community, i.e. those who clean, are generally treated as non-persons.

Although avoidance tends to be mutual, there is a clear imbalance in this mode of behaviour at the expense of Muslims, for they are the ones who are more frequently dependent on the other sector of society as clients and subordinates. Civil servants at the counters of public service offices frequently pretend not to see Muslim clients, who are then forced into making humiliating attempts to attract attention. Avoidance behaviour practised by Catholics follows the same pattern as 'joking,' and communicates that *moro* is an inferior category and that *moros* are not accepted as full co-citizens.

While exchanges of goods and services do create ties between Christians, Jews, Muslims and Hindus, these tend to remain contractual. There are hardly any inter-ethnic bonds generated in the realms of friendship, sociability, marriage or kinship. Nor are there spontaneous — that is non-ritualised — involvements of people of various ethnic backgrounds in focused social activities. In the last chapter we will deal with a striking exception to this basic principle of inter-ethnic communication in Melilla.

Chapter 9

Hindus and Muslims

Kesho Ram Tiwari was born in Hyderabad (Sind), a year after the partition of the Indian subcontinent. He was the first son of a prosperous cloth merchant of Brahman status, who, in view of the dramatic events taking place around him, decided that his future looked bleak in a Muslim state. Just after Kesho Ram's first haircut, the family left for Suez where his father had distant relatives and business contacts. One of these kinsmen advised him to try his fortune in Melilla, where he had a business partner. At the age of two Kesho Ram arrived at Melilla with his parents and sister. The head of family resumed trading in cloth and also began to import gold and silverware from Sind. In the mid 1950s he rented a building on the main avenue and opened a shop. Four other children were born and business went well.

In the course of the 1950s more families from Sind arrived in Melilla. Kesho Ram was one of the first Hindus who entered the prestigious Salesian college. But in the mid-1960s his father's business began to fail — according to gossip because of heavy gambling — and he committed suicide. Kesho Ram had to leave high school just before the end of his studies in order to take over what was left of his father's enterprise. Within a decade the young man had built up the strongest commercial empire in Melilla. He was the first of its merchants to see the potential of transit trade in electronic commodities from the Far East and established pioneer contacts in Japan, Hong Kong and Singapore. When I first met him, Kesho Ram was a rather stout, though energetic, man with gold-capped teeth. He had recently divorced his wife from Bombay and was still childless. He spent most of his time travelling between his stores in Melilla, Las Palmas and Gran Canaria, Madrid, Valencia and Bombay, Tokyo, Hong Kong and Singapore.

Kesho Ram is one of the founding members of the Hindu Community of Melilla, of which he has been President since it

152

was officially established in 1977. In that year he also became the president and major sponsor of the local football team and initiated the annual galas of Sanyo and Honda for which he contracted major Spanish and international artists, like Julio Iglesias and Demis Roussos, the receipts going to the local Red Cross. Moreover, Kesho Ram is a Maecenas for almost any social and cultural activity. Some years ago he acted as the personal guide to the Spanish King and Queen on their state visit to India. In 1982 King Carlos had an interview with him about the possible consequences of the opening up of the frontier between Gibraltar and Spain, a topic on which he also exchanged opinions with the Spanish Foreign Minister.[1]

When his mother died in Bombay, the entire Hindu Community of Melilla mourned for one year, during which Kesho Ram suspended all public appearances apart from business. Tiwari House, which he runs together with his two younger brothers, employs thirty people in Melilla alone, and holds monopoly rights over the import of Sanyo equipment and Honda cars into Spain. Kesho Ram also helps to promote tourism in Melilla, having spread the slogan: 'Come to Melilla, paradise for shopping!'. At only forty years of age, his name — always linked to Honda, Sanyo and Citizen — has become a legend and has given rise to many a Dallas-type story. One of these holds that when he married the woman from Bombay whom he had met on an airplane, he spent over 100 million pesetas on a wedding party that lasted for several days on board a yacht.

Ismael Mohatar is a paradigmatic representative of the large Muslim population of Melilla. He was born in 1935 in the tribe of Ait Bu Gafar. Before he reached his first birthday his father died in an accident in the ore mines of Wixan. His young mother moved with her four children to a husband's brother in Melilla where they shared a *chabola* (hovel) and took in washing for Catholics. Then the Civil War broke out, bringing years of famine and hardship. The Mohatar family, who lacked documents of any kind, was first listed in the municipal census (*empadronado*) in 1940.

As a small boy Ismael from time to time received meals in the soup-kitchen run by local Falangists. He began to hang around the barracks of the Civil Guard in the barrio of Mantelete where he gained the confidence of the guards who used him as an errand-boy. At the age of six he began to work as a shoe-shine boy. At the end of the 1940s his family moved out of his uncle's hut to the Muslim ghetto of Cañada de la Muerte where his mother rented a room. At that time Ismael became a luggage porter in the port district. In 1954 his mother found a bride for him, the daughter of a sergeant in the Protectorate army and a distant matrilateral relative in the Ait Bu Gafar. At first Ismael opposed this marriage, because 'I did not have money to sustain a family', as he put it, but finally gave in to his mother's wish.

With a loan from his father-in-law and the help of 'Pepe the Gypsy' he built a small dwelling in the Cañada. His first child, a girl, turned out to be mentally retarded. 'My wife took her to all the major marabouts in Nador, we prayed and slaughtered chickens, but all this was to no avail.' Another daughter and three sons were born. One of them became a cripple when he was shot in the knee by a legionnaire after having climbed the barbed wire which surrounds the Cañada. He sells lottery tickets in the main avenue.

Ismael was a peddler of old silver coins when I first met him in one of Melilla's market-places. He is a tall, slightly built, calm and talkative man, who knows a lot of local people and who is liked for his talent for telling stories. His meagre income is supplemented with remittances sent to him by his daughter who works as a domestic servant in Madrid and a son who works in the construction trade in Catalonia. His life so far has been a continuous struggle with the bureaucracy of Melilla. When Morocco gained independence in 1956, personal documentation became an important issue. In 1964 he wished to join the swelling wave of Muslim migrant workers to Western Europe. For this he needed a Spanish or Moroccan passport. 'In Nador they did not know me, because my mother never registered my birth, while here the civil servant told me that I was a temporary resident, although I have been living here since I was a baby.'

Through friends of friends Ismael managed to get hold of a safe conduct pass with which he could travel to Barcelona. With 1,000 pesetas in his pocket he took the ferry to Málaga and a bus to Catalonia. After a month his pass expired. The police told him to return to Melilla, but at the Moroccan consulate he succeeded in 'buying' a provisional Moroccan passport. A Muslim friend in Melilla sent him Moroccan leatherwork which he peddled in Barcelona. But then the police arrested him for not having a work permit and a *carnet* for peddling. After much trouble he managed to get a trading licence. Having roamed the streets of Barcelona for six months he travelled back to Melilla. In the meantime his 'statistical card' — a kind of unofficial card of residence, only valid in Melilla — had expired and because of his provisional Moroccan passport he was expelled. He returned to Melilla illegally.

Two years later Ismael and his wife Ttleitmas were expelled again, while their children were allowed to remain behind. 'How could we live in Nador, while our children were in Melilla? I do not belong to Nador, Farkhana or Drius, I belong to Melilla.' Once again he returned illegally. His second daughter who worked as an assistant in a Jewish store, managed to get a new 'statistical card' for her parents through a friend of her boss who was a lawyer. At present he and his wife are still considered as temporary residents. They are stateless, belong nowhere, and simply do not exist in administrative terms. 'I have lived much longer in Melilla than most of those bazaar-owners in the Poligono who have the money to buy the necessary papers. The streets belong to everybody, the police only arrest innocent people like me who work and are not really interested in catching criminals. Let them shove those documents into their mother's cunt.'

Kesho Ram and Ismael are exemplars of two types of inhabitant who are separated from each other by the widest economic, ethnic and cultural gap possible in Melilla. Although the former is in administrative terms a temporary resident like Ismael, he has never had any problem about this status. The Hindu and Muslim communities of Melilla are worlds apart. Although they are two ethnic minorities in a Spanish enclave, they are each other's opposite in every respect. The Hindus constitute the smallest ethnic minority while the Muslims are becoming the majority. The former are highly literate, belong to the upper class, maintain long-distance networks of kin, friends and business partners, while the latter are mostly illiterate, find themselves in the lumpenproletariat, and are more or less imprisoned in the small enclave. The Hindus have a high level of self-respect and pride in their culture which they doggedly preserve, while most Muslims lack a positive frame of reference. The Hindus despise Muslims whom they see only as servants and buyers of their products. Outside the economic domain the two groups have little contact. The Muslims, however, have one advantage over the other ethnic groups — their staying power and numerical strength. Recently, they have become increasingly aware of this strength as we will see below.

Brahmans as Compradores

The Hindus constitute one of the smallest but most powerful ethnic minorities of Spain. Together they number approximately 5,500 individuals, of whom 2,000 live in Las Palmas de Gran Canaria, 1,000 in Tenerife, 300 in Ceuta and the rest in Melilla, Valencia and Madrid.[2] They nearly all originate from Hyderabad (Sind), an important communication, commercial and industrial centre in Pakistan.[3] Their mother tongue is Sindi which they speak among themselves. Most of them are merchants who claim Brahman status. In the late 1970s the Hindu colonies founded 'Hindu Community Associations' and a Spanish-wide umbrella association, thereby formalising a pre-existing informal organisational structure. The vast majority of them hold British or Indian passports and a Spanish *autorización de residencia*, which gives them unrestricted freedom of movement and commercial action.

The 110 Hindus who live in Melilla constitute twenty nuclear family units. The average number of children per family is two. The Hindu presence in the enclave dates back to the late nineteenth century, the census of 1895 listing three merchants from Bombay who had arrived two years earlier. They were single and lived under the same roof. Three more Hindus arrived in 1900. In 1918 seventeen 'Indians' (all men) were listed in the census, but ten years later all had left.[4] The present Hindu inhabitants, the first generation of whom arrived between 1940 and 1950 and more than half of whom are born in Melilla, know nothing about their predecessors. The colony began with sixteen members in 1940 and grew to seventy-three in 1965 and 110 in 1983.[5]

Krishan Chand Chatturvedi is one of the few left of those who arrived in 1940. He was born into a Hyderabad merchant family in 1932. He recalls how he disembarked in Melilla with his parents and two older sisters after a passage on an overcrowded ferry. The Second World War had just broken out and there were two German frigates in the port of Melilla:

> I will never forget how during the first weeks of our life in this city we were constantly being gaped at by Muslims and Christians who

probably assumed that we came from a different planet. We were the only three Indians among the Catholic and Jewish pupils at the Don Bosco Salesian College and we were frequently teased by the Spanish boys. The war years were pretty hard. My father had invested his capital in a partnership with a Hindu merchant in Ceuta dealing mainly in cloth. In 1949 he opened up his own shop in O'Donnell street. In secondary school we were taught English by an American who had been a sergeant in the North African invasion army and married a Spanish woman. This English class was only attended by Jews and our people.

Krishan's eldest sister married a Hindu merchant in Las Palmas, and the other married a trader in Poona. He himself entered into matrimony at the age of twenty-eight. His wife, five years his junior, is a distant paternal relative, who arrived at Melilla just after the end of the Second World War. Shortly after his marriage Krishan took over his father's shop, while his parents returned to India to live with their daughter.[6] Krishan and his wife, who are both Indian nationals, have three children, two boys born in 1961 and 1963 respectively, and a daughter born in 1973. His oldest son is destined to take over the store which Krishan has transformed into a prosperous *bazaar* on the main avenue. He is generally known among the Catholic inhabitants as 'Pepe el Indio'. Almost every year they spend their holiday in Poona.

The only Hindu who has married outside his ethnic group is Ram Prashad who came from Hyderabad to Melilla as a twenty-year-old to work as a book-keeper for the Tiwari-House. While he was working in Tenerife he met a Spanish woman from Valladolid who was a schoolteacher. They married in 1966 and began a household in Melilla where Ram started wholesale trading in his own right. The mixed couple and their five children are active members in the Hindu Community, of which Ram is the treasurer. Their children carry mixed Indian-Spanish names, Kamlu Angeles and Kishu José. After the birth of the last child, Ram's wife resumed her work as a teacher. She is the only woman married to a Hindu who works outside her home.

Joint families are exceptional as residential units.[7] One bazaar-owner employs a nephew who was born and raised in Tangier and also provides him with board and residence. A manager in the Tiwari-House brought over a cousin from Madras to work as a clerk for his patron, and two brothers share both a household and business.

Thirty-one Hindus are inscribed in the Register of the Chamber of Commerce as wholesale merchants, a dozen of whom are absentee owners.[8] They combine wholesale business with retail trading, employing over 200 people, the vast majority of them Spanish shop-assistants. Non-Hindus are excluded from administrative jobs. As we have seen, the merchants often employ kinsmen in managerial or administrative posts.

Hindu trading is marked by its commercial aggression, active advertisement campaigns, and its near monopoly over trade with the Far East. Hindus control over 60 percent of the imports of bazaar commodities (watches, TV sets, radio-cassettes, jewellery, chinaware, automobiles, cameras, videos, personal computers and software), while they represent only 5 percent of all importers in Melilla. They are the most outstanding innovators, inventing the formula of the bazaar-store in electronic merchandise at a time when Japan and Hong Kong began to dump huge cargoes of their products in external markets; at the same time they create a nineteenth-century ambience by burning incense in their shops, receiving their clients with hospitality, and allowing bargaining, which especially appeals to the Muslim clients. Since the late 1960s dozens of Catholic, Jewish and Muslim merchants have emulated the Hindu example but none of them have succeeded in superseding the pioneers.

The Hindus constitute a closed community, that is, closed to Catholics, Muslims and Jews, yet open to other Hindu communities with which they form a large commercium and connubium. They carefully cultivate an image of political non-commitment and as dispensers of charity and sponsors of all kinds of cultural and social events. Two Hindus hold visible public posts; one sits on the board of management of the Chamber of Commerce, while the other is a member of the Red Cross committee. Many Catholic and Muslim inhabitants, however, are convinced that the leading members of the Hindu Community wield considerable back-stage political power. In the past there have been allusions in the press to the power of the 'Hindu mafia' and its large-scale involvement in illegal transit trade with Morocco. The president of the Hindu Community Association vehemently denies such allegations:

> We devote ourselves exclusively to trade, and aim at maintaining good relations with all local politicians, civil servants as well as with the citizens in the streets, that is all.

What he does not deny is that the greater part of Hindu imports flow illegally to Morocco through Muslim middlemen. Indeed the practice of 'smuggling' is so widespread in Melilla that it has almost lost its meaning of illegality, notwithstanding continuous demands on Spanish governments by their Moroccan counterparts to enforce customs regulations and intensify vigilance at the border.[9] Hindu merchants seem to be experts in handling the twilight boundary between bribery and business gifts. Several politicians and civil servants openly display small luxury commodities on their desks bearing inscriptions such as 'With the compliments of Ram Ghamandas'.

Apart from sponsoring all kinds of sociocultural events, the Hindu Community Council occasionally organises grand Indian spectacles to which they invite all important local authorities, businessmen, intellectuals and leading members of the umbrella Hindu Association. One of these 'grand galas' featured a famous classical music-and-dance company from Orissa contracted for the occasion by the Indian Embassy and the local Hindu Association in a joint venture to promote both India and the business interests of local Hindus. Members of the Association welcomed all guests personally, presenting the ladies with a carnation, and carefully guiding the most important guests to seats of honour in the first two rows. The Governor and his spouse were seated in the centre of the first row, flanked by Kesho Ram Tiwari and the mayor. Then followed the supreme military commander, government representatives, councillors, leading members of all local political parties, the president of the Chamber of Commerce, of the Jewish Community, and other high officials. Prominent Muslims, however, were conspicuously absent. It was one of the few occasions at which the spouses of Hindu merchants, dressed in their white saris, appeared in public. On the stage stood a statue of Vishnu with an incense burner. Kesho Ram Tiwari spoke a few words of welcome, emphasising the city's positive ambience and inter-cultural exchanges, after which he gave the floor to the embassy's cultural attaché who briefly explained the themes and symbolism of the pieces to be performed.

Many Spanish guests left during the break of the three-hour spectacle, among them the representative of the Ministry of Culture and the Secretary-General of the Spanish Socialist Worker's Party. Some days later the Ministry representative confided to me that he had found the performance too long and boring (*demasiado pesado*), claiming Spanish opera to be superior to Indian dance and music. On such occasions the Hindu community carefully presents its self-image to a wider audience and cultivates its relationship with the top leaders of local society.

From this ceremonial event and interviews with members of the Hindu community emerges the following self-image. The main components of this self-perception and presentation are a rich and ancient cultural heritage, superior Brahman status and a long tradition of trading. As Brahmans they claim to observe their religious duties strictly, avoiding the consumption of beef and eggs, fish, and meat on Mondays and during full moon. They maintain the major rites and customs of their land of origin of which they talk proudly. The following rites, which are standard rites of orthodox Hinduism, were enumerated to me several times.[10] The wedding ceremony is focused on a sacred fire which the couple has to circumambulate seven times. The second major act, which they stressed, is the washing of the bridegroom's feet by one of the bride's brothers, a rite of respect, expressing the inferior status of wife-givers. The third act is the breaking of a coconut by smashing it on the threshold of the new couple's house, which they explained to me as symbolising the defloration of the bride, and the bridegroom's sexual potency and fertility. The initiation of newborn males into the community involves a first hair cut forty days after birth and the washing of the head in the sea. Finally, they stress the importance of the proper cremation of the corpse of a deceased person on a pile of wood, oil, perfume and butter. They bring over priests from India to preside over post-cremation rites.

These rites of passage are intimate family and communal occasions to which no outsiders are admitted, with the exception of weddings, and then only to a formal reception specially held for acquaintances belonging to the Catholic and Jewish segments of local society. These rites thus act as markers *par excellence* of the boundaries of the Hindu community. Diwali, the major communal festival celebrated by Melilla Hindus, serves the same function of promoting internal cohesion and demarcating the outer group boundaries. For this 'Festival of the Light' celebrated in honour of Lakshmi, the goddess of wealth and fertility who is particularly linked to the merchant caste,[11] the Hindu Association hires a luxurious restaurant on the boulevard. Here the Hindu community gathers to rejoice in close intimacy. The festival is concluded with a firework display on the beach.

With regard to their identification with India and Melilla, I noted down the following statements:

> Generally and also personally, we do not have plans to return to India, although our motherland continues to have a central place in our hearts and we will always love India. But we also feel ourselves to be part of Melilla and, by implication, also of Spain and it is hard to imagine returning to India and leaving Melilla behind as long as the circumstances are normal here. (President of the Hindu Community Association)

> Our loyalty to this city is strong; we feel accepted here. I have lived in Las Palmas and Ceuta, but nowhere did I feel the *convivencia* inherent in this city. (a middle-aged merchant)

> Of course, our national sentiments are strong and we maintain intimate contacts with kith and kin in our motherland. What can you expect? Our grandparents and parents were born there. But at the same time, I feel a strong attachment to this soil. (a manager in his mid-twenties)

It is significant to note that only a handful of Hindus have died in Melilla; the overwhelming majority return to India on retiring from business. In this respect their attitude towards Melilla very much resembles that displayed by members of the Jewish Community Association who also consider their residence in the enclave as temporary, notwithstanding the fact that they have been living for generations in this corner of the Mediterranean world. Their tie with Melilla is almost entirely an economic one. In this regard the phrase in the Hindu leader's statement — 'as long as the circumstances are normal' — is revealing. What he meant to express is that they will continue to live in the enclave as long as conditions are favourable for their trade and Catholics and Muslims allow them to live in peace.

The similarity in the structural position of Hindus and Jews is striking in other regards as well. Like the first Jewish merchants who came from Tetuan, they moved away from a Muslim environment, which hampered their economic and cultural aspirations, to a transitional place that offered new economic opportunities. They brought with them a rich cultural heritage, an innate sense of superiority, a wide network of commercial ties, language skills, and a strong drive for self-reliance. They typically occupied an interstitial niche as brokers. Their success as innovators followed almost naturally from their basically ambiguous position in the host society. Both Hindus and Jews combined an expansive commercial stance with keeping their ethnic ranks closed to outsiders. It is not surprising that the attitude displayed towards them by the dominant segments of the host society is equally ambivalent. Catholics and Muslims both admire and envy the Hindus' commercial success, and both respect and despise their way of life. The intra-ethnic dynamics of the Hindu community and their management of ethnic boundaries are put into sharper relief if we contrast their situation with that of the Muslims.

From Tribe to Ghetto

The officially registered Muslim population totals one third of the city's inhabitants.[12] However, the Muslim imprint on public life is greater than this number suggests as there are thousands of illegal, more or less permanent residents in addition, while an estimated 8,000 to 10,000 border-dwellers commute daily to Melilla. Muslims thus very much dominate public space in a visual sense, the more so as they virtually monopolise ambulant and market-place trade in the food sector.

The overwhelming majority are *dhamaziqht*-speaking Berbers who come from the Iqar'ayen and other tribes in the province of Nador, where their parents and grandparents were sedentary peasants. Language, religion and origin are the main markers of their identity. They present themselves by these over-arching criteria, and the other ethnic groups use the same criteria in addition to real or assumed racial traits to identify them. Thus for the Catholic inhabitants *moro* and Muslim are synonymous.

The tribal divisions of the pre-Protectorate era have largely given way to a broader self-awareness of being Rifians and Muslims. If you ask a Muslim resident where he or she was born, nine out of ten will reply Nador, the provincial entity created by the Moroccan state after independence, which is largely coterminous with the eastern Rif. If you ask for more information people rarely give the names of tribes or tribal divisions but rather the names of hamlets and villages, which, indeed, formerly largely coincided with the boundaries of patri-lineal groups. In the context of the enclave the older agnatic divisions have almost completely lost their meaning.

Today the Muslim population is far more fragmented and heterogeneous than its origin would suggest. Roughly speaking, the main lines of division within the Muslim collectivity are nationality and length of residence,[13] social class, degree of religious involvement, and political orientation, which partly overlap as markers of internal differentiation. Of prime importance is the distinction between those who hold Spanish nationality and those who do not. Within the first category, which constitutes approximately one quarter of the total Muslim population, are the economically and culturally most powerful Muslims, the ethnic elite. They are the literate and established merchants and property-owners, who frequently have a dual nationality and own land and houses in Nador province. They are descended from the first Muslims who settled in Melilla between 1910 and 1930. Their forebears belonged to the tribal elite who were given privileged treatment by the Spaniards. They exploit the advantages of their dual nationality, are fairly well integrated into the enclave society and are at the same time royalists who identify themselves with the regime of King Hassan II. They are also custodians of the Islamic tradition.

The Muslim middle and lower-middle classes are of a very heterogeneous composition. These strata largely consist of retail traders,[14] but also include civil servants, shop assistants, artisans, and skilled workers. They cannot be clearly defined in terms of the criteria mentioned above, in contrast to the proletarian Muslims who constitute the largest category.

The lumpenproletarian Berber immigrants are illiterate, unskilled, largely undocumented or stateless, only marginally involved in Islam, and live in the margin of Melilla, in a state of residential and social apartheid. Most of them came to Melilla just before or soon after Morocco's independence.[15] Muslim women who work as domestic servants mainly belong to this category. Their men are unemployed most of the time and are prepared to hire themselves out for any menial odd job. They crowd the large informal or parallel economic sector as small street traders and small-scale smugglers and are continuously seeking ways to make a living. They dwell in overcrowded ghettos such as Cabrerizas Altas, Cañada de la Muerte, Barrio Hebreo, and Barrio Reina Regente (popularly called Barrio Cuernos, 'quarter of the Horns'). The total number of Muslims living in these outlying ghettos is about 7,000.

Religious affiliation is the overriding marker of ethnic identity. People are identified by the label of religion regardless of their actual degree of identification with its ethos and participation in its rituals. In theory, Islam touches almost every aspect of daily life. In reality, Islamic doctrines and rites play only a marginal role in the lives of the great majority of Muslims. The elaborate Islamic ritual cycle includes the five daily ritual prayers, the communal Friday service, Ramadan, the Great and the Little Feast, and the pilgrimage to Mecca. In Melilla, as in Morocco, only a small minority of Muslims regularly observe these ritual obligations and they are mainly middle-aged and elderly men from the upper and middle classes.

The exception to this rule is the month of fasting which is observed by almost the entire Muslim population. Ramadan sums up what it means to be a Muslim. In this month Islam is most consciously acted out in daily life (Eickelman 1976: 137). In a multiethnic society dominated by a Catholic majority, the celebration of Ramadan is invested with extra significance. It ritualises Muslim identity and highlights the Muslim ideal of religious *communitas*. In particular the reversal of day and night during Ramadan sets the Muslims apart as a collectivity in a highly visible way. The peculiar rhythm of fasting leaves a clear mark on the public life of Melilla at large, and the other ethnic groups are forced to adapt themselves to this rhythm. Bar attendance drops dramatically during the day and streets and shops are far less crowded. Between sunset and sunrise, which are marked by loud signals, the Muslim collectivity fully comes to life. The streets and popular bars of the Poligono quarter fill up with an animated Muslim crowd after the 'breakfast' (*fatur*) and many men stay there until the last meal before daybreak. Many more men than usual dress in jellabas and perform the ritual prayers. The climax in the celebration of Muslim identity is the Little Feast, which breaks the fast with a day of conspicuous consumption during which Melilla is flooded by Moroccans.

'The Ravine of Death'

I would now like to consider the case of one particular Muslim ghetto, the Cañada de la Muerte. Its sinister name refers to a battle in 1893 between the Melilla garrison and tribesmen in which the Spanish suffered a bloody defeat. Barrio-dwellers often refer to the barrio as 'Camello' ('Camel') or simply 'the Muslim barrio'. It is set apart from the rest of the city by a tract of wasteland, edged off by a road that runs to a border post and by barbed wire from the grounds of the Foreign Legion barracks. Its small cube-shaped houses in white, pale-blue and green have been built by their inhabitants according to the model of a traditional Rifian dwelling. This self-contained Muslim microcosm, compactly and erratically constructed along the ravine on the slope of a hill, is crowned by a new mosque with a pale green minaret which was built and financed by its inhabitants. An intricate maze of alleys connects the houses with each other.

The barrio originated in the pacification campaigns of 1909 and 1919–1922 when the Military Governor forced Muslim residents to move to an internment camp. When in 1922 Melilla's hinterland had been pacified, the deportees were permitted to leave and the wooden sheds were then occupied by Rifian soldiers of the Protectorate Army with their families. The newcomers gradually transformed the sheds into mud-and-stone dwellings. In 1930 there were fifty-two such houses in the Cañada de la Muerte.[16] The municipal census of 1940 yields the following sociographic data. The total number of inhabitants amounted to 1,192, 108 Catholics included. One quarter of them were listed as economically active. The distribution of occupations is shown in table 9.1.

The strong presence of professional Rifian soldiers indicates the military origin of the barrio. All but six Muslims were illiterate. Unskilled labour and peddling were economically the second most important subsistence activities. It has to be noted that women made up a remarkable 20 percent of those who earned a living, a fact that is intimately linked to the composition of households. Almost 30 percent of all households were run by widows; probably most of them were war widows who had to supplement a meagre pension with labour. Since traditional Rifian society did not offer employment opportunities to unattached women, they depended on the urban society for work.[17] About one fifth of all households were extended arrangements, ranging from nuclear families with one cohabitating relative to polygamous households, which made up 4 per cent. The most extreme case of an extended household was that of a fifty-seven-year-old ambulant trader from Ait Sidar who had moved to the barrio in 1934. He had three wives aged thirty-five, twenty-three, and twenty-two, eleven sons ranging in age from two to twenty-five — four of them listed as street vendors — and seven daughters. On the whole, however, polygamy was exceptional among these people of very modest economic means.

Table 9.1 Occupational structure of the barrio Cañada de la Muerte (Muslims)

Ragman	10
Laundress	19
Domestic servant	37
Fisherman	5
Soldier	84
Street vendor	52
Teacher	2
Artisan/construction	33
Religious teacher (*fqih*)	6
Boot-black (children)	22
Casual labourer	23
Peasant	4
Goatherd	2
total	299

Source: Padrón Municipal, 1940

Comparing these data with the census of 1980, we can detect little structural change. The same occupations recur, with unskilled workers and street peddlers predominating. The situation remains as it was in 1940 when one quarter of the barrio population had some regular source of income, pensions of retired soldiers included. Even more women — 25 percent — are now economically active as laundresses, domestic servants and seamstresses. Seven women have found employment in a tin factory.

Take the case of Sulika, who was born in Ait Shikar in 1922. She moved to Melilla when she was thirteen years old, to be married to a soldier in the native regiment of the Protectorate Army. She is now widowed and lives with her five unmarried children in a two-roomed dwelling. Apart from her small pension, her household lives on the wages earned by two daughters of thirty and thirty-one in a tinned-food factory. A daughter of fifteen and a son of fourteen are unemployed. Another son is an invalid and sells lottery tickets. The whole family is illiterate and holds semi-official cards of residence.

All Catholic residents have now moved out of the Cañada de la Muerte. Whereas forty years ago all Muslim residents had been born in the territory of the Iqar'ayen, today 65 percent of

Table 9.2 Administrative status of people living in the Cañada

Individual inhabitants		Families	
Holding Spanish nationality	169	All members holding Spanish nationality	3
Possessing statistical card*	616	All members possessing a statistical card	56
Moroccan nationality	1	With one member a Spanish citizen	196
Undocumented	290	Undocumented	101
Inhabitants under 14	606		
Total	1.682	Total	356

Source: Padrón 1984
* Indicating that the holder has been registered by the municipality as an illegal immigrant.

them were actually born in Melilla. The level of illiteracy has remained the same with 98 percent of the barrio-dwellers unable to read and write. This lack of access to school education dramatically highlights the marginality of the barrio. That it is a world apart from mainstream Melilla is further indicated by the administrative status of the 1,682 inhabitants, as table 9.2 clearly indicates.

Only 10 percent of all inhabitants have no problems with official documentation, whereas almost all families have to cope with problems of this kind. The story of Ismael Mohatar applies in fact to the vast majority of the barrio-dwellers.

Housing conditions illustrate the precarious existence of the Cañada Muslims. All dwellings have been constructed illegally on military terrain. Eighty-five percent of the houses are owned by the families who live in them, but only four dwellings are registered in the municipal office of real property, which means that legally the barrio does not exist. The rest of the houses are rented by their occupants, again without any written contract. On the whole, the quality of the houses is poor and they are very small. One quarter of all families have to share a house with another family, which means that they have to live in one room barely sixteen metres square. On the other hand, thirteen families occupy more than one dwelling. Small variations in housing conditions, administrative status, and the pooling of different sources of income in individual households, indicate slight differences in the shared experience of marginality.

Until the late 1970s the Cañada lacked public amenities of any kind. Only from 1980 onwards did the municipal government begin to acknowledge the existence of the barrio. Twelve public fountains were installed and most houses were supplied with electricity. An improvised primary school for a maximum of 130 pupils was opened and two nuns set up a small Red Cross dispensary. The inhabitants built a mosque with their own labour and funds, and this house of prayer has become the object of barrio pride. The fountains are foci of female sociability, while the men gather in the square of the mosque and in the barrio's two tea-houses. The households have elected an informal community leader, a *moqaddem*, who is backed by the respected barrio elders and acts as a *primus inter pares*, mainly settling internal disputes and acting as the barrio's representative to the outside world. This informal political arrangement is, in fact, very similar to the traditional village council as it operated in the Rif prior to the establishment of the Spanish Protectorate.

With regard to general socioeconomic and political conditions the Cañada Muslims differ little from the majority of Muslim residents in Melilla. However, the barrio is exceptional in one important respect: it constitutes a tightly-knit village community with a strong sense of collective identity, co-operative spirit and communal pride. It is the only exclusively Muslim residential unit in which ethnicity and locality are entirely coterminous. The spatial and social discreteness of the Cañada makes it a highly visible entity in the enclave. It is not surprising then that it has become the main target of Catholic racist stereotypes and prejudices. Popular opinion among Catholics, for instance, claims that the population of the Cañada amounts to at least 5,000 *moros*, a figure that is used to support the image of a Muslim invasion and the stereotype that 'they breed like rabbits'. Catholic inhabitants also frequently evoke images of threat and danger when they refer to the barrio: 'If you enter that place you will end up with a knife in your back'. In accordance with these highly negative stereotypes, the barrio has on several occasions been the target of unlicensed violence by foreign legionnaires.

On the other hand, this Muslim barrio has also become the main vehicle of Muslim identity and pride in Melilla, and has simultaneously been used by Muslim political leaders and critical Spanish journalists as an exemplar of Muslim marginalisation.

From an outsider's point of view, however, Muslim ghettos such as Cabrerizas Altas and Barrio Cuernos are materially far worse off and enjoy little communal organisation. This unique combination of marginality and communal coherence, pride and self-help makes the Cañada de la Muerte a prominent symbol in the confrontation between Catholics and Muslims.

Although the Cañada represents only 5 percent of the total Muslim population of Melilla, it has become a powerful image of the potential tactical strength of Muslims. The infrastructural improvements in the barrio of the early 1980s were mainly due to the collective efforts and solidarity of the barrio-dwellers themselves. And the first large-scale demonstration held by Muslims in Melilla in fifty years was organised and led by Cañada Muslims.

Organising Muslim Ethnicity

One of the basic problems of the Muslims of Melilla is how to transform numerical strength into power and bring ethnic identity into political play.

The first formal Muslim organisation dates back to 1937 and was founded by one of the most powerful Rifians of this century. General Mohand Ameziane Belkacen, born into a lineage of Imazujen leaders, was the first Rifian to enter a Spanish military academy. He made a spectacular career as an officer in the Spanish army, fought with Franco in the Civil War, became one of the dictator's confidants, and was appointed Captain-General of La Coruña and Barcelona. After Morocco's independence he became a Marshal in the Moroccan army and an influential member of several governments.

The Muslim Community organisation he founded served as an instrument of control rather than a vehicle for Muslim emancipation. It monitored the public behaviour of Muslims, settled disputes, issued charity cards and wielded patronage in order to keep Muslims in their subordinate position. This organisation, which was never meant to become a political instrument for the Muslims themselves, was dissolved in 1956 when a border was erected between Melilla and Morocco.

Eight years later a prominent religious leader and six Muslim merchants created the *Asociación Musulmana* (Muslim Association) with the approval of the local authorities and the endorsement of the government in Madrid. Si Muhammad Musa, the originator and the first president of the Association, was the son of the chief of the Ait Shikar who became Spain's most loyal ally in 1911, and as a reward was appointed chief *caid* of the Iqar'ayen confederacy in 1912. Musa received a religious education and later became the spiritual leader of the Muslims in Melilla. From the very start the *Asociación Musulmana*, the overt aim of which was purely religious, represented mainly the interests of the Spanish Muslims.

In the early 1980s a small group of young, educated Spanish Muslims launched the first serious effort to create an overall Muslim organisation. Led by the economist Ahmed Moh they convoked a meeting in the Great Mosque in September 1982 where they presented their plan and nomination for an executive council of the proposed *Comunidad Musulmana* to a gathering of some hundreds of Muslims.[18] During the meeting Moh's candidacy for president was challenged by an elderly informal leader. After a brief pause, during which the evening prayer was performed, Moh and his four main followers were elected as the leadership of the new organisation.

At this very first meeting a basic divide within the Muslim collectivity became visible. Mohand Amar, Moh's opponent, represented the religiously-oriented traditionalist section of the Muslim population. A man in his fifties who is a retired corporal of the Protectorate Army, a trader, and an active member in the local lodge of the Alawiya brotherhood, Amar stood for a conservative political orientation and defended close cooperation with the Spanish authorities. He had a following in Barrio Cuernos where he lived for part of his life. The opposition between his faction and Moh's was largely due to a generational, educational and religious divide.

Two days after the meeting the Governor of Melilla published a communiqué in the local newspaper in which he declared the meeting and the *Communidad Musulmana* illegal.[19] He pointed out that the meeting had not been authorised, nor had the regulations of the new organisation been submitted to the government for approval. The Governor argued that an organisation of Spaniards of Moroccan origin infringed an article in the Spanish Constitution which prohibits discrimination against Spaniards on the grounds of sex, race, birth, or religion. Finally, he declared that the *Asociación Musulmana* founded by Musa was the only legal Muslim organisation in Melilla.

Meanwhile the struggle for power in the Muslim collectivity continued. Early 1983, Amar held a counter-meeting at which a few hundred Muslims from the ghettos elected him as their leader. Moh reacted by collecting about 2,000 signatures among his followers which he offered to the Governor as proof that he was the legitimate leader. The latter, however, persisted in his decision not to authorize the new organisation. Then the struggle for leadership began to take the form of mutual public insinuations. Moh accused Amar of being a police informer who turned illegal residents over to the Spanish Civil Guard. Amar retaliated by declaring that Moh was a bewitched atheist who possessed the evil eye and who swindled his illiterate clients. The dispute finally became still more aggravated over the issue of the control of the communal hearse, thus becoming extended into the moral, ritual and religious domain. The hearse was registered on behalf of the Muslim collectivity in the names of three Muslims, one of whom was Amar, who usually acted as its driver. It was (and still is) used to transport corpses to Moroccan cemeteries as Melilla lacks a Muslim burial ground, a very delicate issue in Catholic-Muslim relations. When Amar did not turn up on time for one funeral, Moh took the hearse from the garage of the Great Mosque and transported the corpse to Morocco. Amar reacted by denouncing his enemy to the police for stealing the hearse and a lawsuit ensued.[20]

Moh gained the upper hand over his rival when he succeeded in gaining the support of the president of the *Asociación Musulmana*, to whom he proposed a merger with the still illegal organisation. Musa accepted on the condition that he would become vice-president. This meant a major victory for Moh in three respects. He further isolated his main rival, gained access to religious legitimisation, and forced the Governor to authorise the new *Comunidad Musulmana*.

The politics of ethnicity in Melilla took an unexpected and dramatic turn because of an external event. In the autumn of 1985, the Spanish Parliament passed an Aliens Act that considerably restricted the residence of foreigners, introduced new obstacles in the procedure for acquiring the Spanish nationality, and provided the police with a new instrument for expelling foreign residents. Not surprisingly, the new law provoked strong emotions in the enclave. The Catholic inhabitants of Melilla loudly welcomed it as a blessing, for it gave them the means to curb and even reverse the influx of Rifians. The Muslim population was shocked as the law made the majority of them liable to expulsion. This serious external threat mitigated the divisions within the Muslim collectivity by giving them a common cause. Moh, who had nothing to fear because of his Spanish nationality, cleverly exploited the hysteria by channeling the resistance to the law into a broad emancipation movement of which he became the undisputed leader for the next two years. Within six months he had set up networks of barrio committees, a female section of the *Comunidad*, and a new Muslim political party.

The first collective action took place one night in late October when thousands of Muslims in several barrios deprived the city of its sleep by incessantly beating pots and pans.[21] Peaceful demonstrations were held in the city centre. In November the Muslim leaders of Ceuta and Melilla agreed to coordinate their actions. The ethnic situation became increasingly grave after the political parties had staged a huge march, in which about 25,000 Catholic inhabitants took part, to the Governor's office to demand a more rapid application of the new law. Muslims considered this demonstration to be a provocation and from then on inter-ethnic relations rapidly deteriorated.

In January 1986 Moh called a general strike of Muslims which forced the Spanish government to extend the deadline for Muslims to put their documents in order. In March the police stopped a peaceful demonstration of veiled Muslim women and their children with tear-gas and batons, wounding several women. Moh exploited this serious incident, a most direct violation of the Muslim sense of integrity and honour, to gain the support of *El Pais*, the largest and most prestigious Spanish national newspaper. Moreover this incident provoked outrage in Morocco.[22] In response to national and international pressure to find a way out of the crisis, the Spanish government decided to set up a commission composed of the Muslim leaders of Melilla and Ceuta and high-ranking officials of the Ministry of the Interior. The government promised temporary residence permits to those Muslims with roots in the enclave until a solution could be found.

While the Muslim leaders were negotiating with the central government to improve the civil status and social conditions of the Muslim population, the irritation of the Catholics in Melilla grew because their political parties had been completely passed over by the government in Madrid. The slogan that Muslims were 'Morocco's Trojan horse in Melilla' was proclaimed more loudly every day. In June 1986 Moh accused the local authorities of illegally expelling four Muslim residents and of harassing many more Muslims. Six days prior to Spain's general election, the leader announced that Muslims with a right to vote would boycott this major political event and that shadow elections would be held in protest at Madrid's failure to grant Spanish nationality to the 4,200 Muslims who had applied for it.

Three days later militant Catholic nationalists gathered outside Moh's home after a Spanish football victory in the World Cup in Mexico, waving Spanish flags, sounding horns and throwing stones at his windows. They shouted cries such as 'Long live Spain!', 'Moros out!', 'We have come to cut your throat, Moh, son of a bitch!' Alarmed Muslims arrived armed with knives and clubs to protect their leader. An elderly man started to cry 'Allah Akbar', whereupon some of the Muslims attacked the aggressors. Only with the greatest effort did the police succeed in separating the two bands. That same night the Muslim leader and the Governor made a tour around the barrios appealing to the inhabitants not to yield to provocation.

As a gesture of goodwill the Governor then allowed the Muslims to hold an informal election in the mosques on the day of the Spanish one. He provided police protection to Moh, the only candidate, who got more than 9,000 votes. This tolerant attitude of the Governor provoked a series of violent demonstrations by militant Catholics demanding that the Governor relinquish his office, calling him a traitor and *cabrón* (billy-goat).[23] Anti-Muslim militants founded a clandestine group called 'Struggle for the Liberation of Melilla', whose leader was arrested for hiring a criminal to plant a bomb in the Governor's office. Then the central government decided the time was ripe for the appointment of a new Governor, a confidant of the Prime Minister and former director of the security service of the Royal Family. This former police officer, who had served several years in Melilla, received a mandate to restore public order. However, he perpetrated a political blunder by not inviting Muslim representatives to his inauguration ceremony, which was felt as a serious affront by the Muslim leaders.

The arrival of the new Governor almost coincided with an offer by the central government to Moh to become an advisor on minority problems to the Minister of the Interior. Moh accepted this offer, although at the cost of conflict with the radicals within his movement who accused him of having sold out to the enemy. In Moh's absence this radical wing took over command, organised a mass-meeting at the beginning of November where a motion was passed to call Moh back from Madrid and to declare Melilla 'an Arab and Maghribian city'. The Muslim leader leader resigned expressing his disappointment with the Spanish bureaucracy: 'I did not come to Madrid for words but rather for deeds'. On his return to the enclave he publicly appealed to his followers to withdraw their applications for Spanish nationality.

While Moh was in Madrid the Muslims of Melilla had gone through a rapid process of radicalisation which was partly a reaction to the indiscriminate beatings-up of Muslims by street gangs of Spanish militants. Simultaneously, Islamic slogans and symbols began to play a more prominent role in their demonstrations. At the close of 1986, Moh for the first time began to seek direct contacts with Moroccan officials and made a statement in the local newspaper that 'Melilla is a Moroccan city'. In January 1987 his brother-in-law, a high-ranking customs officer for Nador province and advisor to the Moroccan government on matters regarding Melilla, was declared *persona non grata* by the Governor and expelled. In the meantime the Spanish government rejected a proposal by King Hassan II to set up a joint commission, 'to reflect on peaceful and appropriate means to settle the territorial dispute over Melilla and Ceuta'.

At the end of the month Moh fled to Nador, just in time to escape arrest for inciting rebellion. On 31 January, Muslim shopkeepers closed their businesses in support of their leader. That same night serious race riots broke out in the streets of the enclave. After two days of fighting, local and national newspapers drew up the following balance-sheet:[24] seven men of the riot police treated in hospital, four Muslims seriously wounded by bullets, cars burnt, houses looted, and twenty-seven Muslims arrested, almost the entire leadership of the Muslim Community. The seven most prominent leaders were charged with sedition against the state and transferred to a prison in Almeria, Andalusia. Three days later one of the Muslim victims, shot by a Spanish watchman during the riots, succumbed to his wounds. Musa, the only leader not in jail, defied his house-arrest and led the funeral which resulted in a mass demonstration. As the funeral procession slowly moved from the deceased's house to the Great Mosque and then on to the Moroccan cemetery across the border, the crowd incessantly shouted: 'There is only one God for all, for all only one God'. The 8,000 people who attended the interment were addressed by Moh, who tried to coordinate the revolt from his base in Nador, calling for unity, but at the same time accusing Musa of double-dealing with the Governor.[25]

In the course of February 1987 collective action dwindled and the Muslim movement disintegrated once again into competing factions.[26] At the end of that month nine leaders, who had been arrested during the clashes, were released from custody, after they had publicly declared their intention of breaking with Moh. Most of them retired from politics, while Moh's right hand man founded a new political party. Moh himself had lost most of his credibility among his followers by fleeing to Morocco and remaining there.

The struggle for emancipation by the Melilla Muslims should also be considered within a wider context. On the one hand, it is one of the many instances of the explosion of ethnic minorities in the Middle East since the 1960s. It is a characteristic of ethnic movements that they are often led by young educated members of the subordinate group, professionals whose careers are handicapped by their origins (cf. Horowitz 1985: 33). The young Muslim leadership in Melilla belonged to this category; they had profited from a Spanish education but were frustrated in their attempts to become upwardly mobile by their Rifian background. A second characteristic of the ethnic *réveil* is that it is often a direct response to actions by the dominant group to expel long-term residents of the subordinate group. In Melilla a new Aliens Law provided the *cause célèbre* of Muslim mobilisation, organisation and opposition. The external threat was needed to overcome internal fragmentation and factionalism. Thirdly, ethnic protest is frequently clothed in religious symbolism, because this kind of symbolism bases material claims in moral ideas that go beyond the local conflict.

Moh's movement partly drew inspiration from the wider movement of Islamic revivalism, which, consisting of ideas and aims of a higher order, had to serve as a means to mask internal divisions. However, in the context of the enclave, this appeal to a higher encompassing moral order was not effective because, for the majority of Muslims in Melilla, Islam is not so much a matter of faith and rites, binding individuals to the local community of believers, as a context-bound ascriptive affiliation in an amorphous collectivity. High levels of illiteracy and civil insecurity, as well as economic weakness and highly individualist ways of making a living constitute great obstacles to the transformation of the Muslim collectivity into a politically effective ethnic organisation.

Chapter 10

Marginality, Bodily Discourse and Blurred Ethnicity

This chapter deals with a barrio in the margins of Melilla where individuals of different ethnic origins have merged into a single community with distinctive cultural characteristics. It is in particular the prominent role of the body in interaction that sets this community apart from the wider society.

The Making of a Community of Marginals

Cabrerizas Altas is the most outlying neighbourhood of Melilla. It is located on a hill at the edge of the enclave's territory. The barrio of flat-roofed and single-storey houses is laid out like a chess-board. It is separated from the city by a large vacant lot, which is occasionally used as a military parade ground. A road, coming up from Melilla, separates the barrio from the first of the enclave's two barracks of the Spanish Foreign Legion. Not far from Cabrerizas the road branches off into a track that leads to a minor border-post. The main road runs through a small wood of pine trees, past the second barracks of the Legion where it sharply descends towards the sea. Cabrerizas, which literally means goat pens, was the name that the inhabitants of ancient Melilla gave to some clusters of Berber houses scattered over the plateau. As a consequence of the 1863 treaty that ended the war between Spain and Morocco, the Rifian inhabitants had to abandon the place and cede it to the Christians. The Spanish army tore the dwellings down and constructed a fort on this site,[1] but preserved its name.

The civilian settlement originates from the boom period brought about by the military occupation of Melilla's hinterland, the mining and railway construction, and the pacification campaigns of

177

1909–1911. The explosive urban growth characteristic of this period has been pointed out in chapter 2.[2] One of the barrios that sprang up in those years was Cabrerizas Altas. In 1917 there were 200 men and 230 women living here.[3]

The war of pacification (1919–1927) further fuelled the growth of Melilla. In 1921 Berber hillmen, rallied by 'Abd al-Krim, overran the line of poorly defended outposts of the Spanish army all the way up to Melilla. The town was rescued by 4,500 troops rushed over from the western part of the Protectorate. Among them were two battalions of the Spanish Foreign Legion (*Tercio de Extranjeros*, or simply, *La Legión* or *El Tercio*). The first battalion was led by Francisco Franco, the future dictator of Spain,[4] and became part of the permanent garrison still quartered at Cabrerizas Altas.

From 1923–4 the famous Spanish novelist Ramón Sender spent the larger part of his military service in the quarters facing Cabrerizas Altas. He has bequeathed us a penetrating portrait of life in the barrio.[5] The inhabitants were a poor, hurt and resentful people. Among them were several ex-convicts from the former penal settlement of Melilla, who could be recognised by special tattoos on their arms. These people had neither hope nor ambition. Their world-view can be summarised in such current sayings as 'life is rubbish', 'poverty is dog faced', and 'humanity is a swine that fattens'. The inhabitants, among them Rifians dressed in the Spanish fashion, derived their main source of income from services to the barracks. Widows earned a meagre living by repairing and washing uniforms. A former gunsmith repaired watches and clocks, while his daughter worked as a prostitute. An elderly woman made a living as an abortionist. A man, born from a Berber father and Spanish mother, claimed to be a healer using incantations. An ex-cornet sold cocaine in the brothels. A former chaplain derived an income from selling drugs to prostitutes and their clients. From time to time he got drunk and then consecrated the wine according to the Catholic rite while the prostitutes knelt down to play their part in this parody of the mass. These were the memorable characters in the barrio. The majority peddled all kinds of articles to the soldiers. Both soldiers and inhabitants shared the stigma of being beyond the pale.

An Enclave within the Enclave

Today the barrio population fluctuates around 250, which is half the number of people who lived there at the time of Sender's military service. The wooden shacks have now been replaced by brick-and-mortar houses, although only half a dozen stand out as well kept among the majority which are in a state of dilapidation. At the edge of the barrio, people share their living space with chickens and goats. On the whole the barrio is a depressed and ugly place, and remains one of the lowest-income neighbourhoods of the enclave, with the highest rates of unemployment and illiteracy. But while there are other parts of Melilla that are poor and peripheral, nowhere does peripheral location so forcefully express the marginality of the inhabitants as in this barrio. This is clearly revealed by the terms of reference for the area used by the inhabitants of the central sectors of the city: *el poblado, barrio de sinvergüenzas* and *wild west*. The first name, 'the settlement', suggests that the barrio is something alien to the city, a world apart. *Poblado* also has pejorative rural connotations. The second term, 'neighbourhood of the shameless ones', means that the inhabitants are beyond the pale. 'Wild west' expresses the barrio's reputation of violent behaviour. All the inhabitants are lumped together in these descriptions. People in established society feel embarrassed about the barrio and avoid the place, while the police only go there when a serious crime has been committed.

The inhabitants comprise eighty households.[6] While in the other parts of the city single-person households are rare, in the barrio they make up a quarter of all the households. There are nine single women, three of whom are young Moroccan prostitutes and the others Spanish women now in their fifties who work as cooks, or washing and cleaning women. One of these runs a cheap boarding-house. Among the men who live alone retired legionnaires prevail.

There are also several single-parent families, invariably women, mostly ex-prostitutes, with their children. Take the case of Ttleitmas. She is a Moroccan widow in her late fifties whose husband served in the Spanish Protectorate army. She receives a small pension which she complements with money earned by washing the uniforms of legionnaires. She lives with two of her unmarried sons who are unemployed and hang around in downtown Melilla where they sell hashish to soldiers and tourists. This family came to the enclave in the early 1960s and lacks the necessary Spanish or Moroccan documents.

Dolores Mohamedi is a special case. She is the widow of a Spanish grocer who has continued to run the shop since her husband's death. She is the only women of Berber origin in the barrio who knows how to read and write. Her four children have been baptised and have Christian names. The oldest son works in Barcelona as a clerk. Clearly, this family is relatively well off.

Whereas in the rest of Melilla inter-ethnic sexual alliances are exceptional, in Cabrerizas they predominate. Almost 60 percent of all cohabiting pairs are ethnically mixed and most of these are legionnaires allied to Moroccan women.[7] Antonio's case is paradigmatic. He was born in Córdoba in the early 1940s.[8] When he was nineteen he joined the Foreign Legion in order, as he put it, 'to avoid trouble with the police'. Until 1975 he served in the Spanish Sahara where he was promoted to the rank of sergeant. He was transferred to Melilla when Spain abandoned that colony. In his late thirties he started his own household (he used the term *casar*, to marry) with a Moroccan girl of fifteen who was raised in Melilla by a brother of her deceased father. Antonio met her uncle in a bar and after several talks the man agreed to give him his niece 'in exchange for some money'.[9] The couple live in a three-room dwelling with their three children.

The other mixed couples are lower-class Spaniards living with Rifian women. Of these four are unemployed, one is a house-painter, another is a baker, and there are also a mechanic and a bartender. Manolo was born in Málaga and first came to Melilla to work for a construction firm. After he lost his first wife, he married to Moroccan woman thirty years his junior. They have three children who all have been given Christian names. Since Manolo lost his job, the family depends on municipal welfare for its survival. Federico and Irene are their neighbours, and own one of the barrio's taverns. Federico originally came from Sevilla and worked for some years in a Swiss factory. He left his first wife when he discovered that she was having an affair with another man. While working at the Costa del Sor he met Subida, a divorced woman in her twenties from Nador, who worked as a cleaning woman in a hotel. Before they married, she was baptised and changed her name to Irene. They took the ferry to Melilla and with their savings started a bar in Cabrerizas. When I met him he told me that he had enough of barrio life and was now trying to sell the tavern.

Almost all inhabitants of Moroccan origin are illegal residents who lack documents of any kind. Once every year the Civil Guard raids the barrio, picks up some illegal residents, mostly unmarried women and their children, and expels them to Morocco. Sandra is a young prostitute with two small children. She was born in a *bidonville* of Marrakesh. Like so many girls from the Moroccan underclasses — in Melilla there are prostitutes from Oujda, Casablanca, Tangier, Rabat, Fez and Meknes — she ended up in his profession because her male relatives failed to provide for her. She was taken to Melilla by a souteneur and worked in a local whiskey-bar until a retired legionnaire bought her out. After the birth of her second child this man married her but died soon afterwards, forcing her to resume her former calling. Neighbours care for her children while she is away from home. But a woman alone is vulnerable and, since her husband's death, she has twice been expelled.

Like Sandra, prostitutes sometimes manage to bind the men who make them pregnant. Non-commissioned officers of the Legion and retired legionnaires tend to take these women as concubines or wives, although sooner or later they also fail to provide for them and their offspring. Often these women do the laundry and mending for the garrison in order to have an extra and independent source of income.

That a person should take care of himself is a basic dictum of barrio life. This holds true for both men and women, young and old, married and unmarried. The combination of the prevalence of incomplete families and single-person households, the tendency towards matrifocality and the ethos of self-sufficiency is not surprising given the precarious conditions under which most barrio dwellers live. Flexibility is a vital quality in the face of existential insecurity. That household stability is closely tied to economic security is proved by the barrio's 'respectable' families. The three grocers, three of the four bar-owners, the tobacconist, and some skilled workers all have a regular income and are the heads of the barrio's most stable households.[10]

In spite of the emphasis on autonomy, people depend upon each other in several respects. The barrio is as strongly female-centred as the households. Women pay each other visits, borrow from and help one another, and exchange the latest news. Networks of female reciprocity hold the barrio together. Only 'free' prostitutes like Sandra spend much time away from the barrio. There is even a sense of barrio chauvinism based on common residence, fate and lifestyle. Both barrio men and many of the women are identified by their nicknames.[11]

Most barrio dwellers think that life in Melilla is a misery, or, as they themselves put it, a shit (*una mierda*). They keep out of local politics. While most of the other neighbourhoods have formal associations representing the interests of the inhabitants to the city government, Cabrerizas has none. They are cynical about the benefits of democratic politics and suspicious of local authorities and their agents whom they associate with the dominant segment (the *gordos* or 'fat ones'). On the other hand, they try to manipulate civil servants in order to obtain residence cards and municipal benefits. Although they use some of the religious symbols used by the wider society, such as Christ on the Cross, the Madonna, the *khamsa* and other amulets with words from the Quran, they are indifferent or hostile towards religion. As one informant put it: 'In this barrio, no religion. Well, I do believe in a God for there must be someone who is to be blamed for the misery. But you might also call him the Devil.' People know that they must rely on their own force and cunning in order to survive, yet at the same time they recognise that their lives are subject to forces beyond their control.

With sharp contradictions between the wider society's standards of family life, economic and social behaviour, and social worth, on the one hand and conditions of barrio life on the other, counter-values have come into being. Petty crime is accepted as just one way of making a living. Masculinity, bravery, and aggression are greatly admired. Abuse of alcohol and drugs, and illicit sex are more prominent than in other neighbourhoods. These counter-values have been crystallised in the confrontations between legionnaires, barrio toughs and prostitutes. Their way of life also determines the barrio's image to the wider society.[12]

Prowess and Prostitution

Legionnaires and barrio dwellers are part of the same community. The barrio and the quarters of the Legion came into existence almost simultaneously and have been tied to one another ever since. Not only does a sizeable number of legionnaires and retired NCOs live in the barrio, many more visit it daily to purchase food, liquor, cigarettes, drugs and sex, and to engage in sociability on street corners and in taverns. The military quarters and barrio are mutually interdependent. Their inhabitants share a similar outlook on life and style of interaction.

The formal ethos of the Foreign Legion is simple and explicit. It celebrates death, toughness, discipline, suffering, and fellow-ship in arms.[13] Its battle cry, as we have mentioned before, is 'Long Live Death'. The ram, which symbolises toughness and endurance in many parts of the Mediterranean area, is its mascot.[14] 'Christ of the Good Death' is its patron and 'The Betrothed of Death' its anthem.

The Legion is justly notorious for its violence. Its men are trained to it. They represent the roughest and toughest unit in the Spanish army. However, it is also ridden with paradoxes. While it embodies the state's monopoly over the use of violence, its men are hard to control and quick to use unlicensed violence among themselves and against civilians, particularly against *moros*.[15] This paradox helps to explain the ambivalent attitude of civilians towards the Legion. Catholic inhabitants often praise and romanticise it as a military unit. Parades and other public ceremonies by the Legion are very popular spectacles.

On the other hand, individual legionnaires are often despised and avoided, although a few among them have been celebrated as heroes. 'Johnny the Negro', for instance, was a champion of two generations of Christian inhabitants. Born in the early 1920s in Dallas (Texas), John Shirley Gee arrived at the close of the Second World War with the American invasion army in Casa-blanca. Having deserted, he roamed about Morocco until he finally came to Melilla where he joined the Foreign Legion. Tall, heavy, strong and a good boxer he was respected for his strength and grace. He promoted boxing among the young and played the role of black king in the yearly Epiphany parade. He was reputed to spend his money generously on alcohol, drugs and whores. After more than thirty years of service he died of excessive drinking and became a legend. One informant com-mented upon his reputation as follows: 'Here in Melilla he was somebody, while in America he would have been nobody. People liked his graceful yet clumsy manners.' He embodied the ideal male: strong, tough, generous and fun-loving. Legion-naires rarely live up to this ideal.

Most of them are reputed to 'shoot first and talk afterwards', as an informant put it. They are justly held to be quarrelsome, volatile and violent. A few examples will suffice to illustrate this point.[16]

In the Autumn of 1975 tensions between Morocco and Spain ran high because of the 'Green March' on the Sahara. A bomb exploded in one of the most prestigious bars, causing several casualties. Bands of uncontrolled legionnaires began to roam the streets cornering Muslims and meting out serious beatings and thrashings. Many Moroccans fled over the border or locked themselves up in their houses. The Legion's terrorising behaviour went on for several days until the military authorities put a stop to it. In the summer of 1980 a band of sixteen legionnaires armed with clubs raided the Muslim ghetto, the Cañada de la Muerte, to avenge a comrade who had been beaten up the day before by Moroccan toughs at the fountain of Cabrerizas where Moroccan girls fetch water and wash clothes. Fifteen men were wounded in the brawl and the interior of a Muslim tea-house was left completely destroyed.

There are also many instances of intra-group violence. The smoking of hashish and marijuana is so widespread among legionnaires that their officers are forced to close their eyes to it. One evening a small group had assembled to share hashish in a barracks room. One of the men at first refused to accept the 'joint' that was passed round, but when he was finally persuaded to accept and ready to take a blow one of the men jokingly snapped it away from him. The victim of this horseplay worked himself into a towering rage, grabbed a gun and mowed down his fellows, killing one. Boredom and liquor dominate the life of legionnaires, leading to many a café brawl. Usually these arguments are settled with bare fists, but sometimes get out of hand as in the spring of 1980 when a legionnaire was stabbed to death in a barrio tavern.

Legionnaires consider themselves fighters *pur sang*. Like the prostitutes with whom they mix, they live by and for their bodies; in fact they devote themselves to the cult of the body. Corporal punishment and the energetic, brusque movements which mark the Legion's salutes and drills, have moulded the soldier's body so that there is always nervous tension in their movements. Staring fixedly at people, which is considered offensive in the wider society, is part of the Legion's behavioural code. Legionnaires are proud of their leathery countenances and expose their sun-tanned chests and tattooed biceps. They can be easily identified when they are in mufti. Cropped hair, full beards, wide-open shirts, an arrogant way of moving and the typical tattoos — depictions of Christ on the Cross, naked girls, death's-heads, and pierced hearts — these are the distinctive elements of their presentation. It is a code that conveys their explosive demeanor.

Legionnaires are expected to remain unmarried and to satisfy their sexual needs outside marriage; consequently, they receive free medical treatment for venereal diseases. Older NCOs who may opt to live outside the barracks often take Moroccan prostitutes as their concubines. As their bodies rapidly waste away through over-indulgence, the aspects of life which most interest them are connected with the body — strength, sex, health and illness.

The barrio is frequently the scene of violent confrontations between legionnaires and the young local men, who are mostly the progeny of Moroccan and ethnically mixed parents (*mulatos*). They consider each other natural enemies in competition for the same spoils, that is, reputations of toughness and womanising. At the same time they are dependent upon each other as the sellers and buyers of drugs. The barrio is one of the centres for drug distribution. The dealers, overwhelmingly young Moroccan men and prostitutes, openly and proudly talk about their trade. As one of them told me: 'We have to do something in order to earn our keep. If you get involved you should carry the risks like a man.' Disputes among these peddlars and their clients break out frequently.[17]

One of the most notorious homicides of the last decade was committed in the barrio in 1983. Although an extreme case, I cite it at some length because it penetratingly conveys the social atmosphere of the barrio. A Spanish woman, aged fifty-seven and unmarried, who had been living in Cabrerizas for more than twenty years as a prostitute, was beaten to death in her bedroom. The author of the crime was identified as a Moroccan fisherman of twenty-seven who lived with his mother in the Cañada de la Muerte. The newspaper report reads as follows:

> Later that evening the murderer went, in a state of intoxication, to the victim's house. He had maintained an amorous relation with her for the last few months, living with her several times. He wanted to bed her and started to pull off her clothes. The woman tried to stop him and demanded that he first went out to buy a bottle of her favourite liquor. When he refused she clutched him firmly by the testicles. Then the Moroccan began to hit her so hard with such heavy blows that she died on the spot.[18]

But the use of violence is not limited to men. Barrio women also become physically involved in male brawls occasionally. They are as capable and ready to use violence as their male counterparts, as is shown by the case of another woman. She was the concubine of Herbert Hermann, a German corporal of the Foreign Legion. When she found out that her partner had left her for a younger prostitute she set fire to the corporal's house.

This is not to say that the use of violence as an interactive mode and way of solving problems is always so prominent and widespread among *all* barrio dwellers. For many it is a means of last resort. Men who are quick to rely on physical force are respected but not admired by everybody. That there is a violent undertone in the interaction of the barrio is an undeniable fact; one cannot avoid being aware of the undercurrent of excitement, of the shouting and cries, of angry voices interspersed with coarse laughter. When women are angered they gesture like men. I heard them shout at each other: 'You've got no balls', a serious insult among men. Physical performance in communication is indeed direct and obtrusive. Men are smitten upon the back, poked in the ribs, wrung by the hand, but also embraced about the neck and kissed on the cheeks. Dominance and subordination in relationships are established through threatening behaviour and the use of violence. And subordination is seen and felt as a loss of bodily integrity.

Children learn this discourse of force at an early age, and by ten years they are streetwise. Boys adopt fierce stances and frequently embark on games which test their agility and strength, emulating the Kung Fu they see in the cinemas and on television. José's career is more or less paradigmatic for barrio boys. He was born in Cabrerizas in the early 1960s. At that time his mother was living with a sergeant of the Legion, José's supposed father. At the age of eleven he dropped out of school, and his mother bought him a shoe-black box with which he roamed the shopping district of Melilla. He literally had to muscle himself into the trade. After three years of polishing shoes, he considered himself too old for this job, and took to washing cars in the Plaza de España. He soon found out that the trafficking of hashish was a more lucrative and manly activity. When he was short of money he broke into cars. On one occasion he was caught in the act and jailed for six months. Meanwhile his mother was expelled from the enclave. José now lives with a girl in a rented room in Cabrerizas and earns his living by selling the drugs which his girlfriend smuggles into Melilla. I first met him in the central park where he spotted me as a potential client. Like most of his peers he hates Melilla, and frequently talks about leaving for the Peninsula. As an illegitimate child of a Moroccan prostitute he lacks all the legal requisites for obtaining the national identity card which would enable him to leave.

The limited interaction between legionnaires and women precludes any form of communication except for sexual intercourse. They are bound to each other by illicit sex and caught up in a web of dependence that is ridden with contradictions. Access to a prostitute's body is not only seen as essential for their well-being but also for the maintenance of masculinity, part of which consists of sexual prowess. However, the dependence of legionnaires and young barrio toughs upon the scarce services of prostitutes and the latter's sexually aggressive stance contradict the independence stressed in the code of masculinity.[19] Prostitutes undermine the legionnaire's sense of dominance. When NCOs establish more permanent ties with these public women by taking them as concubines and domesticating them, they do so in order to escape the contradiction inherent in the prostitute-client relation. But then they stumble over another contradiction, for the Legion's ethos and way of life precludes domestic life. These contradictions certainly help to explain the violent attitude of legionnaires towards prostitutes.

Prostitutes, in their turn, depend upon legionnaires and young toughs for their living. They earn money with their bodies but pay the price of loss of shame, loss of male protection. Their behaviour is, of course, the polar opposite of that of the ideal woman (a concept shared by Christians, Muslims and Jews alike), who learns bodily modesty at an early age and whose sexuality is controlled within the domestic domain. As sexually and economically active women, prostitutes do not fit the gender categories prevalent in the wider society. In many respects they have taken over male symbols, manners, and prerogatives.[20] Like legionnaires and young toughs, the prostitute's most important means of communication consists of gestures and postures. Like their male counterparts they sell the integrity of their body for money. Unlike respectable women, they openly advertise their bodies in order to attract men, and they continually transgress the boundaries of male space. Moreover, their presence is imposing, their postures and eye-contact are defiant and audacious. They take initiatives and stand leaning on the counter in taverns like men, cigarette in one hand, a glass of beer or whiskey in the other. They walk about the streets chewing gum. They relieve themselves in the street quite unashamedly as men do. When two or more of them are together they are prone to mock men openly. And when angered they are ready to react violently. In short their behaviour is more masculine than feminine yet it fits neither category. They function in a transitional realm in the margins of society, where they always run the risk of violent confrontations with men. In order to reduce this danger, prostitutes tend to seek more permanent unions with legionnaires, especially when they grow older and the market value of their services decreases.

Legionnaires, prostitutes and young barrio men are engaged in interactions that hinge upon the body, force and sexuality. In the eyes of the established ethnic communities the inhabitants of Cabrerizas Altas are brutalised, part of the underbelly of local society. Historically, their way of life has been shaped out of the violent confrontation between colonisers and colonised. On one level, Spanish legionnaires and Moroccan prostitutes represent opposites in the colonial constellation. The former are instruments of domination, while the latter are the most apparent victims, political, economic as well as sexual. The young men of the barrio are in a literal sense the products of this confrontation. They are neither Spanish nor Moroccan. Administratively they just do not exist. On another level, two soldiers of the Foreign Legion are as marginal as their concubines and offspring. They are socially uprooted men who have drifted away from their communities and cultures of origin. Relegated to the margins of society, they have become part of a distinct community.

Conclusions

Melilla is a unique society, simultaneously European and North African, and on the frontier between the First and Third Worlds. It is also however a Mediterranean city, marked by the intersection and long co-existence of the three main religious and cultural traditions of the wider area. Seen from a global and long-term perspective, the Mediterranean world itself is a zone of transition between Europe, Africa and Asia, a zone that has been created by two millennia of warfare and conquest, trading, and cultural diffusion, confrontation and accommodation. The local history of Melilla represents these processes on a microcosmic level. As a boundary phenomenon Melilla is an inherently complex and conflict-ridden society. It serves as a mediating bridge between Latin Europe and North Africa, partaking of the qualities of both. Yet it also draws attention to a basic internal division within the western Mediterranean area. Melilla's border is open, yet there is a striking closedness about this society. Many inhabitants look across the sea to metropolitan Spain yet their survival depends upon regular communication with the Moroccan hinterland. This fundamental ambivalence pervades life in the enclave.

The selected themes of the enclave's history and ethnography cluster around the axis boundary-ethnicity-ritual-power. Although I have attempted to let historical and ethnographic detail and discussion speak for themselves, it is now necessary to sum up the findings in more general terms.

Frontier as Interactive Process

Melilla has been neither a rigid nor a wide-open frontier. A close study of local history over four centuries reveals a pattern of oscillation between periods of Christian-Muslim confrontation

189

via mutual *razzia* and sieges during which religious differences became exacerbated, and periods of intense cross-frontier trade and service exchange during which they were muted. Desertion and apostasy were important mechanisms of cultural transfer of ideas, information, values, technical skills, and vocabulary across the frontier. A wide gap existed between central state ideology and frontier praxis. Seen from the standpoint of the central authorities in Spain and Morocco, Melilla was part of a strict divide between civilisation and barbarism, a barrier that was largely defined in religious terms. Between the fifteenth and nineteenth centuries the Spanish as well as the Moroccan state did its best to maintain this ideological divide. But in daily life the Hispano-African frontier was a zone of interaction rather than a divide. In the light of the Melilla experience, both Braudel's and Hess's views of the frontier are overstated. My findings are in accordance with earlier studies of frontier societies elsewhere which show frontiers as zones of interchange between the invader's culture and the culture of the invaded, and, as a process rather than a fixed line of division.[1]

When in the course of the nineteenth century Morocco was increasingly being drawn into the orbit of European imperialism, Melilla served as a spearhead of commercial penetration and later military intrusion. Between 1907 and 1927 the military pacification of the Rif, which met with fierce Berber resistance, was ideologically represented as a 'civilising mission'. Its aim was the erasure of the Hispano-African frontier. The ethnographic mapping of Rifian society and culture, which followed in the wake of military pacification, was an integral part of Spanish domination. Textual and pictorial representations may be seen as attempts to domesticate the Berbers at a symbolic level. The incorporation of northern Morocco into the Spanish state replaced the external frontier with internal ethnic boundaries. The ethnic identities which emerged within one polity were the result of inclusion and interaction rather than of separation.

In the first three decades of this century, which constituted the apex of European colonialism, life in Melilla was hectic and harsh. Primitive capitalism became the rule, geared to the exploitation of cheap native labour, the extraction of the mineral wealth of the Rif, and the dumping of goods produced by metropolitan Spain. The massive immigration of unskilled labourers resulted in erratic urbanisation, poverty and social misery. The history of the Jewish colony illustrates several of these features of uncontrolled expansion. These first non-Spanish and thus non-Christian residents of Melilla were specialists in trans-frontier communication and as such played a vital role in the explosive growth of the enclave. But, paradoxically, by taking up permanent residence in Melilla they contributed to the era-sure of the frontier, though they managed to continue playing a broking role in the colonisation of northern Morocco. In spite of pronounced internal differences in origin, wealth, education and lifestyle, the Jewish collectivity defined itself, and was defined by Christians and Muslims, primarily in terms of ethnicity, in which religion remained a core element. On the whole, ethnic loyalties and identification were stronger in Melilla than class consciousness and organisation. The labour movement that sprang up in the 1920s largely recruited its members from the dominant ethnic group.

The transformation of Melilla from a *presidio* into a trading port and regional capital also left deep marks upon Rifian society and culture. Land and labour became market commodi-ties. Many Rifians were forced out of subsistence agriculture into wage labour and peddling. Seasonal migration to the large colonial estates of Western Algeria became an increasingly important source of income from the 1870s onwards, while the Spanish Protectorate Army, the ore mines and public works largely depended on cheap Rifian manpower. The organisation of production and distribution along modern lines, together with Spanish reforms, undermined traditional patterns of power and authority, which were based on lineage, access to land, and on the numerical strength of the agnatic group. Territoriality was becoming steadily more important than patrilineality. Mounting demographic pressure on the means of subsistence further accelerated these changes, which meant that more and more Rifians became dependent on Melilla. From the late 1920s Berber Muslims, mainly lumpenproletarians, became a permanent pres-ence in Melilla.

The case of the barrio Cabrerizas Altas shows how dropouts of different ethnic backgrounds react similarly to conditions of marginality and deprivation. They have developed a style of interaction that contains a high degree of physical performance and a low degree of resistance to emotional outbursts.[2] The widespread abuse of drugs and alcohol contributes to a decrease in bodily control. The syntax of body language is simpler than

that of the ritualised interactive modes dealt with in Chapter 8.[3]
This is not to say that violent behaviour in Cabrerizas is completely devoid of symbolic function. It might be argued that the
violent tone of interaction is a statement of opposition to or
rejection of the values of the established ethnic groups (cf.
Riches 1986: 19–20).

Violent masculinity has more or less vanished in the wider
society as a means of establishing and maintaining relations of
dominance and subordination in daily life, although the game of
masculinity has not lost its importance. However, it has to a
large extent become verbalised and ritualised, a matter of rhetoric rather than deeds. In other words, threats to act violently
still occur, while the actual use of violence has become rare.[4] In
the barrio the reverse is true. Legionnaires and young men are
constantly claiming, showing and proving to themselves and
others that they have *cojones* (balls) and are truly *macho*. Real
men get drunk, beat up women, and bully other men. In
Cabrerizas masculinity is still primarily expressed physically.

The main categorical divide in the enclave, that between
Muslims and Catholics, has become blurred in the barrio. The
body language so prominent in barrio life is a cross-ethnic
discursive mode. There is a point for comparative urban research in the Cabrerizas case. The barrio is a twilight zone in
many respects similar to ethnically homogeneous ghettos in
other parts of the Mediterranean area. The way of life of these
marginal people, for instance, bears a strong resemblance to that
of the underclasses of Naples or the backstreet poor of Cairo (cf.
Belmonte, 1979 and Wikan, 1981).

The juxtaposition of the smallest and the largest minorities
reveals much of the politics of ethnicity in Melilla. Hindus and
Muslims are each other's opposites in almost every respect. The
economic power of the Hindus enables them to remain aloof
from formal local politics, while their low political profile helps
them to protect their commercial strength. Hindu ethnic identity
and cohesion is greatly enhanced by their money as well as by
the elaborate performance and conservation of family and communal rites, from which outsiders are excluded. Their strongest
bonds are with the other Hindu communities of Spain. At the
same time they preserve positive and close relations with their
motherland. Although they participate in the *agasajo* circuit and
invest large sums of money in social and recreational funds,
their identification with Melilla is ambivalent. As I have pointed

out, this ambiguity and their role as economic brokers are predicated upon each other. Their experience and management of ethnicity closely resembles that of the other colony of middle-men, the Jews.

The vast majority of the Muslim inhabitants lack economic power, while the well-to-do tend to dissociate themselves from the mass of their poor brethren-in-faith. The latter need political power in order to be able to embark on a process of emancipation. Their basic problem is how to transform their numerical strength into real power. Recently, some organisational progress has been achieved at the barrio level. Muslim identification with their country of origin is weak and largely negative, while at the same time they lack a positive identity as inhabitants of the enclave. Most Muslims aspire to acquire Spanish nationality. When a new Aliens law blocked this aspiration the Muslims rose *en masse*. Educated Muslims of Spanish citizenship frustrated in their careers by discrimination tried to channel the discontent and fear into a broad emancipatory movement, the first of its kind since Muslims had settled in Melilla. When the direct external threat disappeared, this movement split up into competing factions and once again the Muslims became a loose and fragmented collectivity. I have suggested that a high level of illiteracy and insecurity, as well as economic weakness and highly individualistic ways of making a living, are largely responsible for the political failure of Muslim ethnicity.

Rites of Power and the Power of Rites

While the study of ritual cannot explain the distribution of power in society, it can demonstrate how power actually works. Power is often hedged about with ritual and ceremonial. This is not to say that rites merely act as the frills of power. On the contrary, it is my view that ritual itself generates power that can be tapped for different purposes.

The flag ceremony discussed in Chapter 6 displays the well-known functions which anthropologists and sociologists since Durkheim have attributed to ritual and ceremonial in nation-states. The blessing and presentation of a new national flag to the Foreign Legion mobilised the overwhelming majority of the Spanish-Catholic inhabitants. The new flag acted as a symbol of rebirth of the Spanish nation in the image of the family. The

Foreign Legion was represented as both the protector of the boundaries of the nation and of the family. 'Christ of the Good Death', placed in between the old and new flags, mediated the rebirth of democratic Spain and sanctioned the renewal of the covenant between Spain and the enclave. The flag ceremony thus delineated the boundaries of Spanishness in this multi-ethnic society; it induced communal feeling by evoking shared symbols; it strengthened and reaffirmed identification with the higher collectivity; it expressed primordial sentiments of belonging, and it released the tensions which had been generated by internal division and strife. It explicitly aimed at overriding internal divisions within the Catholic population simply by denying them and by employing symbols that alluded to a higher order, the nation-state and the divine realm.

The cult of the Catholic cemetery fulfils similar functions. Funerals and post-funerary rites, which are stronger among the Catholics than among the Muslims and Jews, are among the main markers of ethnic boundaries. By celebrating their bond with the ancestors, the Catholic inhabitants express and legitimate the claim that Melilla is their patrimony and simultaneously cement the bonds among the living. The cult of the cemetery thus not only expresses the anxieties of the Catholic population, it is also instrumental in alleviating them and transforming them into solidarity.

The *fiesta de la galleta* ('festival of the biscuit') or *mimuna* offers a particularly illuminating case with regard to the connections between ritual, power and ethnicity. Ambiguity is one of the centrepieces in this festival, reflecting Jewish sentiment about the contradictions and ironies of their situation. Passover is essentially a time of segregation, largely because of dietary restrictions. It mainly represents the annual re-living of the formation of Jewish nationhood primarily within the stronghold of the Jewish home. The greenery that is used for decoration, connoting the power of fertility, well-being and growth, is brought in from the outside by the people from whom Jews have secluded themselves during the preceding seven days. The theme of interdependence is clearly expressed in this ritual occasion. The Jews are dependent on Catholics and Muslims for power. But during the ritual they become hosts and return power to their guests via the prepared foods which are symbolically imbued with the powers of growth. The *fiesta de la galleta* is thus pervaded by ambivalence. On the one hand, the Jews' ideal expressed in Passover is exclusion and uniqueness. The reality, however, is that power outside is held by the Catholic and Muslim Communities and the Jewish community cannot survive without maintaining stable relationships with the outside world. Through ritual, the Jews play out, and thereby come to terms with, the ambiguities ingrained in their position.

The *agasajo* presents an interesting contrast with the *fiesta de la galleta*. Where the latter accentuates the contradictions of inter-ethnicity, the former plays ethnicity down and stresses social class. Food plays a remarkable role in both occasions. In daily life food is often used to mark ethnic boundaries, whereas in inter-ethnic ritual events it is employed to open closed boundaries. Note that in the 'festival of the biscuit' Jewish food is offered to Catholic and Muslim guests, while in the *agasajo* there is a tendency to serve 'neutral' food, mainly fish and chicken, fruits and sweets.[5]

Both the ceremonial gatherings of the ethnic elites and the quasi-joking and avoidance relations which middle and lower-class Catholics maintain with Muslims are instances of ritualised behaviour. However, they differ from one another in one fundamental respect. While the elite gatherings simply deny that there are power differentials involved in these events, at the lower level competitive hostility is clearly expressed and to create differences is an explicit aim. In Chapter 9 I discussed a case of de-ritualisation, that is the breakdown of ritual forms of interaction in a situation of extreme conflict when the Muslims challenged the legitimacy of Spanish-Catholic dominance.

Finally, it may be possible to discern a break between the expressive and the instrumental in the ritual forms and occasions discussed in this book. It has recently been argued that the rituals of so-called 'traditional' societies are largely concerned with problems of making change take place through the design and media of the rituals themselves. They are supposed to bring about transformation. Such transformative change is primarily reproductive of cosmic and social orders. Rituals of transformation are purposive in their design; they are teleological and predictive; they have built-in contradictions and uncertainty; they are organised as relatively simple and closed systems; they are self-regulating to a high degree. On the other hand, the rituals of the modern state are mainly expressive of particular versions of moral and social order and explicity intended to reinforce feelings about them. They have nothing to do with making change happen through their own operations. In sum, these rituals are pre-eminently concerned with experience, expression and affect.[6]

Having looked closely at the situation in Melilla, I find this sharp dichotomy between 'traditional' and 'modern' society, between 'affect' and 'effect', 'expressive' and 'effective' or instrumental too sweeping to be of analytic value. I would suggest that the ritual forms and events described in the previous chapters are not merely expressive and concerned with generating and strengthening sentiments. They may not be transformative in the sense that their enactment brings about purposely intended changes, but they are certainly effective in terms of power in a variety of ways. Ritual generates power or reflects, expresses and otherwise fits the power structure. It legitimises, strengthens or challenges the existing distribution of power resources. It can also deny, conceal or distort the realities of power, class and ethnicity. Power inheres in ritual and the use of power is often ritualised.

Epilogue

Can anthropologists make sound predictions? One summer evening of 1984 I was leaning on the railing of the ferry to Málaga and musing on the future of the people I left behind while the city of Melilla slowly vanished beyond the horizon. My intuition and understanding told me that there were violent clashes in the offing given the pent-up racial frictions, the sparks of which I had felt continuously during my stay in the enclave. Two years later unrest turned violent. Aware of the international repercussions of this conflict between 'Christians' and 'Muslims', the Socialist government of Felipe Gonzalez intervened rapidly and forcefully. Calm was restored by a combination of repression and promises.

The immediate cause of the dispute was removed by an agreement to speed up the granting of Spanish nationality to Rifians with roots in the city. In 1986 there were more than 17,000 of them registered as 'undocumented'. By the beginning of 1990 this number had been reduced to less than 1,000. A second measure by the central government was the injection of the huge amount of 32,000 million pesetas into the enclave in the years 1986–90. A panacea, a means to secure the 'Muslim' vote, or was it a rapid way of lifting the city's face? The professed idea behind this public investment was to implement a policy of ethnic integration. Three years later, the money had been spent on improvements of streets and the port, on the construction of new public buildings — a district hospital, a post office, a swimming-pool, a sports hall, a nautical port, and three schools. There are still plans to improve communication by air and water and, at last, to construct a Muslim cemetery. These public projects also attracted private investment. Since 1987 three new hotels, an apartment block, a barrio of *chalets*, and a shopping centre have been built. Three of the ten schools are now predominantly Muslim which reflects and reinforces ethnic segregation. The Cañada de la Muerte now boasts the urban comforts of paved streets, piped water, and electricity. These are the attainments of the uprising. However, serious problems remain with regard to health, employment, education and discrimination.

During my fieldwork inhabitants regardless of ethnic background kept telling me that Melilla was a forgotten place. The incidents of 1986 and 1987 put their city in the limelight. The general elections of October 1989 again made the enclave headline news. It was discovered that the Socialists had committed large-scale vote rigging in Melilla, in particular with Muslim votes. A party member was caught red-handed with dozens of ballot papers of Muslim residents; Socialists had intimidated Muslim voters at the entrance of polling-stations; and the total number of votes cast exceeded the voter-rolls by 3,000.

The elections were annulled on appeal. The second poll in March 1990 was of wider significance because had the Socialists been able to gain Melilla's seat in the Cortes they would have achieved an absolute majority (176 out of 350 seats). A day before the election pamphlets were found which advised Muslims to stay home because 'the Christians have not changed since Franco.' The turn-out was indeed low, with only 50 percent turning up to vote.

The Centre-Right not only won the Cortes seat but also the two Senate seats, thanks to the votes of the racist anti-Muslim party which had taken 10 percent of the votes in the 1989 elections. Given the relative strength of these extremists and the increasing power of the Muslim electorate, which will double in the census of 1990, it is to be expected that the campaigns for the local elections to be held in 1991 will have a strong racial overtone. A Spanish-Berber Party has been founded by radical Muslim inhabitants. A pro-Iraq demonstration during the Gulf War attracted about 1,000 Muslim inhabitants (5 percent of the total Muslim population). The large-scale granting of Spanish nationality to Muslim residents has done nothing to mitigate the ethnic divide. The labels of Christian and Muslim persist as markers of ethnic-political identity. Ethnic integration remains to a large extent political rhetoric.

Declarations on the future of the enclave by Spanish and Moroccan leaders are made with ritualistic regularity. In March 1990, during the struggle for the Cortes seat, the Prime Minister denied allegations by the Opposition that the Socialists envision a transference of Ceuta and Melilla to Morocco in the year 2000. On the other hand, a spokesman of King Hassan declared on the occasion of the independence of Namibia that the two Spanish enclaves are the last 'European colonies in Africa, museums of colonialism'. It cannot be denied that there is a core of truth in this statement.

What does the coming of the 'New Europe' and the opening of Eastern Europe mean to the Mediterranean area in general and the Spanish enclaves in particular? There are indications that this new Europe is going to close its southern borders to the threat of Islamic fundamentalism and the illegal immigrants from Africa, thereby turning the Mediterranean sea into a super Rio Grande. The Gulf War accelerated the shifting of NATO security concerns towards the Mediterranean. In this light political tranquillity in Melilla and Ceuta has become more important than ever.

Not all confrontations between residents of Rifian and Spanish origin are negative. As in the past, the domains of ritual and economics continue to offer examples of constructive cooperation. There are clear indications that the young use the cultural differences of the past to fashion new cultural forms. This may be detected in the work of several Melilla painters. This point was also brought home to me (in a literal sense) when three young musicians from Melilla came to perform in the Dutch city where I work and live. Their music, 'rif-flamenco', was advertised as 'unique' and 'exotic'. The two guitar-players of Rifian origin and the bassist of Spanish parentage had created a new genre by combining motifs drawn from flamenco and traditional Rifian music. The songs were announced in Spanish, the lyrics sung in Rifi and the themes were a mixture of the local (the beauties of Melilla and the Moroccan landscape) and the universal (freedom, love, and justice). The audience was Dutch, among them three boys, belonging to the sizeable second generation of Moroccan immigrants, who were thrilled by the music and lyrics and shouted responses in their native language. Like Nigerian juju or Algerian *rai* this music travelled a long distance to be performed in an ambience of cultural cosmopolitanism.

Glossary

The cumbersome use of diacritics in the transcription of Arabic, Hebrew and Rifian terms has been avoided for purely practical reasons. Abbreviations: S, Spanish; A, Arabic; H, Hebrew; R, Rifian.

acaparador (S) hoarder; person involved in black market operations.

Africanismo (S) ideological movement which emerged in the second half of the nineteenth century to promote scientific and other interests of Spain in Africa; *africanista*: student of African culture, protagonist of Spain's interests in Africa.

agasajo (S) banquet, party, entertainment; in local usage it denotes ethnically mixed social gatherings among the elite.

amghar (R) adult man, member of communal council; man of means and influence.

bandera de parlamento (S) flag of parley; *bandera de paz*, flag of truce.

barmitzvah (H) rite of passage by which boy becomes a mature member of the religious and social community at the age of thirteen.

baraka (A) divine blessing or grace; ability of holy men to work miracles.

barrio (S) quarter, district, neighbourhood

berberisco (S) berber.

bled al-makhzan (A) land of government as opposed to *bled as-siba*: land of dissidence.

cabrón (S) billy-goat, cuckold.

campo moro (S) Moorish country, land beyond the enclave; *campo infiel*: infidel country.

campo santo (S) literally holy land, cemetery.

carnet (S) permit, license, identity card.

cena-baile (S) full-dress supper party.

chabola (S) hut, hovel.

Communidad (S) group of people and interests; used in Melilla to refer to a formal association of Jews, Gypsies, Muslims and Hindus, recognised by the Spanish government.

confidente (S) spy, informer, confidant.

convivencia (S) cohabitation; local usage to refer to the (desired) peaceful co-existence of ethnic groups.

cultura (S)   good breeding and manners, refinement; Spanish ideology of civilisation.

desterrado (S)   exiled convict.

dhaqbitsh (R)   tribe.

dirham (A)   Moroccan coin, monetary unit.

djazzat (R)   Spanish spelling of *dhazttat*: protection money paid by a traveller to a powerful man for safe passage through land belonging to another tribe (cf. Hart 1976: 457).

dshar (R)   local community of scattered dwellings centred on a mosque (Spanish spelling: *dchur*); also used for localised patrilineage.

fqih (A)   teacher of the Quran; gives the Friday sermon at noon.

gamberro (S)   libertine, criminal; often used locally to refer to unemployed Muslim youth.

gente fino (S)   refined people, elite.

ghusl (A)   major ritual ablution.

gordo (S)   literally, fat; a rich man, a man of position.

guerra divina (S)   holy war, crusade.

Haketia (H?)   a mixture of ancient Castilian, Hebrew and Moroccan Arabic spoken by the descendants of Spanish Jews in Morocco until the beginning of the Protectorate.

harca (S)   derived from *harka* (Moroccan Arabic) used to describe a band of tribal warriors and its military expeditions.

hillula (H)   festival commemorating the anniversary of the death of a holy man, including a pilgrimage to his shrine.

hombre de prestigio (S)   man of prestige; used to denote local Rifian leaders sought out by the Spaniards for collaboration.

huerta (S)   garden, irrigated plot of land, vegetable garden.

interventor local (S)   inspector; local Spanish administrator during the Protectorate.

jma'a (A)   Spanish spelling *Yemáa*; administrative unit corresponding to tribal section.

jnun (A)   plural of *jinn*: spirit.

jornada (S)   foraging expedition, raid (*razzia*).

jura de bandera (S)   the pledge of allegiance to the Spanish flag; rite of incorporation into the army after a period of basic training.

kalb (A)   dog; an insulting way of referring to Christians.

khamsa (A)   literally five, referring to an amulet in the form of an open hand used against the evil eye.

liff (A)   group of people, involvement; 'an alliance between social or political units at any level, from that of the individual or nuclear family, virtually, to that of the tribe, an alliance which is more than capable of breaking the bonds created by the segmentary system' (Hart 1976: 461).

ma'ariv (H)   Jewish evening prayer.

macho (S)   masculine, a real man.

megorashim   see *toshavim*

melillense (S)   used by and for the Spanish Catholic inhabitants of the
   enclave belonging to *familias de arraigo* (families with genealogical
   roots in the city); *melillismo*: local patriotism among the Catholic
   inhabitants.

mellah (A)   Jewish quarter of Moroccan towns.

mimuna (A)   festival of Moroccan Jews including a visit to a saint's
   shrine after Passover; known in Melilla as *fiesta de la galleta* (festival of
   the biscuit).

moqaddem (A)   caretaker, headman in charge of *jma'a* (subordinate to
   a *shaikh*).

Morisco (S)   Muslim under Christian rule, converted to Christianity.

moro (S)   Muslim, unbaptized (pejorative term); *moro fronterizo*: Rifian
   frontiersman; *moro del rey*: Rifian or Arab under Sultan's rule; *moro de
   paz*: peaceful Moor; *moro de guerra*: hostile Moor.

padrón (S)   municipal census rolls.

paisano (S)   civilian compatriot; soldier in civilian clothes; *paisa*: used
   by Rifians as a term of address for Spaniards.

paseo (S)   evening stroll; street or square where stroll takes place.

patria chica (S)   'little fatherland', localism.

perro (S)   dog; insult used to describe Muslims (see also *kalb*).

Plaza (S)   stronghold, fortified town; *plaza*: square.

pleito homenaje (S)   installation ceremony of high *presidio* officials.

poblado (S)   settlement; often used pejoratively to describe a small
   outlying place.

presidio (S)   garrison, fortress, citadel, penitentiary settlement.

pueblo (S)   town, people, nation, working classes.

qabila (A)   administrative unit corresponding to tribe; Spanish spelling *kábila*.

qadi (A)   judge in Koranic law.

qaid (A)   local administrator.

razzia   see *jornada*.

Regulares (S)   special unit of the Spanish army; during the Protectorate it consisted of Rifian soldiers.

rifi (A)   Rifian (male), Rifian language (*dhamazight*, R).

romeria (S)   pilgrimage, festival held at a saint's shrine.

shaikh (A)   local official, subordinate to *qaid*.

Shari'a (A)   corpus of Islamic Law.

sharif (A)   descendant of the Prophet, religious leader; holy man.

sinvergüenza (S)   shameless, rogue.

soltera (S)   unmarried woman.

suq (A)   market.

tapa (S)   snack, assortment of appetizers served with beer or wine in
   bars.

tbila (H)   immersion in a ritual bath.

tendero (S)   shopkeeper.

Tercio (S)   literally, third; Spanish infantry regiment in the sixteenth and seventeenth centuries; Spanish Foreign Legion (*Tercio de Extranjeros, El Tercio, La Legión*).

tertulia (S)   social gathering of friends at regular times in a public place.

toshavim (H)   native Moroccan Jews, as opposed to *megorashim*: exiled Jews from Spain.

washun (R)   homestead, household.

zawiya (A)   sacred place, lodge of a religious order.

Notes

Chapter 1

1. See for a discussion regarding urban research in the Mediterranean area, Gilmore (1982) and Kenny & Kertzer (1983).
2. Excellent recent discussions on the use of history in anthropology are Ortner (1984) and Moore (1987). For an overview of recent trends in the use of history, both as consciousness and process, in ethnography see Driessen (1988). The many different ways in which time is represented and historical material employed in research and writing, point to the fragmentation of the diachronic perspective. A common conceptual framework, coherent research agenda, and shared goals are lacking. In spite of the increasing frequency with which the label of 'historical anthropology' is now being used, such a specialism in fact does not exist. It is even doubtful whether a new specialism is desirable, since history should inform any anthropological analysis.
3. An exception is Seddon (1981) who fully acknowledges the impact of Melilla on the political economy and culture of the Rif Berbers.
4. See Barth (1969) for the simple yet seminal idea that ethnic boundary formation is not dependent upon cultural isolation or segregation but rather the result of interaction.
5. This has recently been done in a fine study of Armenians in London (Talai 1986).
6. For a thorough discussion of this basic point see Moore & Myerhoff (1977), Burke (1987: 223–39), Cannadine (1987: 2–3), Kertzer (1988). I owe much to Handelman's provocative paper (1988). This point will be revisited in the conclusion.
7. In 1984 the *de jure* and *de facto* population amounted to 58,711 and 63,507 respectively. These data were provided to me by the *Servicio Estadistica Municipal*.
8. These figures proceed from the *Delegación del Gobierno de Melilla*. In 1983, 2,500 illegal Moroccan residents were returned to Morocco.
9. The enclave's hinterland covers a large part of the province of Nador, which is one of the most depressed areas of Morocco. The

Moroccan government is fully aware of the fact that tens of thousands of Rifians depend on Melilla for their work as domestic servants, peasants, fishermen, ambulant traders, smugglers and drug-dealers.

10. A pun on 'Green March'. In 1975 King Hassan II forced the issue of the Spanish Western Sahara by organising an impressive march of hundreds of thousands of Moroccans into the disputed territory, while Franco was dying and Madrid not prepared nor willing to fight a distant colonial war. When Spain surrendered control over this area to Morocco and Mauritania, the Spanish inhabitants of Melilla were shocked, fearing a similar fate for their city in the near future.

11. Several new books relevant to this study appeared after I finished the script. Unfortunately, I cannot take them into account here. Fouad Zaïm (1990) considers the history of Mediterranean Morocco as a 'histoire manquée'. His book is very useful as he develops a Moroccan perspective on the history of the enclaves based on some new sources.

   In Melilla a new generation of local historians established itself in the second half of the 1980s. They are prolific and committed to the plight of the Spanish enclave. The heightened awareness of Melilla's predicament seems to boost historical production. Interesting work is being done by Vicente Moga Romero, Antonio Bravo Nieto, Juan Diez Sanchez, and Francisco Saro Gandarillas among others. Once in a while the scholarly journal *Aldaba* devotes special issues to local history. The municipality and the 'Fundación Municipal Sociocultural' set up two new series called 'Historia de Melilla' and 'La Biblioteca de Melilla'. A photo album (*album de cromos*) and comic book about local history have been published in order to heighten the historical consciousness of the (Catholic) inhabitants.

Chapter 2

1. The Spanish state was built on reconquest. At this time state formation rested heavily on religion; indeed, Catholicism provided the cement for binding together the heterogeneous regions under the crowns of Castile and Aragón.

2. We find the following phrase in Isabel's testament: '(. . .) and that they do not abandon the conquest of Africa and fight for Our Faith against the Infidels' (cited in Garcia Figueras 1944: 59).

3. See Driessen (1985: 107–8) for a summary of this long-term process and for relevant literature.

4. See de Castries' monumental source book (1921:I, x).

5. See the most recent local history of Melilla by Mir Berlanga (1983),

who deals at length with the legal aspects of enclave life.

6. The most important secondary sources for an ethnographic history of the enclave are two anthologies from journals written by parish priests over more than four centuries. These collections were published by the local historian Gabriel de Morales in 1909 and 1920. This is the richest source on daily life in the *presidio*. Braudel and Hess are the major authorities on the Ibero-African frontier.

7. See Seddon (1981: xiii–xiv).

8. For a historical ethnography of the Rif see Hart (1976) and for an ethnography of the Iqar'ayen area Jamous (1981).

9. These events are cited in all local histories. They all go back to Estrada y Paredes (1769).

10. See de Morales (1920: 210).

11. More than a century later this miraculous version turned up in Estrada y Paredes (1769).

12. See de Morales (1909:90). Fourteen Rifians of both sexes were taken prisoner in this raid, while seven Spanish soldiers died and six were wounded.

13. This siege by Sultan Mulay Abdallah lasted one hundred days. See Mir Berlanga (1983: 79–86).

14. Taken from de Morales (1920: 172).

15. Idem (1909: 544–5).

16. Cited in de Morales (1909: 97).

17. See the excellent study on Spanish captives in North Africa by Friedman (1983).

18. See de Morales (1909: 604–18).

19. Idem (1920: 50).

20. On this point also see Friedman (1983: 47 ff.)

21. Taken from de Morales (1920: 43, 32).

22. Idem, 99.

23. Idem, 156.

24. Taken from an article in the *Telegrama de Melilla*, 25/12/1979.

25. Taken from 'Documentos Sueltos, Cronista de la Ciudad', 1820–1855, Legajos 9–11, Archivo Municipal de Melilla (A.M.M.).

26. *Campo infiel* literally means infidel country. This and the second case are based on 'Documentos Sueltos, Cronista de la Ciudad', 1820–24, documento 4, folios 141–54, legajo 7; and, doc. 3, folios 38–84, legajo 8, A.M.M.

27. Taken from de Morales (1920: 16, 87, 92–3, 195).

28. Idem, (1909: 179).

29. The policies of Madrid more often than not clashed with the ideas, wishes and realities of the *presidio*.

30. Legajo 11, 1853–61, 'Notario', doc. 193, folios 425–8; Legajo 12, 1862–61, 'Notario', doc. 34, folios 84–89.

31. See the article in the *Telegrama de Melilla*, 28/8/1976.

32. Taken from de Morales (1920: 156).
33. Idem, 200.
34. Idem, 96.
35. Idem, 147.
36. Idem, 228.

Chapter 3

1. Very little is known about the history of the Rif prior to 1900. See Seddon (1981), Hart (1976) and Ayache (1981, 1983) for useful overviews at the local and regional level.
2. The daily newspaper *El Telegrama del Rif*, founded in 1902, is a valuable source of information, especially for the Spanish view of Rifian history. It acted as the mouthpiece of *Africanismo*. The founder saw the newspaper as an 'independent daily and defender of Spanish interests in Morocco.'
3. Lobera Girela (1912: 29). This influential africanist was one of the architects of Spanish colonial policy.
4. Much of his life belongs to oral tradition, only his final years have been documented. See Ayache (1981: 137–52) and Jamous (1981: 197–8) for a life history based on both Spanish and Moroccan sources.
5. The daily newspaper made fun of this belief and presented it as a proof of Rifian fanaticism and superstition.
6. In 1911 Spain founded the *Fuerzas Regulares Indigenas*, originally comprised of 800 Rifian soldiers and a squadron of 100 horses (cf. de Morales 1920: 117).
7. Not surprisingly, Rifian epic history gives a radically different account of the marabout's death, a version that is consistent with the image of Sidi Mohand as heroic warrior saint. This account claims that one summer day the saint and his escort arrived at a village in Ait Sidar territory. They decided to spend the night there. A spy advised the military commander in Melilla and under cover of the night 'thousands' (meaning many) of Spanish soldiers were able to surround the village. When Sidi Mohand discovered what had happened, he gathered his men and asked them whether they were willing to die with him in his last battle. Nobody refused. They spent the rest of the night praying and the next day fought till the last man. The end of this account has several variations. One story has it that the enemy found a horse weeping at the side of the saint's body. The Spaniards were unable to separate the animal from his master's corpse. Another story relates that angels descended from heaven to take him directly to paradise. And yet another version points out that after the saint's death nothing

would grow in the battlefield because nature was inconsolable. All these variants show the special bond between the saint, nature and heaven.

8. See Hart's excellent chapter on 'Abd al-Krim and the Rif War (1976: 269–403). One of the best Spanish accounts is Goded (1932). Pennell's recent study (1986) by far outshines Woolman (1968) and Ayache (1981).

9. Source: *Padrón de habitantes*, (*de jure* population.) 1880, A.M.M.

10. Idem, 1885 (*de jure*).

11. Idem, 1900 (*de jure*).

12. These events have been drawn from respective editions of *El Telegrama del Rif*, A.M.M.

13. Idem, 29/4/1905.

14. Figures taken from: *Junta Municipal de Melilla. Memorias sobre su actuatión. 1927–1930*, p. 281, B.M.M. and, the *Padrón* of 1935.

15. Data derived from *Anuarios Estadisticos Zona del Protectorado y de los Territorios de Soberania de España en el Norte de Africa, 1940–1955*, B.M.M.

16. Extracted from the *Padrón* of 1882 and 1907.

17. *El Telegrama del Rif*, 28/5/1905.

18. Taken from the section 'Diversas Noticias'.

19. Derived from *Memorias*, p. 237. These figures were not broken down by creed and nationality, and other descriptive labels were used for crimes. I lumped together all physical offences (manslaughter included). Unfortunately, I do not have similar figures for a town of the same size in Spain. All these drawbacks, of course, reduce the comparative value of these data.

20. *Junta de Arbitrios. Su qestión durante los años 1917–1918.* B.M.M.

21. *Memorias*, pp. 115–, 130, 177.

22. *El Telegrama del Rif*, 22/2/1921, also 4/3, 6/3, and 6/4/1921.

23. See Choukri's autobiographical novel *Le pain nu* for an impressive account of these years.

24. *Memorias*, p. 177. Many buildings in the city centre were designed by Gaudi's student Enrique Nieto y Nieto, who took up residence in Melilla.

25. The Rifian population kept strictly aloof from the Spanish labour movement. They perceived socialists and communists as atheist, who aimed at the destruction of both Catholicism and Islam (cf. Fleming 1983). Not surprisingly, they gave complete support to Franco's revolt and enlisted en masse in the Nationalist forces. Rifian troops in Spain were scandalised by the desecration of religious images by the 'Reds' and reacted cruelly (cf. Fraser 1979: 154–5). In fact, the garrison of Melilla initiated the uprising of the Nationalists on 17 July 1936. The military office where the revolt was proclaimed became a 'pilgrimage' shrine during the Franco regime.

26. Based on *El Telegrama del Rif*, 5/5 and 19/5/1905. Others went overland. These Rifian migrants were highly regarded by the French *colons* for being hard workers.
27. See Troin's (1975) quantitative-geographical study of Moroccan markets. Also see Hart's important general observations (1976: 64–72) and Geertz (1979).
28. Sources: *Memorias*, p. 281; Morales Lezcano (1984: 83).
29. *Anuario Estadistico*, 1940.
30. Sources: *Anuario Estadistico*, 1955; *Royaume du Maroc, Ministre du Plan Annuaire Statistique du Maroc*, Rabat: Direction de la Statistique, 1983. The population of Nador province increased by almost 25 percent over the 1970s. In 1982 the population density per square kilometre amounted to 96.8. The number of people per household was 6.2 (in Nador city 5.5). On emigration see Heinemeijer (1976: 53–4, 85). Cammaert (1985) offers a qualitative analysis of the effects of emigration from a female perspective.
31. Prior to the pacification campaign of 1909, Nador was a small village with a Quranic school, a public bath-house, a mosque and a *suq*. It was largely destroyed during the campaign and rebuilt as a military and administrative centre. In the course of the Protectorate it developed into the main satellite of Melilla. Towards the end of Spanish domination its population numbered 22,000, of whom 13,300 were Muslims, 200 Jews, and 8,500 Spaniards (*Anuario Estadistico*, 1955).
32. In spite of the fact that the cultivated area of northern Morocco doubled during Spanish domination, the Rifians lived under constant threat of famine (cf. Mikesell 1961: 93). Today, only a quarter of the Nador province consists of cultivated land. More than half of the total amount of food has to be imported from elsewhere (cf. Cammaert 1985: 20).

Chapter 4

1. Elsewhere (Driessen 1987) I have dealt with pictorial representations of Rifian society under Spanish colonialism.
2. One of the few works worth mentioning is the travel book by Domingo Badia y Leblich (1816), who travelled from Morocco to Mecca disguised as a *hajj*. For an overview of early Spanish travel accounts see Morales Lezcano (1984: appendix II).
3. See the undated and unsigned historical account (probably written in the early 1920s) *Historia. El Garet, El Rif y Guelaia*, B.M.M., p. 54.
4. This is the image of the traditional Moroccan state with its two poles of *bled al-makhzan* ('land of government') and *bled-as siba* ('land of dissidence'). For an excellent discussion of this stereotype see Seddon (1981: 28 ff.).

5. Corporal punishments are stipulated in the *shariʿa* and today are still meted out in Islamic countries such as Iran, Sudan, Pakistan, and Saudi Arabia. Acts of ritual mutilation and defilement were frequently performed on Spanish soldiers.

6. The mixed Arab-Rifian terms and transliterations are Lobera's.

7. *Guía del Norte de Africa y Sur de España, 1917.* Madrid: Guías Internacionales Ortega. This guide contains a mixture of tourist information and statistical and cultural data.

8. The following reports were examined: *Cuestionarios de Kábilas,* Beni Sicar (65 p.), Mazuza (101 p.), Beni Bu Ifrur (55 p.), Beni Sidel (6 p.), Beni Bu Gafar (108 p.), Carbon copies in B.M.M. The names of tribes, divisions, institutions, places etc. are given in Arabic, which reflects the low regard Spanish had for *Rifi.*

9. For instance, in 1912 the Spanish settled 248 blood-feuds in Ait Shikar, some of them going back more than forty years (*Historia. El Garet, El Rif y Guelaia,* p. 106). In 1920 seven cases of blood-feud were brought before the local commissioner of the Ait Shikar. That year 1,836 land disputes were reported (Ait Shikar, p. 53).

10. See Hart (1976: chapter 12) for a discussion of the blood-feud within the context of the segmentary lineage system.

11. See Caro Baroja (1970) for a discussion of the 'national character' concept and myth.

12. This view is prominent in the work of García Figueras (1944, 1947).

13. See Hart (1958) for a discussion of one of the best representatives of this military ethnographic tradition. See also his annotated bibliography (1976).

14. See the brief notes on Westermarck in Davis (1977:2) and Eickelman (1981: 45, fn. 1).

15. The most famous case is, of course, Malinowski's diary. For a recent flourishing of the confessional literature see Marcus & Cushman (1982).

16. On this point see Turnbull (1973), Sheenan (1980), Blok (1982), and Taussig (1987).

17. For a critique of diffusionism and its culture area concept see Harris (1968: 375–76).

18. Apart from the fact that France already had an established tradition of anthropological research, Berber ethnography was also stimulated by the colonial policy of dividing Berbers and Arabs (cf. Burke 1973).

19. This is the main point of criticism in El Guindi's review of the book (1979).

20. See in particular the summaries in Davis (1977: 110–26) and Eickelman (1981: 85–105) who hold opposing points of view. For a more recent discussion and reconsideration of the debate see Combs-Schilling (1985), Hart (1989) and Munson (1989).

21. Apart from obvious differences in theoretical perspective (function-alism versus an interpretative approach, a holistic versus problem-oriented stance), the positions in the debate can also be partly attributed to different fieldwork locations (mountainous areas in-habited by Berber peasants and labourers, as opposed to the towns with a predominantly Arab and Arabised Berber population). Finally, there are slight but important differences in the periods of field research (the 1950s versus the late 1960s and early 1970s, with social change accelerating during the latter period).

Chapter 5

1. See the monographs reviewed in the preceding chapter. Exceptions are Rosen (1972) and Geertz (1979) on the Sefrou Jews. Hardly anything is known about the Jews who lived among the tribes. It is not surprising then that Davis (1977: 38–9) confines himself to a short summary of the conventional wisdom about North African Jews. Recently, these Jews have been the subject of a growing number of scholarly writings (cf. *Actes du Colloque*, 1980). This interest fits well into the accelerating growth of studies in ethnicity and of Mediterranean societies. There is also a recent search for their past by Maghribian Jews now living in France, Israel, the United States and Canada (cf. Stillman 1978, Deshen & Shokeid 1974).
2. See for striking parallels the myths of origin of the Jerban Jews (Udovitch & Valensi 1985: 8–9).
3. According to Leo Africanus this happened in 1487.
4. Ben-Ami's account of the legend (1980: 107) differs from mine in several respects. In his version the rabbi arrived at Melilla and let the Jewish authorities know through a Muslim messenger that he was going to die and thus asked for all necessary services. The authorities refused whereupon the rabbi got furious and called down a curse upon them: 'Your women will be numerous, your men few, and there won't be any contact between the families'. This came to pass; Jewish women were unable to find a husband. The saint then requested Muslim assistance. After having taken his ritual bath in tears of sadness which flowed from his eyes, he wrapped himself in the funeral shroud and announced to the Muslims that his house would burn down, and that he and his descendants would become guardians of the shrine, on the con-dition that they would ask no more than one *dirham* per pilgrim. When he died a tempest broke out and a huge stone covered his grave. Ben-Ami does not mention his source. In another article (1981) he points out that there exists among Moroccan Jews a legend about the arrival of seven rabbis from the Holy Land, who

after their death were venerated as saints. Note that in Judaism seven is a number of completion. The first rabbi of Melilla, grand rabbi Abraham Cohen, is also venerated as a holy man.

5. On the whole, the official Moroccan attitude towards the Jews who continue living in Morocco has been tolerant. This attitude was voiced by a cousin of Hassan II, minister of State and chief editor of the government's daily newspaper *Le Matin du Sahara*, as follows: 'For centuries Morocco has proved that coexistence between Jews and Muslims is not only possible, but has also resulted in mutual understanding, harmony, and fraternity.'

6. *Documentos sueltos, Cronista de la Ciudad*, legajo 7, doc. 196, folios 435–6, A.M.M.

7. *Doc. sueltos, Cronista de la Ciudad*, legajo 7, doc. 66, folios 266–76, 1874. A.M.M. Similar notary acts were made for Halfon Hachuel Cohen, merchant and rabbi who lived in Melilla since 1865 (idem, doc. 64, folios 300–310), Judah Israel Abensur and Isaac Salama Bennaen from Tetuan, living in Melilla since 1871 (idem doc. 68, folios 289–99).

8. *Padrón de 1880*, A.M.M.

9. The most detailed history of North African Jews is Chouraqui (1985).

10. Data derived from the 1884 *Padrón*, A.M.M.

11. The most common names for men were Yacub, Yousef, Moises, Abraham, Salomon, Samuel, Simon, Judah, Elias, David, Mesod and Israel. For women, Nona, Sultana, Zohra, Nana, Luna, Sol, Ameja, Lisa, Yamina, Mesauda, Reina, Aluisa, Saida, and an occasional Rachel and Ester. These names were followed by *bent* (daughter of). In subsequent censuses we note a considerable castilianisation of Jewish first and family names. Mainly Jews of urban origin changed their first names into a Spanish equivalent, Yousef became José, Abraham became Alberto, etc.

12. Compare Goitein (1978: 314–9) on this point.

13. Also see Jamous (1981: 206) who reports that 'No real man would attack a Jew without losing his honour'. Jews were simply excluded from the game of power and honour.

14. Oral communication from Jesus Salafranca.

15. Idem. The increasing activity of Jews in the ports of Tangier, Melilla, Ceuta and Gibraltar caused the commercial decline of Tetuan at the beginning of this century (cf. Cohn 1927: 8).

16. *Ponencia de Africa, sección Commandancia General de Melilla*, Servicio Histórico Militar, Madrid, legajo 62, carpeta 5, 1910.

17. Computed from *Padrón de 1900*, A.M.M.

18. *Padrón de 1928, 1936; Anuario Estadistico*, 1946, Zona de Protectorado y de los Territorios de Soberania de España en el Norte de Africa; *Reseña Estadistica de Ceuta y Melilla*, 1972, A.M.M.

19. For instance, the campaigns of 1909–11 (*Servico Histórico Militar*, Madrid, legajo 70, carpeta 4, 1911.)
20. Data derived from the *Guia del Norte de Africa y Sur de España*, Madrid: Tipografía Moderna, 1917, pp. 617–21, 628, 645. The big merchants used a number of small itinerant traders who travelled about the countryside on donkeys together with their wares. Geertz (1979: 170–2) refers to this patron-client type of arrangement in Sefrou in terms of 'sitting Jews' and 'riding Jews'.
21. Jewish accounts were born out by a Catholic informant who as a boy participated in these occasions.
22. The account that follows is based on interviews and on the *Guia Oficial de Marruecos y del Norte de Africa Española*, Madrid, Compañia Ibero-Americana de Publicaciones, 1931: 1018, 1033–4, 1051. A.M.M.
23. *El Telegrama del Rif*, 28/4/1931.
24. The Jewish community in the sociological sense of the term (a cohabiting ethnic group) is not completely co-terminous with the Community, the official association of Jewish residents. However, most of the Jews are members of the Community.
25. Derived from the *Guia Comercial e Industrial de Melilla*, 1983. Cámara de Comercio, Industría, y Navegación.
26. Derived from the 1984 *Padrón*.
27. Very little work has been done on this ritual. The best account so far is Goldberg (1978) who applies a structuralist analysis to miscellaneous data derived from published sources. Also see Chouraqui (1985: 216–8) on the *mimuna*. North African Jews also keep this tradition alive in Israel.

Chapter 6

1. *El Telegrama de Melilla*, 3/8/1983.
2. Idem, 7/8/1983.
3. Idem, 8/3/1984. I also used the issues of 14/3/1984, 16/3/1984, and 17/3/1984 for references and descriptions of events that are reconstructed in this section.
4. Needham's thesis that 'there is a significant connection between percussion and transition' (1967: 613) has provoked much criticism. The link is too general to be significant and stripping percussion of all connections to rhythm makes it valueless (cf. Sturtevant 1968 and Jackson 1968). In this ceremony we see a peculiar mixture of what Rouget (1985), in his seminal study on music and trance, called emotive and communal trance.
5. During my research in Andalusia I stumbled upon a similar flag ceremony in an entirely different context, which was held in a small

rural town in 1920. In spite of differences in detail, the structure of the two flag ceremonies was strikingly similar (the prominent role of god-parenthood, the symbolism of baptism and marriage, the decor, the pillars of social order). The ceremony was performed after a period of class struggle and aimed at the restoration of the status quo.

6. Bloch (1986) deals with a similar development in his monograph on state ritual in Madagascar.

7. The discourse of ethnicity is in many different cultural and historical settings that of kinship.

8. See for similar conclusions on the links between power and ritual Evans-Pritchard (1949), Geertz (1980), Cohen (1981), Bloch (1986, 1987). Flag ceremonies seem to be much more frequent in Melilla than in metropolitan Spain. This is connected with the colonial and contested status of the enclave and with feelings of isolation and insecurity among the Catholic inhabitants. Whenever there is a crisis in which the Spanishness of the enclave is at stake, they take to the streets with the national colours. More than 20,000 of them did so in the spring of 1984 after a leading Spanish socialist had accused the inhabitants of racism. Such demonstrations were repeated several times in successive years.

Chapter 7

1. For Western Europe see Praz (1970) and Ariès (1978).

2. Cf. Gorer (1965) for a discussion of the taboos surrounding death in Great Britain. Ariès (1976) points out the process by which the 'familiar' and 'tamed' death of the Middle Ages and early modern period became increasingly 'shameful and forbidden', transformed from an occasion of ritual ceremony into a technical phenomenon. Emotions of grief and mourning have become repugnant and death has been displaced from the home to the hospital. While in the nineteenth century death was still omnipresent, now it has become concealed and 'unnameable'. For similar conclusions see Elias (1980) on the 'loneliness of the dying' in modern Western Europe.

3. Bloch and Parry (1982) offer an example of a symbolic approach to death cut off from the wider ethnography. To be sure, their focus on the symbolism of funerary rites is perfectly legitimate. However, their promise to deal with the social implications of these rites is not fulfilled. Their notion of 'social order' is as reified as Herz's which they reject. What kind of society is it in which the Indian householder pursues a 'good death' as a sacrificial act through which the deceased, time and the cosmos are regenerated? (Parry 1982: 74–111).

4. In 1880 only three families had settled down in the less secure second precinct, while four families lived in the third where the tiny gardens were located. Source: Padrón de Melilla de 1880, A.M.M..

5. According to Berber oral history, Spanish sources deny that this act of desecration took place.

6. This rite intends to achieve the opposite of a mortuary ritual, namely the dehumanisation of the corpse.

7. Padrón de Melilla de 1900, A.M.M.

8. Actas de la Junta Local de deslindes y amojonamientos, 1866, A.M.M.

9. The funeral of a Muslim killed by a Catholic in the race riots of early 1987 was turned into a political demonstration (see Chapter 9).

10. This is not the place for a systematic comparison of local beliefs and rituals surrounding death among Jews, Christians, Hindus and Muslims. Of course, Hinduism with its polytheism, its belief in reincarnation and practice of cremation, presents a contrast with the three religions of the Book. In spite of basic similarities in beliefs, mortuary practices vary considerably among Jews, Christians and Muslims. For instance, the widespread Catholic custom of interment in niches and the use of iconographic imagery is prohibited by Muslim and Jewish law.

11. Statistical data were provided by the administrator of the cemetery. It is hard to say whether the number of visitors is high since comparative data are not available. There are approximately 30,000 nominal Catholics in Melilla. Usually there is one member in a family who specialises in tending the graves of the deceased, often an elderly woman. This point will be dealt with in a separate section below.

12. See de Pina Cabral (1980) for northern Portugal. Also see Bloch & Parry (1982: 22) for a discussion of this image in the context of the belief that female sexuality is the cause of the corruption of the flesh.

13. On this point see Huntington & Metcalf (1975: 45).

14. Unfortunately I was not able to witness All Saints' and All Souls' celebration in Melilla. This account is based on interviews and newspaper reports.

15. See Christian (1972), Mernissi (1975) and Jansen (1987) on this point.

16. Similar experiences of Muslim women at graveyards are pointed out by Mernissi (1975: 101–6) and Munson (1984: 155–6).

17. See Myerhoff (1982b) on 'Re-membering' among the elderly.

18. The *paseo* is an important institution in Spanish society. Strolling up and down the main avenue, the participants in this ritualised pastime expose themselves to the public eye. People put on their

best clothes for the occasion. On weekend evenings families go out together arm in arm to join the milling crowd congesting the main avenue. People walk about in an exhibitionistic and at the same time voyeuristic way. They are clearly performing on the public stage. Also see Gilmore on the evening stroll (1987: 160).

19. *El Telegrama de Melilla*, front page, 7/10/1983. The use of the term *gamberro* is a subtle insinuating device. It is invariably used in connection with crimes committed in Melilla, which, according to the police are the work of Muslims in 98 percent of the cases. Consequently, the term *gamberro* has almost become a synonym for *moro*. Also see *El Telegrama de Melilla*, 8/10/83 and 27/10/1983.

20. This slogan was invented by the founder of the Spanish Foreign Legion, Millán Astray, nicknamed 'the glorious mutilated one' after his many battle mutilations.

21. There is an ambivalence in the attitudes of the Catholic inhabitants towards the Legion. As a military unit it is often praised and romanticised. In oral history many references are made to the 'heroism' of the Legion. Parades and other ceremonial performances by the Legion are popular. On the other hand, individual legionnaires are generally despised and avoided for their brutal conduct.

22. A recent exception is a book by a Dutch art historian on the politics of death during the French Revolution (van Helsdingen 1987). Also see Etlin (1984).

23. Data taken from post-war census returns (*padrones*) and their summaries, A.M.M.

Chapter 8

1. See Wolf's useful typology of coalitions (1966: 81–95). In a single-stranded bond people are tied together by a single interest.

2. On the other hand, there are also ethnic riots that can be attributed to working-class economic competition (cf. Horowitz 1985: 99).

3. *El Telegrama del Rif*, 18/4/1905.

4. In 1916, for instance, numerous Spanish guests were invited to participate in the celebration of an important marriage, linking the lineages of two influential, pro-Spanish leaders (cf. Driessen 1987: 59–60).

5. *El Telegrama del Rif*, 29/3/1921.

6. Ibid., 15/3/1921.

7. An *agasajo* alliance resembles both a clique and an action-set (cf. Boissevain 1974: 171–9).

8. See Simmel's seminal and still relevant essay on the sociological importance of quantitative aspects: 'But the more persons come

together, the less it is probable that they converge in the more valuable and intimate sides of their natures, and the lower, therefore lies the point that is common to their impulses and interests' (1950: 112).

9. There is an extensive literature in anthropology on commensality. Pitt-Rivers (1977: 110) in his essay on the law of hospitality in the Mediterranean area writes: 'Food and drink always have ritual value, for the ingestion together of a common substance creates a bond. Commensality is the basis of community . . .'

10. Compare Veblen's still relevant statements on the cultivation of habits of decorum in the leisure class (1899: 48–50).

11. Cf. Goffman (1967: 57, 62–3, 71).

12. Until the 1950s asymmetrical 'joking' was also quite common in the encounters of lower-class Catholics and Jews. Today, as a result of emigration, there are hardly any lower-class Jews left in Melilla.

13. For a general discussion and overview of the literature on this phenomenon see Apte (1985: chapter 1; also see chapter 4 on ethnic jokes). Handelman & Kapferer (1972) make a useful distinction between 'setting-specific joking' and 'category-routinised joking'. Both types are recognisable in the examples offered. Since expressed agreement of the participants in 'joking' encounters is lacking, I use the concept between inverted commas.

14. One of the most serious riots took place during a match in January 1984 between a local Catholic team and a team from the Algerian city of Tlemcen. What had started as a friendly match degenerated into an outright battle between the Algerian players and the audience. Five players were seriously injured.

15. See Apte (1985: 32) for a discussion of this point.

16. See Simmel's famous essay on the stranger (1950: 402–8).

Chapter 9

1. Cf. *El Telegrama de Melilla*, 7/2/1982.

2. These figures were provided by the President of the Hindu Community Council.

3. Traditional Sindi communities have a reputation for their business acumen throughout India (Personal communication by Jonathan Parry).

4. These Hindus only left traces in the municipal census.

5. Data derived from the *Padrones* of 1940, 1965 and 1980, A.M.M.

6. Parents living with their daughter and son-in-law is rather unusual in the Indian context, for it runs counter to the ideology of *kanya dan* ('the free gift of the virgin') which prevents a high-status Brahman from eating in the house of his married daughter (cf. Parry 1979:

162). In this case the daughter lived in a separate house on her parents' property.

7. The practice of living in nuclear families contradicts the ideal of joint living which was still avowed by informants. In India household arrangements are also rather variable and their composition is ambiguous (cf. Parry 1979: 159).

8. Data derived from the *Guía Comercial e Industrial de Melilla 1983*.

9. Once every while the Civil Guard undertakes some token action against smuggling which is largely done with speedboats. Spanish border control has been intensified somewhat since 1985, following high-level agreements between the Spanish and Moroccan governments. This has taken the form of preventing it from being done too openly. If official regulations against illegal exports were to be observed, Melilla would soon be dead economically.

10. During my fieldwork the only Hindu ceremony I able to attend was a wedding.

11. This festival is celebrated in the month of Karttih in most towns of Northern India and it is basically a seasonal rite of passage. It is an occasion of gambling (personal communication by Jonathan Parry).

12. The *Delegación del Gobierno* provided the following figures for 1984:

Muslims with Spanish nationality:	2,500
Their children under 18	4,500
Muslims with residence cards	5,902
Their children under 18	6,000
Entirely undocumented Muslims	2,520
Total	21,422

The *Comunidad Musulmana* claimed an overall figure of 30,000 Muslim inhabitants.

13. See Elias & Scotson (1965: 149 ff, 154 ff) on the sociological concept of 'oldness'.

14. Of a total number of commercial enterprises, 502 were in the hands of Moroccans and 104 were run by Spaniards of Moroccan origin. Figures provided by the *Guía Comercial e Industrial de Melilla*, 1983.

15. Muslim settlement in Melilla did not exceed 8,000 residents prior to 1955. Source: *Anuarios Estadisticos* 1940–1955.

16. This is oral history borne out by both Muslims and Catholics. The figure of fifty-two *barracas* is derived from *Junta Municipal de Melilla. Memorias sobre su actuación, 1927–1930*, p. 177.

17. Compare Jansen (1987) for an analysis of the structural position of women without men in an Algerian city.

18. A Spanish source (*El Telegrama de Melilla*, 17/9/1982) claimed that only 100 attended, while Moh and Musa stated that there were at least 1,000.

19. *El Telegrama de Melilla*, 19/9/1982.
20. The two rivals also sought support within the Spanish Socialist Labour Party. Moh, who had recently become a member of this party, forged an alliance with some radical members; this group was led by the government's representative for cultural affairs, an outsider who since his appointment in Melilla had decried the discrimination of Muslims, a stance which local Socialist politicians strongly resented. Amar received the support of the deputy mayor and his faction who were busy trying to oust the acting mayor from office. In this way the struggle for Muslim leadership became entangled with factional strife within the Socialist Party. In 1984 it turned out that both Moh and Amar had bet on the wrong horse. The government's representative for cultural affairs, a radical socialist, was transferred back to Spain, while the deputy mayor was called to order by a Party convention, which also decided to expel Moh from the Party on the ground of disloyalty and agitation. This act which was prompted by a fear of too much Muslim influence in local politics, sealed a definite estrangement between the major political party and the largest ethnic minority.
21. The chronology of events that follows is mainly based on Driessen (1986).
22. One month earlier, more than 1,000 Moroccans had already demonstrated in Nador in support of the Muslims of Melilla and against Spanish 'colonial domination'. This demonstration and those that would follow, were staged by Buceta's nationalist Istliqal Party.
23. *Cabrón*, billy-goat, is a serious term of abuse in Spain. It refers to a man deceived sexually by his wife. Such a man, who is not a true man, is the object of public scorn.
24. *El País*, 2/2/1987, front page.
25. Idem, 8/2/1987.
26. Meanwhile both Moh and Musa continued to make overtures to the Moroccan king. After the annual swearing of loyalty to the king in 1987, Hassan II met the two Muslim leaders for the first time.

Chapter 10

1. Cf. de Morales (1920: 65).
2. Between 1905 and 1915 the civil population of Melilla quadrupled (from 9,200 to 36,700), while the garrison increased from 2,700 to 36,700. Source *Junta Municipal de Melilla. Memorias sobre su actuación 1927–1930*, A.M.M.
3. *Padrón Municipal de 1917*, A.M.M.
4. For useful overviews of the Rifian war see Payne (1967), Woolman (1968), Ayache (1981) and Pennell (1986).

5. See his novel *Cabrerizas Altas*, which belongs to the literary tradition of social realism. The municipality of Melilla republished this novel in 1990 together with Sender's articles for the local newspaper.

6. The figures in this section have been drawn from the *Padrón Municipal de 1981* (corrections and mutations included up to 1984), *Servicio Estadistica Municipal*.

7. Note that these are all instances of Spanish men living with Moroccan women. The reverse is rare.

8. To talk with legionnaires about their past is to ask them why they joined the Legion, which is taboo and bad form. However, when Antonio learned that I had lived in Córdoba, he took a liking to me and told me his story.

9. The custom of brideprice is used here in a new context for different ends.

10. This could be ascertained by tracing the households in the *padrones* over a period of 25 years.

11. Compare Brandes (1975) who has noted that nicknames thrive in communities that are small, egalitarian and traditional. I would replace 'traditional' by relative isolation *vis-à-vis* the wider society. Nicknames also occur in contexts where there are power differences among the people who nickname each other. In the barrio most of the women, notably prostitutes, bear nicknames for the simple fact that they are much more public than women in other sectors of Melilla.

12. Elias and Scotson's model of established-outsiders relationships is useful in this context. The image which the established have of themselves tends to be modelled on 'the minority of the best', while the image they project onto the outsiders is modelled on the 'minority of the worst' (1965: 7). One of the conclusions of this study is that 'civilising differentials' (higher degree of self-constraint and stricter morals) play an important part in the making and perpetuation of power differentials. This principle also operates in the relationships between the established sectors of local society and the fringe people.

13. Founded in 1920, the Spanish Foreign Legion was modelled after the French. It rapidly became the toughest force within the Spanish army. Although it was intimately tied to colonial expansion in Africa, it was also used to intervene in civil affairs at home. In 1936, for instance, it played a decisive role in the rebellion that triggered off the Civil War (1936–9). After the decolonisation of Western Sahara in 1976, it was subjected to drastic reform. One of its regiments (*tercios*) was disbanded. Another was sent to Fuerteventura (Canary Islands). The remaining two are posted in Melilla and Ceuta. Legionnaires have been involved in serious incidents in all these places. Today, the majority of its soldiers are conscripts (who

may opt for service in the Legion; they are not placed in the unit against their will). But there are still many volunteers, including foreigners, mainly from Portugal, West Germany, Romania, and former Spanish Guinea, especially in the ranks of non-commissioned officers.

14. See Blok (1981) on the role of rams in the symbolism of masculinity and honour.

15. The Legion is also an anachronism as there are no more colonial wars to be fought. Its organisational structure is highly ambiguous. As a 'total institution' (cf. Goffman 1968) it is both a residential male community and a formal organisation. The same ambivalence holds true for its ethos. On the one hand, legionnaires are trained to submit blindly to the unit and its leaders, yet at the same time they celebrate fellowship in arms, and equality in the face of danger. The officers use violence to breed violence in the legion-naires. However, this violent stance is at odds with the values of the wider society where a strong emphasis is put on the control of aggressive impulses. All these paradoxical characteristics make the Legion a phenomenon of special ethnographic interest. To my knowledge there are very few ethnographic studies of military communities available.

16. The incidents that follow are mainly reconstructions based on local newspaper clippings and interviews.

17. I noted down the following incidents for the first half of 1984. (1) A young Moroccan was found severely wounded in one of the barrio streets. The police arrested another young Moroccan and a prosti-tute and found hashish in the latter's room. (2) A local tough was stabbed to death by a rival during a row about drugs in the barrio. (3) Malika, a young Moroccan prostitute with a room in Cabrerizas, not only sells her body but also drugs. The police arrested a man from Huelva after finding hashish on his body when he was about to embark the ferry to Málaga. The information squeezed out of him led the Civil Guard to Malika. (4) A couple of weeks later the Civil Guard also found drugs in the room of a Moroccan prostitute, known in the barrio as the 'Tattooed'.

18. Cited from the *Telegrama de Melilla*, 8/11/1983, front page.

19. The dominant gender hierarchy in which men are expected to initiate sexual contact and women are supposed to submit is re-versed. In the wider society Catholics, Jews and Muslims share the idea that women are by nature lecherous and fear that their sexual-ity disrupts the social order.

20. This section on prostitutes has profited much from discussions with Willy Jansen. See Arnold (1977) and Jansen (1987) for similar observations on the structural position of prostitutes in Peru and Algeria respectively.

Conclusion

1. See, for instance, the seminal work by Owen Lattimore (1962).
2. Firth (1973: 311), Mauss (1979: 122) and Douglas (1978: 114) made pertinent statements about the link between status and amount of physical performance in human interaction.
3. See Leach (1976: 11) on this point.
4. Compare Driessen (1983) and Gilmore (1987) on the cult of masculinity in southern Spain.
5. I am particularly grateful to Don Handelman and Lea Shamgar-Handelman for valuable suggestions with regard to the *mimuna* and *agasajo*.
6. See Handelman (1988). These ideas are elaborated in his book, *Models and Mirrors: Towards an Anthropology of Public Events*.

References

Abun Nasr, Jamil 1971 *A History of the Maghreb.* Cambridge: Cambridge University Press.

Actes du Colloque International sur la communauté juive marocaine 1980 *Juifs du Maroc. Identité et Dialogue.* Paris: Pensée Sauvage.

Adams, William 1981 Dispersed Minorities of the Middle East. A Comparison and a Lesson, in George P. Castile & Gilbert Kushner (eds.), *Persistent People. Cultural Enclaves in Perspective.* Tucson, Arizona: University of Arizona Press, 3–25.

Apte, Mahadeve L. 1985 *Humor and Laughter. An Anthropological Approach.* Ithaca/London: Cornell University Press.

Ariès, Philippe 1976 *Western Attitudes toward Death: From the Middle Ages to the Present.* London: Marion Boyars.

—— 1978 *L'Homme devant la Mort.* Paris: Editions du Seuil.

Arnold, Katherine 1977 The Introduction of Poses to a Peruvian Brothel and Changing Images of Male and Female, in John Blacking (ed.), *The Anthropology of the Body*, A.S.A. monographs 15, London: Academic Press, 179–98.

Artbauer, Otto 1911 *Die Rif Piraten und ihre Heimat. Erste Kunde aus verschlossenem Welt.* Stuttgart: Strecker und Schröder.

Ayache, Germain 1981 *Les origines de la guerre du Rif.* Paris/Rabat: Publications de la Sorbonne/S.M.E.R.

—— 1983 *Etude d'histoire marocaine*, 2nd ed. Rabat: Société des Editeurs Réunis.

Badia y Leblich, Domingo (pseudonym Ali Bey el Abbassi) 1816 *Travels of Ali Bey in Morocco, Tripoli, Cyprus, Egypt, Arabia, Syria and Turkey between 1803 and 1807.* 2 Vols. London: Longman, Hurst, Rees, Orme & Browne.

Barley, Nigel 1983 *The Innocent Anthropologist: Notes from a Mud Hut.* London: British Museum Publications.

Barth, Frederik 1969 Introduction to Frederik Barth (ed.), *Ethnic Groups and Boundaries: The Social Organisation of Cultural Differences.* London: George Allen & Unwin, 9–38.

Belmonte, Thomas 1979 *The Broken Fountain.* New York: Columbia University Press.

Ben-Ami, Issachar 1980 Le culte des saints chez les juifs et les musulmans au Maroc. In: CNRS, *Les relations entre juifs et musulmans en afrique du nord, XIX–XX siècles.* Paris: Editions du CNRS, 104–9.

—— 1981 Folk-Veneration of Saints among the Moroccan Jews. Tradition, Continuity and Change: The Case of the Holy Man Rabbi David u-Moshe. In: Shelomo Morag, Issachar Ben-Ami & Norman A. Stillman (eds.), *Studies in Judaism and Islam. Presented to Shelomo Dor Goitein.* Jerusalem: The Magnes Press/Hebrew University, 283–344.

Blasco López, José Luis 1987 La vida cotidiana de los capuchinos en Melilla en el siglo XVII, *Trapana, Revista de la Asociación de Estudios Melillenses,* 1, 20–22.

Bloch, Maurice 1986 *From Blessing to Violence: History and Ideology in the Circumcision Ritual of the Merina of Madagascar.* Cambridge: Cambridge University Press.

—— 1987 The Ritual of the Royal Bath in Madagascar: the Dissolution of Death, Birth and Fertility into Authority, in David Cannadine & Simon Price (eds.), *Rituals of Royalty. Power and Ceremonial in Traditional Societies.* Cambridge: Cambridge University Press, 271–293.

Bloch, Maurice & Jonathan Parry 1982 Introduction to Maurice Bloch & Jonathan Parry (eds.), *Death and the Regeneration of Life.* Cambridge: Cambridge University Press, 1–45.

Blok, Anton 1981 Rams and Billy-Goats: A Key to the Mediterranean Code of Honor. *Man* (N.S.), 16, 427–40.

—— 1982 Primitief en geciviliseerd, *Sociologische Gids,* XXIX, 197–210.

Boissevain, Jeremy 1974 *Friends of Friends. Networks, Manipulators and Coalitions.* Oxford: Basil Blackwell.

Bowie, Leland 1976 An Aspect of Muslim-Jewish Relations in Late Nineteenth-Century Morocco: A European Diplomatic View. *International Journal of Middle East Studies,* 7, 3–19.

Brandes, Stanley 1975 The Structural and Demographic Implications of Nick-names in Navanogal, Spain. *American Ethnologist,* 2, 139–48.

Braudel, Fernand 1976 *The Mediterranean and the Mediterranean World in the Age of Philip II,* 2 vols. Glasgow: Fontana/Collins.

Bravo Nieto, Antonio 1987 La iglesia de la purísima concepción en Melilla la vieja, *Trapana, Revista de la Asociación de Estudios Melillenses,* 1, 22–29.

Brignon, Jean *et al.* 1967 *Histoire du Maroc.* Paris/Casablanca: Hatier/Librairie Nationale.

Burke, Edmund III 1973 The Image of the Moroccan State in French Ethnological Literature: A New Look at the Origin of Lyautey's Berber Policy, in Ernest Gellner & Charles Micaud (eds.), *Arabs and Berbers: From Tribe to Nation in North Africa.* London: Duckworth, 175–200.

Burke, Peter 1987 *The Historical Anthropology of Early Modern Italy. Essays on Perception and Communication.* Cambridge: Cambridge University Press.

Cammaert, Marie-France 1985 *Migranten en Thuisblijvers: een Confrontatie. De leefwereld van Marokkaanse Berbervrouwen.* Assen/Maastricht/Leuven: Universitaire Pers Leuven/van Gorcum.

Cannadine, David 1987 Introduction: Divine Rites of Kings, in David Cannadine & Simon Price (eds.), *Rituals of Royalty. Power and Ceremonial in Traditional Societies.* Cambridge: Cambridge University Press, 1–19.

Caro Baroja, Julio 1970 *El mito del caracter nacional: Meditaciones a contrapelo.* Madrid: Seminarios y Ediciones.

Castries, Henri de 1921 *Les sources inédites de l'histoire du Maroc* Vol. I, II, Paris/Madrid: Ed. Leroux/Ruiz Hermanos.

Caulkins, Douglas 1980 Contemporary American Subcultures. Ethnography in the 1970's. *Choice,* 17, 29–40.

Choukri, Mohamed 1981 *Le pain nu.* Paris: Seuil.

Chouraqui, André 1985 *Histoire des Juifs en Afrique du Nord.* Paris: Hachette.

Christian, William A. Jr. 1972 *Person and God in a Spanish Valley.* New York: Seminar Press.

Clifford, James & George Marcus (eds.) 1986 *Writing Culture. The Poetics and Politics of Ethnography.* Berkeley: University of California Press.

Cohen, Abner 1974 Introduction: The Lesson of Ethnicity, in Abner Cohen (ed.), *Urban Ethnicity.* London: Tavistock.

—— 1981a *The Politics of Elite Culture. Explorations in the Dramaturgy of Power in Modern African Society.* Berkeley: University of California Press.

—— 1981b Variables in Ethnicity, in Charles F. Keyes (ed.), *Ethnic Change,* Seattle & London: University of Washington Press.

Cohn, Hermann 1927 *Moeurs des Juifs et des Arabes de Tétuan (Maroc).* Paris: Libraire Lipschutz.

Combs-Schilling, Elaine 1985 Family and Friend in a Moroccan Boom Town: The Segmentary Debate Reconsidered, *American Ethnologist,* 12, 659–75.

Coon, Carleton S. 1931 *Tribes of the Rif.* Cambridge (Mass.): Peabody Museum of Harvard University, Harvard African Studies, Vol. IX.

—— 1932 *Flesh of the Wild Ox: A Riffian Chronicle of High Valleys and Long Rifles.* New York: William Morrow.

—— 1934 *The Riffian.* London: Cape.

Crapanzano, Victor 1980 *Tuhami. Portrait of a Moroccan.* Chicago: University of Chicago Press.

Davis, John 1977 *The People of the Mediterranean: An Essay in Comparative Social Anthropology.* London: Routledge & Kegan Paul.

Delbrel, G. 1911 *Geografía general de la provincia del Rif y kábilas de Guelaia-Kebdana.* Melilla: Imprenta del Telegrama del Rif.

Deshen, Shlomo & Moshe Shokeid 1974 *The Predicament of Homecoming: Cultural and Social Life of North African Immigrants in Israel*. Ithaca and London: Cornell University Press.

Douglas, Mary 1978 *Natural Symbols. Explorations in Cosmology*. Harmondsworth: Penguin Books.

Driessen, Henk 1983 Male Sociability and Rituals of Masculinity in Rural Andalusia, *Anthropological Quarterly*, 56, 125–33.

―― 1985 Mock Battles between Moors and Christians: Playing the Confrontation of Crescent with Cross in Spain's South, *Ethnologia Europeae*, XV, 105–115.

―― 1986 Interetnische confrontatie in Melilla en Ceuta. *Internationale Spectator*, 11, 694–700.

―― 1987 Images of Spanish Colonialism in the Rif. An Essay in Historical Anthropology and Photography, *Critique of Anthropology*, VII, 53–66.

―― 1988 Historisch besef en perspectief in recent etnografisch onderzoek. *Sociologische Gids*, 35, 162–74.

Dwyer, Kevin 1982 *Moroccan Dialogues: Anthropology in Question*. Baltimore & London: Johns Hopkins University Press.

Eickelman, Dale F. 1976 *Moroccan Islam: Tradition and Society in a Pilgrimage Center*. Austin: University of Texas Press.

―― 1981 *The Middle East: An Anthropological Approach*. Englewood Cliffs: Prentice-Hall.

Elias, Norbert & J.L. Scotson 1965 *The Established and the Outsiders. A Sociological Inquiry into Community Problems*. London: Frank Cass.

Elias, Norbert 1980 Over de dood en eenzaamheid van de stervenden in onze tijd, *De Gids*, 143, 451–80.

Epstein, Arnold L. 1978 *Ethos and Identity. Three Studies in Ethnicity*. London: Tavistock.

Estrada y Paredes, J.A. 1769 *Población general de España, sus reynos, y provincias, ciudades, villas, y pueblos, islas adyacentes, y presidios de Africa*, Vol. II, Madrid: Imprenta de Andrés Ramirez.

Etlin, R.A. 1984 *The Architecture of Death. The Transformation of the Cemetery in Eighteenth-Century Paris*. Cambridge (Mass.): The MIT Press.

Evans-Pritchard , E.E. 1949 *The Sanusi of Cyrenaica*. Oxford: Clarendon Press.

Fabian, Johannes 1983 *Time and the Other: How Anthropology Makes its Object*. New York: Columbia University Press.

Fernández de Castro y Pedrera, Rafael 1911 *El Rif. Los Territorios de Guelaia y Quebdana*. Málaga: Zambrana Hermanos.

Firth, Raymond 1975 *Symbols: Public and Private*. London: Allen and Unwin.

Fleming, S.E. 1983 Spanish Morocco and the Alzamiento Nacional, 1936–39. The Military, Economic and Political Mobilization of a Protectorate. *Journal of Contemporary History*, 18, 27–42.

Fogg, Walter 1940 Villages, Tribal Markets and Towns: Some Considerations Concerning Urban Development in the Spanish and International Zones of Morocco. *The Sociological Review*, 32, 85–107.

Foster, George M. 1960 *Culture and Conquest: America's Spanish Heritage*. New York: Wenner Gren.

Fraser, Ronald 1979 *Blood of Spain. The Experiences of the Civil War, 1936–1939*. London: Allen Lane.

Friedman, Ellen G. 1983 *Spanish Captives in North Africa in the Early Modern Age*. Madison: The University of Wisconsin Press.

Gallego Ramos, E. 1909 *La Campaña de Rif (1909), Origenes, desarrollo y consecuencias*. Madrid.

García Figueras, Tomás 1944 *Marruecos. La accion de España en el Norte de Africa*. Madrid: Ediciones Fé.

―― 1947 *Miscelánia de Estudios Africanos*. Larache: Editora Marroqui.

Geertz, Clifford 1973 *The Interpretation of Cultures*. New York: Basic Books.

―― 1979 Suq: the Bazaar Economy in Sefrou. In: Clifford Geertz, Hildred Geertz, and Lawrence Rosen, *Meaning and Order in Moroccan Society. Three Essays in Cultural Analysis*. Cambridge: Cambridge University Press, 123–314.

―― 1981 *Negara: The Theatre State in Nineteenth-Century Bali*. Princeton (New Jersey): Princeton University Press.

Gellner, Ernest 1969 *Saints of the Atlas*. London: Weidenfeld & Nicolson.

Gilmore, David D. 1977 The Social Organization of Space: Class, Cognition, and Residence in a Spanish Town, *American Ethnologist*, 4, 437–52.

―― 1982 Anthropology of the Mediterranean Area. *Annual Review of Anthropology*, 11, 175–205.

―― 1987 *Aggression and Community. Paradoxes of Andalusian Culture*. New Haven: Yale University Press.

Goded, Manuel 1932 *Marruecos. Las etapas de la pacificación*. Madrid/Barcelona/Buenos Aires: Compañia Ibero-Americana de Publicaciones.

Goffman, Irving 1967 *Interaction Ritual. Essays on Face to Face Behavior*. New York: Doubleday.

―― 1968 *Asylums. Essays on the Social Situation of Mental Patients and other Inmates*. Harmondsworth: Penguin Books.

Goitein, Shelomo D. 1978 *A Mediterranean Society: The Jewish Communities of the Arab World as Portrayed in the Documents of the Cairo Geniza. Vol III, The Family*. Berkeley & Los Angeles: University of California Press.

Goldberg, Harvey E. 1978 The Mimuna and the Minority Status of Moroccan Jews, *Ethnology*, 17, 75–87.

―― 1987 Potential Politics: Jewish Saints in the Moroccan Countryside and in Israel, Paper presented at the Conference on Religious Regimes and State Formation, Amsterdam, Free University.

Gorer, G. 1965 *Death, Grief and Mourning in Contemporary Britain.* New York: Doubleday.

Handelman, Don 1988 Affect or Effect? Ritual in Modern and Traditional Societies. Unpublished paper presented at the NIAS Symposium on 'Ritual and the Social Order'. Leiden.

—— 1990 *Models and Mirrors: Towards an Anthropology of Public Events.* Cambridge: Cambridge University Press.

Handelman, Don, & Bruce Kapferer 1972 Forms of Joking Activity: A Comparative Approach, *American Anthropologist*, 74, 484–517.

Hannerz, Ulf 1980 *Exploring the City. Inquiries Towards an Urban Anthropology.* New York: Columbia University Press.

Harris, Marvin 1968 *The Rise of Anthropological Theory: A History of Theories of Culture.* New York: Thomas Y. Crowell.

Hart, David Montgomery 1958 Emilio Blanco Izaga and the Berbers of the Central Rif, *Tamuda*, VI, 171–237.

—— 1976 *The Aith Waryaghar of the Moroccan Rif. An Ethnography and History.* Viking Fund Publications in Anthropology, 55. New York & Tucson: Wenner-Gren Foundation for Anthropological Research, The University of Arizona Press.

—— 1989 Rejoinder to Henry Munson, Jr. *American Anthropologist*, 91, 765–69.

Hastrup, Kirsten 1978 The Semantics of Biology: Virginity, in Shirley Ardener (ed.), *Defining Females: The Nature of Women in Society.* London: Croom Helm, 49–66.

Heinemeijer, W.F. *et al.* 1976 *Weggaan om te blijven. Een onderzoek naar de gevolgen van gastarbeid op het Marokkaanse platteland.* Amsterdam: Sociaal-Geografisch Instituut, Universiteit van Amsterdam, Publicatie no. 2.

Helsdingen, H.W. van 1987 *Politiek van de dood. Het begraven tijdens de Franse Revolutie.* Amsterdam: SUA.

Herzfeld, Michael 1987 *Anthropology Through the Looking-Glass: Critical Ethnography in the Margins of Europe.* Cambridge: Cambridge University Press.

Hess, Andrew C. 1978 *The Forgotten Frontier. A History of the Sixteenth-Century Ibero-African Frontier.* Chicago & London: University of Chicago Press.

Horowitz, David L. 1985 *Ethnic Groups in Conflict.* Berkeley: University of California Press.

Houdas, O.V. 1969 *Le Maroc de 1631 à 1812.* Amsterdam: Philo Press.

Huntington, Richard & Peter Metcalf 1979 *Celebrations of Death: The Anthropology of Mortuary Ritual.* Cambridge: Cambridge University Press.

Jackson, Anthony 1968 Sound and Ritual, *Man*, (N.S.), 3, 293–99.

Jamous, Raymond 1981 *Honneur et Baraka: les structures sociales tradition-elles dans le Rif.* Cambridge/Paris: Cambridge University Press/ Editions de la Maison des Sciences de l'Homme.

Jansen, Willy 1987 *Women Without Men. Gender and Marginality in an Algerian Town.* Leiden: Brill.

Julien, C.A. 1970 *History of North Africa. Tunisia, Algeria and Morocco. From the Arab Conquest to 1830.* London: Routledge & Kegan Paul.

Kedar, Benjamin Z. 1984 *Crusade and Mission. European Approaches toward the Muslims.* Princeton: Princeton University Press.

Kenny, Michael & David I. Kertzer (eds) 1983 *Urban Life in Mediterranean Europe: Anthropological Perspectives.* Urbana: University of Illinois Press.

Kertzer, David I. 1988 *Ritual, Politics and Power.* New Haven and London: Yale University Press.

Kettani, M. Ali 1986 *Muslim Minorities in the World Today.* London: Mansell Publishing.

Lattimore, Owen 1962 *Studies in Frontier History. Collected Papers 1928–1958.* Paris, The Hague: Mouton.

Leach, Edmund 1976 *Culture and Communication. The Logic by which Symbols are Connected.* Cambridge: Cambridge University Press.

Leibovici, Sarah 1984 *Chronique des juifs de Tétouan (1860–1896).* Paris: Maisonneuve et Larosse.

Llanos y Alcaraz, Antonio 1894 *Melilla. Historia de la Campaña de Africa en 1893–94.* Madrid: Velasco.

Lobera Girela, Cándido 1912 *Notas sobre el problema de Melilla.* Melilla: Tip. El Telegramma del Rif.

Marcus, George & Dick Cushman 1982 Ethnographies as Texts. *Annual Review of Anthropology*, 11, 25–69.

Marcus, George & Michael Fischer 1986 *Anthropology as Cultural Critique. An Experimental Moment in the Human Sciences.* Chicago & London: The University of Chicago Press.

Mauss, Marcel 1979 Body Techniques, in Marcel Mauss, *Sociology and Psychology. Essays.* London: Routledge and Kegan Paul, 95–123.

Mernissi, Fatima 1975 *Beyond the Veil: Male-Female Dynamics in a Modern Muslim Society.* New York: Schenkman.

—— 1977 Women, Saints, and Sanctuaries. *Signs*, 3, 101–12.

Mikesell, Marvin W. 1961 *Northern Morocco: A Cultural Geography.* Berkeley and Los Angeles: University of California Press.

Mir Berlanga, Francisco 1983 *Melilla. Floresta de Pequeñas Historias.* Melilla: Ayuntamiento.

Moore, Sally F. 1987 Explaining the Present. Theoretical Dilemmas in Processual Anthropology, *American Ethnologist*, 14, 727–37.

Moore, Sally F. & Barbara G. Myerhoff 1977 Introduction: Secular Ritual: Forms and Meanings. In: Sally F. Moore & Barbara Myerhoff (eds.), *Secular Ritual.* Assen: Van Gorcum, 3–24.

Morales, Gabriel de 1909 *Datos para la historia de Melilla*. Melilla: Tip. el Telegramma del Rif.

—— 1920 *Efemérides y Curiosidades, Melilla, Peñón y Alhucemas*. Melilla: Tip. El Telegramma del Rif.

Morales Lezcano, Victor 1984 *España y el Norte de Africa: El protectorado en Marruecos, 1912–56*. Madrid: U.N.E.D.

Mouliéras, Auguste 1895 *Le Maroc Inconnu, Exploration du Rif*, Vol. I, Paris & Alger: Jourdan, 1895.

Munson, Henry Jr. 1984 *The House of Si Abd Allah. The Oral History of a Moroccan Family*. New Haven: Yale University Press.

—— 1989 On the Irrelevance of the Segmentary Lineage Model in the Moroccan Rif, *American Anthropologist*, 91, 386–400.

Myerhoff, Barbara 1982a Rites of Passage: Process and Paradox, in Victor Turner (ed.), *Celebration: Studies in Festivity and Ritual*, Washington, D.C.: Smithsonian Institution Press, 109–136.

—— 1982b Life History Among the Elderly: Performance, Visibility and Re-Membering, in Jay Ruby (ed.), *A Crack in the Mirror. Reflexive Perspectives in Anthropology*. Philadelphia: University of Pennsylvania Press, 99–118.

Needham, Rodney 1967 Percussion and Transition, *Man*, (N.S.), 2, 606–14.

Ortner, Sherry 1973 On Key Symbols, *American Anthropologist*, 75, 1338–46.

—— 1984 Theory in Anthropology since the Sixties, *Comparative Studies in Society and History*, 26, 126–66.

Parry, Jonathan P. 1979 *Caste and Kinship in Kangra*. London: Routledge & Kegan Paul.

—— 1982 Sacrificial Death and the Necrophagous Ascetic, in: Maurice Bloch & Jonathan Parry (eds.), *Death and the Regeneration of Life*. Cambridge: Cambridge University Press, 74–110.

Payne, Stanley 1967 *Politics and the Military in Modern Spain*. Stanford: Stanford University Press.

Pennell, C.R. 1986 *A Country with a Government and a Flag: The Rif War in Morocco, 1921–26*. London: Menas Press.

Pina Cabral, J. de 1980 Cults of Death in Northwestern Portugal, *JASO*, 9, 1–14.

Pitt-Rivers, Julian 1977 *The Fate of Shechem or the Politics of Sex. Essays in the Anthropology of the Mediterranean*. Cambridge: Cambridge University Press.

Praz, Mario 1970 *The Romantic Agony* sec. ed. Oxford: Oxford University Press.

Rabinow, Paul 1975 *Symbolic Domination. Cultural Form and Historical Change in Morocco*. Chicago/London: The University of Chicago Press.

—— 1977 *Reflections on Fieldwork in Morocco*. Berkeley: University of California Press.

Radcliffe-Brown, A.R. 1952 *Structure and Function in Primitive Society*. London: Cohen & West.

Riches, David (ed.) 1986 *The Anthropology of Violence*. Oxford: Basil Blackwell.

Rosen, Lawrence 1972 Muslim-Jewish Relations in a Moroccan City, *International Journal of Middle East Studies*, 3, 435–49.

Rouget, Gilbert 1985 *Music and Trance. A Theory of the Relations between Music and Possession* (Translation from the French and Revised by Brunhilde Biebuyck in collaboration with the author). Chicago & London: The University of Chicago Press.

Said, Edward 1978 *Orientalism*. London: Routledge & Kegan Paul.

Schneider, Jane & Peter Schneider 1984 Mafia Burlesque: The Profane Mass as a Peace-Making Ritual, in E.R. Wolf (ed.), *Religion, Power and Protest in Local Communities: The Northern Shore of the Mediterranean*. Berlin: Mouton, 117–37.

Seddon, David 1981 *Moroccan Peasants. A Century of Change in the Eastern Rif 1870–1970*. Folkestone, Kent: Dawson.

Sheenan, Bernard 1980 *Savagism and Civility. Indians and Englishmen in Colonial Virginia*. Cambridge: Cambridge University Press.

Sender, Ramón J. 1965 *Cabrerizas Altas*. Mexico: Imprenta Ruiz.

Simmel, Georg 1950 *The Sociology of Georg Simmel*. Translated and Edited and with an Introduction by Kurt H. Wolff. New York: The Free Press.

Stillman, Norman A. 1978 The Moroccan Jewish Experience: A Revisionist View. *The Jerusalem Quarterly*, 9, 111–24.

Sturtevant, William C. 1968 Categories, Percussions and Physiology, *Man*, (N.S.), 3, 133–4.

Talai, Victor 1986 Social Boundaries Within and Between Ethnic Groups: Armenians in London, *Man* (N.S.), 21, 251–71.

Taussig, Michael 1987 *Shamanism, Colonialism and the Wild Man. A Study in Terror and Healing*. Chicago & London: The University of Chicago Press.

Tessler, Mark A. & Linda L. Hawkins 1980 The Political Culture of Jews in Tunisia and Morocco. *International Journal of Middle East Studies*, 11, 59–86.

Thomson, Ann 1987 *Barbary and Enlightenment. European Attitudes towards the Maghreb in the 18th Century*. Leiden: Brill.

Troin, Jean-Francois 1975 *Les souks marocains*. 2 Vols. Aix-en-Provence: Edisud.

Turnbull, Colin 1973 Foreword to Timothy Severin, *Vanishing Primitive Man*. London: Thames & Hudson.

Turner, Victor 1974 *Dramas, Fields and Metaphors: Symbolic Action in Human Society*. Ithaca & London: Cornell University Press.

Udovitch, A.L. & L. Valensi 1985 *The Last Arab Jews: The Communities of Jerba, Tunisia*. New York: Harwood Academic Publishers.

Valderama Martínez, Francisco 1956 *Historia de la acción de España en Marruecos, 1912–1956*. Tetuán: Editora Marroqui.

Veblen, T. 1970 *The Theory of the Leisure Class. An Economic Study of Institutions* (with an introduction by C. Wright Mills). London: Unwin Books.

Westermarck, Edward 1914 *Marriage Ceremonies in Morocco*. London: Macmillan.

—— 1926 *Ritual and Belief in Morocco*, 2 vols. London: Macmillan.

—— 1930 *Wit and Wisdom in Morocco: A Study of Native Proverbs*. London: Routledge & Sons.

Wikan, Unni 1981 *Life Among the Poor in Cairo*. London: Tavistock.

Wolf, Eric R. 1966 *Peasants*. Englewood Cliffs, N.J.: Prentice Hall.

—— 1973 *Peasant Wars of the Twentieth Century*. New York: Harper & Row.

—— 1982 *Europe and the People Without History*. Berkeley: University of California Press.

Woolman, David S. 1968 *Rebels of the Rif: Abd el-Krim and the Rif Rebellion*. Stanford: Stanford University Press.

Zaïm, Fouad 1990 *Le Maroc et son espace méditerranéen. Histoire économique et sociale*. Rabat: Confluences.

Index

'Abd al-Krim, 40–1, 61, 64, 87, 132, 178
Africanismo, 36, 55, 200
  africanistas, 37, 51, 91
agriculture, 45, 51, 53
  colonial image of Rifian, 69
  colonisation, 51
  privatisation of landownership, 60
  scarcity of arable land, 49
Ait Bu Gafar, 27, 153
  Jews from, 85, 88
  population, 53
  report on, 66–7, 69–70, 210n8
Ait Bu Ifrur, 38–9
  ethnography, 76
  population, 53
  report on, 210n8
  Thursday market of, 50
Ait Shikar, 31, 64, 166, 170
  Jews from, 86
  population, 53
  report on, 210n8
  Sunday market of, 49
  traders of, 50
  Wednesday market of, 50
Ait Sidar, 31–2, 165
  Jews from, 83, 85, 90, 99
  population, 53
  report on, 66, 68–9, 210n8
Ait Waryaghar, 27, 40, 52, 71, 75
  Jews, 87
Algeria, 13, 24, 26, 89, 91, 94
  Jewish community of, 106
  Orania, 32, 81
    failure of harvest, 47–8
    grain harvest, 49
Andalusia, 17, 123, 174, 213n5
  immigrants from, 42–3, 47
apostasy, 11, 24–32 *passim*, 190
  see also conversion

baraka, 20, 39, 72, 200

barbarism, 16, 38, 190
Bloch, Maurice, 11, 214n6, 224
bodily discourse, *see* Cabrerizas Altas
Braudel, Fernand, 9, 19, 24, 190, 206n6, 224

Cabrerizas Altas, community of
  marginals, 169, 177–88 *passim*, 191
  bodily communication, 186–8
  body language, 191–2
  cult of the body, 184–8
  households, 179–81
    female-centered, 181
  legionnaires, 182–8 *passim*
  mulatos, 185
  prostitutes, 182–8 *passim*
  see also prostitutes, prostitution
  reputation, 179, 185, 188
cemetery
  Catholic, 124–37 *passim*
  cult of, 12, 122–37, 194
  Jewish, 82, 124, 128
  Moroccan, 171, 174
  Muslim, 197
  proxemics of, 136
  visiting and tending graves at, 130–7 *passim*
ceremony
  and power, 111, 119–20
  Moroccan tea, 140
  of allegiance, 32
  of national flag, 12, 111–21 *passim*, 193–4
    see also flag
  of redress, 113
  pleito homenaje, 22
  see also symbolism
Ceuta, 12, 35–6, 103, 156–7, 172, 174, 199
commerce
  international network of, 35
  see also trade

233